Human Resource Management

Human Resource Management

UGC - NET

(Paper II & III)

Dr Debasish Biswas

KALPAZ

First Published, 2018

Published by

Kalpaz Publications
C-30, Satyawati Nagar,
Delhi – 110052
E-mail: kalpaz@hotmail.com
Ph.: 9212142040

Printed at: G. Print Process, Delhi

Cataloging in Publication Data—DK
Courtesy: D.K. Agencies (P) Ltd. <docinfo@dkagencies.com>

Biswas, Debashis, 1976- **author.**
Human resource management : UGC - NET (paper II & III) / Dr Debasish Biswas.
pages cm
ISBN 9789386397010

1. Personnel management.—Examinations—Study guides. 2. Personnel management—India—Examinations—Study guides. I. Title.

LCC HF5549.B57 2017 | DDC 658.3 23

Contents

Preface 11

Acknowledgements 13

UNIT-I **15**

• Early Approaches to Management • Classical Approach • Scientific Management • Frederick Winslow Taylor • Frank and Lillian Gillbreth • Henry L. Gantt • Administrative Management • Henri Fayol • James D. Mooney (1884-1957) • Mooney and Reily • Lyndall Urwick (1943) • Oliver Sheldon • Bureaucratic Management • Behavioural Approach • Mary Parker Follet • Elton Mayo • The Hawthorne Studies • Contributions of the Hawthorne Experiment • Abraham Maslow • Douglas McGregor • Chris Argyris • Chester Barnard • Management Science • Operations Management • Management Information Systems • Functions of Management • Planning • Types of Planning • Hierarchy of Plans • Steps of Planning • Planning Premises • Organising • McKinney's 7s framework • Staffing • Directing • Controlling • Types of Controlling • Controlling Techniques • Coordinating • Managerial Roles.

UNIT-II **43**

• Personnel Management • Functions of Personnel Management • Managerial Functions • Operative Functions • Models of HRM • Guest Model • Harvard Model • Matching Model • Structure of Personnel Department • Personnel Department in Line Organisation • Personnel Department in Functional Organisation • Personnel Department in Line and Staff Organisation • Personnel Department in a Divisionalised Organisation Structure • Personnel Department in a Matrix Organisation Structure • Difference between Personnel and IR and HRM • Line and Staff • Job Analysis • Job Description • Contents of Job Description • Job Specification • Job Specification Information • Methods of Job Analysis • Manpower Planning • Levels of Human Resource Planning • Process of Human Resource Planning • Problems in HRP • New Challenges of HRM • Recruitment and Selection • Objectives of Recruitment • Sources of Recruitment • Methods of Recruitment • Selection • Selection Test • Interest Test • Process/Steps in Selection • Difference between Recruitment and Selection • Selection Error • The False Negative Error • Placement and Induction • Objectives of Placement • Concept of Induction • Objectives of Induction • Wage and Salary Administration • Wage Concepts • Minimum

Wages • Fair Wages • Living Wages • Need-based Minimum Wage • Objectives of Wage and Salary Administration • Factors Influencing Wage and Salary Structure and Administration • Theories of Wage • Job Evaluation • Methods of Job Evaluation • Methods of Wage Payment • Linking Wages with Productivity • Grievance Handling and Disciplinary Action • Model Grievance Procedure • Discipline and Disciplinary Action • These are discussed one by one • Disciplinary Action • Hot Stove Rule.

UNIT-III **97**

• HRD Concept • Importance • Evolution of HRD • Evolution of HRD in a Chronological Sequence • Functions • Performance Appraisal • Process of Performance Appraisal • Methods of Performance Appraisal • Quality of Work Life • Career Planning • The SODI Career Planning Model • Quality Circles • Important Terms related to Quality • BPM • Training Programmes for Workers • On the Job Training • Off the Job Training • Identifying Training Needs • Management Development Programmes • Evaluation of Training • Types of Evaluation.

UNIT-IV **131**

• Organisational Behaviour • Concept • Elements of Organisational Behaviour • Importance • Evolution • Role • A. Understanding Human Behaviour • Human can be studied from the point of view of the following four levels • Influencing the Human Behaviour • Models of Organisational Behaviour • Autocratic Model • Custodial Model • Supportive Model • Group Dynamics • Theories of Group Formation • Exchange Theory • Group Decision Making Process • Motivation Theories • Theory of Leadership • House's Path Goal Theory • Leadership Styles • Hersey Blanchard Model • Fiedler's Contingency Model • Leader's Trait • Leadership Effectiveness • Continuum of Leadership Behaviour • Transactional Leadership Theory • Leadership-Member Exchange (LMX) Theory • Transformational Leadership Theory • Likert's Management System • Consequences of Low Morale • Fatigue • Types of Fatigue • Causes of Fatigue • Methods of Reducing Fatigue • Monotony • Organisation Change and OD • Organisational Effectiveness.

UNIT - V **183**

• Industrial Relations • Industrial Disputes • Workers Participation in Management • Code of Discipline • Tripartite Bodies • ILO • Industrial Relations and the New Economic Reforms • Concept of Industrial Relations • Industrial Relations versus Employee Relations • Approaches to Industrial Relations • Effects of Poor Industrial Relations • Trends of Industrial Disputes • Methods and Machinery for the Settlement of Industrial Disputes • Conciliation Officer • Board of Conciliation • Prevention of Industrial Disputes • Workers Participation in Management • Code of Discipline • Tripartite Bodies • Conventions • Recommendations • Priority Conventions • New Economic Policy and IR in India.

UNIT-VI **213**

• Meaning • Objectives • Functions • Theories • Structure of Trade Unions • Trade Union Movement in India • Classification based on Agreement • Leadership • Finance • Union Rivalry • Union Politics.

UNIT-VII **227**

• Labour Legislation • Objectives • Principles • Classification • Evolution of Labour Legislation in India • Impact of ILO • Labour Legislation and Indian Constitution • The Factories Act, 1948 • Working Hours of Adult Workers • The Employee State Insurance Act, 1948 • Qualifying Conditions • Extended Sickness Benefit (ESB) • Disablement Benefit • Duration of TDB • Permanent Disablement Benefit (PDB) • Workmen's Compensation Act, 1932 • Restriction on Employment of Pregnant Women.

UNIT-VIII **253**

• Trade Unions Act, 1926 • Composition of Committee/Advisory Board • Payment of Minimum Rates of Wages • Claims and Procedure • Equal Remuneration Act, 1976 • Payment of Wages Act, 1936 • Conditions • The Payment of Bonus Act, 1965 • Applicability of the Act • Calculation of Amount Payable as Bonus • Set-On and Set-Off of Allocable Surplus • Industrial Employment (Standing Orders) Act, 1946 • The Industrial Disputes Act, 1947 • Arbitration • Strikes and Lockouts • Procedure of Strikes • Procedure of Lockouts • Unfair Labour Practices • Fifth Schedule.

UNIT-IX **313**

• Labour Welfare • Statutory and Non-Statutory Labour Welfare • Intra and Extra Mural Welfare • Agencies of Labour Welfare • Meaning of Labour Welfare • Principles and Approaches • Statutory and Non-Statutory Labour Welfare • Intra and Extra Mural Welfare • Agencies for Welfare Work.

UNIT – X **325**

• Labour Market • Concepts of Wages • State Regulation of Wages • Fixation of Wages • Wage Theories • Wage Differentials • Unemployment and Under-employment • Concepts of Wages • State Regulation of Wages • Fixation of Wages • Wage Theories • Wage Differentials.

INDEX **341**

In Memory of My Father

Whose Blessings are My Fountain of Spirit and Inspiration

Preface

I feel great pleasure in placing the first edition of this book before my esteemed readers. It is the outcome of a great deal of encouragement from my colleagues and request from students.

This book is appropriate for management students for appearing NET and all other competitive examinations in the field of Human Resource Management.

My sincere and deliberate efforts have been devoted to give the book comprehensive form. All units have been discussed in a very simple and lucid language so as to make the subject easily understandable to my beloved students.

I am grateful to the esteemed teachers who always provided me with their valuable suggestions from time to time. I am thankful to my students who always shown a keen interest in my publication. I offer my heartfelt congratulations to ……Publications, New Delhi for quick publication of the book.

I welcome suggestions from esteemed teachers and my students for enrichment and improvement of the book in the future.

This book provides detailed information about the human resource related areas with simple language and the concepts have been explained with easy examples.

Dr D. Biswas

Midnapore

First of all, I would like to express

Dr K C Paul, Professor of Commerce and

Universit

up.

Comm

profes

Asso

for th

broth

their

stude

book

I c

differe

work

copy of

Fi

New D

book.

Th

Acknowledgements

First of all, I would like to express my sincere gratitude to Dr K.C Paul, Professor of Commerce and Management, Vidyasagar University, who has been my motivator since the beginning of my write up. He provided me with many helpful suggestions, important advice and constant encouragement during the course of this work.

I am also grateful to Professor Dr Debabrata Mitra, Department of Commerce, North Bengal University for his valuable suggestions.

A special note of appreciation is due to Professor Debasish Sur, professor of Commerce, University of Burdwan and Dr Susanta Mitra, Associate Professor of Commerce, Kaji Nazrul University, West Bengal for their valuable contributions towards enhancing the standard of the book.

I also thank to Dr Abhijit Pakira and Dr Sudin Bag for extending their help in conducting the task. I am also indebted to all of my beloved students and colleagues for their whole hearted co-operation for this book.

I owe a deep gratitude to the authorities of Vidyasagar University, different librarians and all those who inspired and helped me in this work. I must thank Mr. Subhasish Khan for preparing a neat typed copy of the book.

Finally, my sincere thanks to my publisher Kalpaz Publications, New Delhi, for their untiring effort and support in bringing out this book.

The responsibility for errors remains me alone.

Dr D. Biswas

Midnapore

UNIT-I

1. Early Approaches to Management
2. Classical Approach
3. Behavioural Approach
4. Quantitative Approach
5. Modern Approaches to Management
6. Emerging Approaches in Management thought

Functions of Management

Planning

Organising

Directing

Controlling

Coordination

Communication

1. EARLY APPROACHES TO MANAGEMENT

Name	*Period*	*Contribution*
Robert Owen	1771-1858	Proposed legislative reforms to improve working conditions of labour
Charles Babbage	1792-1871	Advocated the concept of 'division of labour'
Andrew Ure	1778-1857	Advocated the study of management
Charles Dupin	1784-1873	Advocated the study of management
Henry R. Towne	1844-1924	Emphasised the need to consider management as separated field of study and the importance of business skills for running a business

2. CLASSICAL APPROACH

Classical Approach	Scientific Management	Administrative Management	Bureaucratic Management

Scientific Management

Scientific Management	Frederick Winslow Taylor	Frank and Lillian Gillbreth	Henry L. Gantt

Frederick Winslow Taylor

Frederick Winslow Taylor is often called the **"father of scientific management."** Taylor believed that organisations should study tasks and develop precise procedures. As an example, in **1898**, Taylor calculated how much iron from rail cars **Bethlehem Steel Plant** workers could be unloading if they were using the correct movements, tools, and steps. The result was an amazing; 47.5 tons per day instead of the mere 12.5 tons each worker had been averaging. In addition, by redesigning the shovels the workers used, Taylor was able to increase the length of work time and therefore decreased the number of people shoveling from 500 to 140. Lastly, he developed an incentive system that paid workers more money for meeting the new standard. Productivity at Bethlehem Steel raised overnight. As a result, many theorists followed Taylor's philosophy when developing their own principles of management.

Frederick Winslow Taylor published a book on **'Shop Management'** in **1903** and **'The Principles of Scientific Management'** in the USA in **1911.**

Taylor also advocated the concepts of **Piece-rate incentive system and Time-and-motion study.**

Frank and Lillian Gillbreth

Frank and Lillian Gillbreth, a husband and wife team, studied job motions. In Frank's early career as an apprentice bricklayer, he was interested in standardisation and method study. He watched bricklayers and saw that some workers were slow and inefficient, while others were very productive. He discovered that each bricklayer used a different set of motions to lay bricks. From his observations, Frank isolated the basic movements necessary to do the job and eliminated unnecessary motions. Workers using these movements raised their output from 1,000 to 2,700 bricks per day. This was the first **motion study** designed to isolate the best possible method of performing a given job. Later, Frank and his wife Lillian studied job motions using a motion picture camera and a splitsecond clock. When her husband died at the age of 56, Lillian continued their work.

Henry L. Gantt

Henry Gantt, an associate of Taylor's, developed the Gantt chart, a bar graph that measures planned and completed work along each stage of production. **It is a simple chart that compares actual and planned performances.** Based on time instead of quantity, volume, or weight, this visual display chart has been a widely used planning and control tool since its development in **1910**. If the worker completed the work fast, i.e., in less than the standard time, he received a **bonus**.

Administrative Management

Administrative Management	Henri Fayol	James D. Mooney	Mooney and Reily	Lyndall Urwick	Oliver Sheldon

Henri Fayol

The first expert of Administrative Management Theory was **Henri Fayol** (1841-1925). Fayol is called the **"Father of Modern**

Management". Henri Fayol was a French industrialist and a management consultant. He started the functional approach to management. Fayol's **five** functions are still relevant to discussion today about management roles and actions. He has proposed that there are five primary functions of management: **planning, organising, commanding, coordinating, and controlling**.

Henri Fayol, a French mining engineer, developed 14 principles of management based on his management experiences.

These principles provide modern day managers with general guidelines on how a supervisor should organise his department and manage his staff. **Henri Fayol** in his book titled **"Industrial and General Administration"** published in **1916**, gave following **14 principles of management**:-

- **Division of work:** Division of work and specialisation produces more and better work with the same effort.
- **Authority and responsibility:** Authority is the right to give orders and the power to exact obedience. A manager has official authority because of his position, as well as personal authority based on individual personality, intelligence, and experience. Authority creates responsibility.
- **Discipline:** Obedience and respect within an organisation are absolutely essential. Good discipline requires managers to apply sanctions whenever violations become apparent.
- **Unity of command:** An employee should receive orders from only one superior.
- **Unity of direction:** Organisational activities must have one central authority and one plan of action.
- **Subordination of individual interest to general interest:** The interests of one employee or group of employees are subordinate to the interests and goals of the organisation.
- **Remuneration of personnel:** The price of services rendered by employees is salary and it should be fair and provide satisfaction both to the employee and employer.

- **Centralisation:** The objective of centralisation is the best utilisation of personnel. The degree of centralisation varies according to the dynamics of each organisation.
- **Scalar chain:** A chain of authority exists from the highest organisational authority to the lowest ranks.
- **Order:** Organisational order for materials and personnel is essential. The right materials and the right employees are necessary for each organisational function and activity.
- **Equity:** In organisations, equity is a combination of kindliness and justice. Both equity and equality of treatment should be considered when dealing with employees.
- **Stability of tenure of personnel:** To attain the maximum productivity of personnel, a stable work force is needed.
- **Initiative:** Thinking out a plan and ensuring its success is an extremely strong motivator. Zeal, energy, and initiative are desired at all levels of the organisational ladder.
- **Esprit de corps:** Teamwork is fundamentally important to an organisation. Work teams and extensive face-to-face verbal communication encourages teamwork.

Henri Fayol also classified the business activities into the following categories:-

1. Technical
2. Commercial
3. Financial
4. Accounting
5. Security, and
6. Managerial Activities.

The Universality of Management: Management is needed in all types and sizes of organisations, at all organisational levels, and in all organisational work areas throughout the world.

James D. Mooney (1884-1957)

Mooney studied mechanical engineering and eventually became a key member of General Motors' top management team. In **1931**, he wrote **'Onward Industry'**. The book is considered by many scholars to be a significant contribution to administrative management theory.

Mooney and Reily

They proposed four principles of organisation:

1. Coordinating Principles
2. Scalar Principles
3. Functional Principles
4. Staff and Line Principles

The exponents of the principles school are bitterly criticized as the prescription of the principle school are based on personal experience and common sense.

Organisation is used in the structure as a designing process. The organisation planner first of all determines the goals of the organisation and then determines the structure in accordance with the goals and while designing a structure certain principles are applied. These principles have developed on the basis of long administrative experiences and observations of administrators and scholars. Some of these important principles are:

1. Hierarchy
2. Span of Control
3. Co-ordination
4. Unity of Command
5. Leadership
6. Authority
7. Delegation
8. Centralisation and Decentralisation
9. Decision Making
10. Planning
11. Supervision and Control

Lyndall Urwick (1943)

Urwick contributed the following principles of management:

1. **The principle of the objective** – the overall purpose of an organisation is its raison d'être.
2. **The principle of specialisation** – one group, one function.
3. **The principle of coordination** – the purpose of organising is to facilitate coordination or unity of effort.
4. **The principle of authority** – in every organised group, supreme authority must be located somewhere, and there should be a clear line of authority to every member of the group.
5. **The principle of responsibility** – a superior may be held accountable for the actions of subordinates.
6. **The principle of definition** – jobs, duties and relationships should be clearly defined.
7. **The principle of correspondence** – in every position, responsibility and authority should correspond with one another.
8. **The principle of span of control** – no person should supervise more than 5–6 line reports whose work is interlocked.
9. **The principle of balance** – it is essential that the various units of an organisation are kept in balance.
10. **The principle of continuity** – reorganisation is a continuous process and provision should be made for it.

He wrote an influential book called **"The Elements of Business Administration"**, published in 1943.

Oliver Sheldon

After graduating from Oxford and completing his military service, he joined Rowntree Company in York, in the UK, in the 1920s. He was closely involved in restructuring the management and organisation of the growing confectionery company at a stage where its growth meant by necessity it had to move away from the personal, family-centered management of its founder. Basically, he concerned himself with the totality of management and its logical position in the community.

He emphasised the ethics or "oughtness" and the human elements of industrial responsibility. His management responsibility to the community grew out of four observations. Those are public interest, growing desire, association of workers in larger groups and scientific approach.

"The philosophy of management" is the best of his books published in 1923.

Bureaucratic Management

In the late 1800s, **Max Weber** disliked that many European organisations were managed on a "personal" family-like basis and that employees were loyal to individual supervisors rather than to the organisation. He believed that organisations should be managed impersonally and that a formal organisational structure, where specific rules were followed, was important. In other words, he didn't think that authority should be based on a person's personality. He thought authority should be something that was part of a person's job and passed from individual to individual as one person left and another took over. This non-personal, objective form of organisation was called a **bureaucracy.** It is also called **Red Tapism**.

Weber believed that all bureaucracies have the following characteristics:

- **A well-defined hierarchy:** All positions within a bureaucracy are structured in a way that permits the higher positions to supervise and control the lower positions. This clear chain of command facilitates control and order throughout the organisation.
- **Division of labour and specialisation:** All responsibilities in an organisation are specialised so that each employee has the necessary expertise to do a particular task.
- **Rules and regulations:** Standard operating procedures govern all organisational activities to provide certainty and facilitate coordination.
- **Impersonal relationships between managers and employees:** Managers should maintain an impersonal

relationship with employees so that favouritism and personal prejudice do not influence decisions.

- **Competence:** Competence, not "who you know," should be the basis for all decisions made in hiring, job assignments, and promotions in order to foster ability and merit as the primary characteristics of a bureaucratic organisation.
- **Records:** A bureaucracy needs to maintain complete files regarding all its activities.

3. BEHAVIOURAL APPROACH

The behavioural management theory is often called the **human relations movement** because it addresses the human dimension of work. Behavioural theorists believed that a better understanding of human behaviour at work, such as motivation, conflict, expectations, and group dynamics, improved productivity.

The theorists who contributed to this school viewed employees as individuals, resources, and assets to be developed and worked with — not as machines, as in the past. Several individuals and experiments contributed to this theory.

Contributions of Behavioural Thinkers to Management Thought

Name	*Period*	*Contribution*
Mary Parker Follet	1868-1933	Advocated the concept of 'power sharing' and integration
Elton Mayo	1868-1933	Foundation for the Human Relations Movement
Abraham Maslow	1908-1970	Motivated by a hierarchy of needs
Douglas McGregor	1906-1964	Theory X and Theory Y
Chris Argyris	-	Classified organisations based on the employees' set of values
Chaster Barnard		Importance of individuals and communication to organisation structure

Mary Parker Follet

Mary Parker Follet stressed the importance of an organisation establishing common goals for its employees. However, she also began to think somewhat differently than the other theorists of her day, discarding command style hierarchical organisations where employees were treated like robots. She began to talk about such things as ethics, power, and leadership. She encouraged managers to allow employees to participate in decision making. She stressed the importance of people rather than techniques — a concept very much before her time. As a result, she was a pioneer and often not taken seriously by management scholars of her time. Innovative ideas from the past suddenly take on new meanings. Much of what managers do today is based on the fundamentals that Follet established more than 80 years ago. Mary Parker Follet: **"the art of getting things done through people"**.

Elton Mayo

The famous **Hawthorne studies** formed the basis of the human relations school, and are described by Roethlisberger and Dickson (1939) and Mayo (1945) and Homans (1950).

The Hawthorne Studies

The term 'Hawthorne effect' was derived from the location where the phenomenon was first witnessed during a series of experiments: Hawthorne, Illinois. The Hawthorne experiments consisted of two studies conducted at the **Western Electric Company's Hawthorne Works**, just outside of Chicago, from 1924 to 1932. The Hawthorne studies were designed to find ways to increase **worker productivity**.

Professor Elton Mayo and his team conducted researches in **five** phases.

- Illumination experiments (1924 – 1927)
- Relay assembly room experiments (1927 – 1928)
- Mass interviewing programme (1928 -1930)
- Bank wiring room study (1931 – 1932)
- Personnel Counseling

1. Illumination Experiment

This experiment was conducted to establish relationship between output and illumination. When the intensity of light was increased, the output also increased. The output showed an upward trend even when the illumination was gradually brought down to the normal level. Therefore, it was concluded that there is no consistent relationship between output of workers and illumination in the factory. There must be some other factor which affected productivity.

2. Relay Assembly Test Room Experiment

This phase aimed at knowing not only the impact of illumination on production but also other factors like length of the working day, rest hours, and other physical conditions. In this experiment, a small homogeneous work-group of six girls was constituted. These girls were friendly to each other and were asked to work in a very informal atmosphere under the supervision of a researcher. Productivity and morale increased considerably during the period of the experiment. Productivity went on increasing and stabilised at a high level even when all the improvements were taken away and the pre-test conditions were reintroduced. The researchers concluded that socio-psychological factors such as feeling of being important, recognition, attention, participation, cohesive work-group, and non-directive supervision held the key for higher productivity.

3. Mass Interview Programme

The objective of this programme was to make a systematic study of the employees' attitudes which would reveal the meaning which their "working situation" has for them. The researchers interviewed a large number of workers with regard to their opinions on work, working conditions and supervision. Initially, a direct approach was used whereby interviews asked questions considered important by managers and researchers. The researchers observed that the replies of the workmen were guarded. Therefore, this approach was replaced by an indirect technique, where the interviewer simply listened to what the workmen had to say. The findings confirmed the importance of social factors at work in the total work environment.

4. Bank Wiring Test Room Experiment

This experiment was conducted by Roethlisberger and Dickson with a view to develop a new method of observation and obtaining more exact information about social groups within a company and also finding out the causes which restrict output. The experiment was conducted to study a group of workers under conditions which were as close as possible to normal. This group comprised of 14 workers. After the experiment, the production records of this group were compared with their earlier production records. It was observed that the group evolved its own production norms for each individual worker, which was made lower than those set by the management. Because of this, workers would produce only that much, thereby defeating the incentive system. Those workers who tried to produce more than the group norms were isolated, harassed or punished by the group.

5. Personnel Counseling

Personnel Counseling Study was needed as the earlier four studies could not yield sufficient information regarding promoting employee relations. The aim of this study was to get a diagnosis of the problems of the employees.

An impartial and non-authoritative agency was created in order to interview the employees and work with the supervisors. Eliminating lack of communication another drawback of the earlier four studies was the second important task of this study. This was very important as it affected production in case the social or informal organisation clashed with the management's organisation.

To achieve these aims each department was assigned personnel counselors who could freely communicate with the employees. This was a very successful move by the management and soon there was marked improvement in supervisor-employee relations, employee-management relations and even in personal adjustments.

The personnel counseling resulted in behaviour and personality changes. It resulted in improving understanding between the employees and their supervisor and greatly helped the management in understanding their employees by communicating effectively with them while formulating company policies and changes.

Personnel counseling greatly helped in reducing the friction between the workers and the management resulting from lack of communication.

The findings of the study are:-

- Each individual was restricting output.
- The group had its own unofficial standards of performance.
- Individual output remained fairly constant over a period of time.
- Informal groups play an important role in the working of an organisation.

Contributions of the Hawthorne Experiment

The important features of the Hawthorne Experiment are:-

1. A business organisation is basically a social system. It is not just a techno-economic system.
2. The employer can be motivated by psychological and social wants because his behaviour is also influenced by feelings, emotions and attitudes. Thus, economic incentives are not the only method to motivate people.
3. Management must learn to develop co-operative attitudes and not rely merely on command.
4. Participation becomes an important instrument in human relations movement. In order to achieve participation, effective two-way communication network is essential.
5. Productivity is linked with employee satisfaction in any business organisation. Therefore, management must take greater interest in employee satisfaction.
6. Group psychology plays an important role in any business organisation. We must therefore rely more on informal group effort.
7. The neo-classical theory emphasises that man is a living machine and he is far more important than the inanimate machine. Hence, the key to higher productivity lies in employee morale. High morale results in higher output.

Abraham Maslow

Abraham Maslow, a practicing psychologist, developed one of the most widely recognised **need theories,** a theory of motivation based upon a consideration of human needs. His theory of human needs had three assumptions:

- Human needs are never completely satisfied.
- Human behaviour is purposeful and is motivated by the need for satisfaction.
- Needs can be classified according to a hierarchical structure of importance, from the lowest to highest.

Maslow broke down the needs hierarchy into five specific areas:

- **Physiological needs:** Maslow grouped all physical needs necessary for maintaining basic human wellbeing, such as food and drink, into this category. After the need is satisfied, however, it is no longer is a motivator.
- **Safety needs:** These needs include the need for basic security, stability, protection, and freedom from fear. A normal state exists for an individual to have all these needs generally satisfied. Otherwise, they become primary motivators.
- **Belonging and love needs:** After the physical and safety needs are satisfied and are no longer motivators, the need for belonging and love emerges as a primary motivator. The individual strives to establish meaningful relationships with others.
- **Esteem needs:** An individual must develop self-confidence and wants to achieve status, reputation, fame, and glory.
- **Self-actualisation needs:** Assuming that all the previous needs in the hierarchy are satisfied, an individual feels a need to find himself.

Douglas McGregor

Douglas McGregor was heavily influenced by both the Hawthorne studies and Maslow. He believed that two basic kinds of managers exist. One type, the Theory X manager, has a negative view of employees and assumes that they are lazy, untrustworthy, and incapable of assuming responsibility. On the other hand, the Theory Y manager assumes that employees are not only trustworthy and capable of assuming responsibility, but also have high levels of motivation.

An important aspect of McGregor's idea was his belief that managers who hold either set of assumptions can create **self-fulfilling prophecies** — that through their behaviour, these managers create situations where subordinates act in ways that confirm the manager's original expectations.

As a group, these theorists discovered that people worked for inner satisfaction and not materialistic rewards, shifting the focus to the role of individuals in an organisation's performance.

Chris Argyris

Chris Argyris's contributions to the behavioural school of thought are extremely important. His contributions are the **maturity-immaturity theory**, the integration of individual and organisational goals, and the Model I and Model II patterns. According to the maturity-immaturity theory, people progress from a stage of immaturity and dependence to a state of maturity and independence.

If organisations keep their employees in a dependent state, they allow them to remain immature and thereby prevent them from achieving their potential. Further, he also contended that a formal organisation develops a rigid structure, compelling people to behave in an immature way. This leads to incongruence between the individual and organisational goals, hinders organisational development, results in failure, and fosters frustration and conflict.

People therefore exhibit signs of aggression, regression, and suppression. Model I and Model II patterns are two different assumptions. Workers in **Model I** type-organisations are motivated by the desire to manipulate others and protect themselves from others, while workers in **Model II** type-organisations are less manipulative and more willing to learn and take risks. Argyris therefore suggested that managers should always try to create a Model II type-organisation.

Chester Barnard

Chester Barnard, who was president of New Jersey Bell Telephone Company, introduced the idea of the **informal organisation** — **cliques** (exclusive groups of people) that naturally form within a company. He felt that these informal organisations provided necessary and vital communication functions for the overall organisation and that they could help the organisation accomplish its goals.

Barnard felt that it was particularly important for managers to develop a sense of common purpose where a willingness to cooperate is strongly encouraged. He is credited with developing the **acceptance theory of management,** which emphasises the willingness of employees to accept that managers have legitimate authority to act. Barnard felt that four factors affected the willingness of employees to accept authority:

- The employees must understand the communication.
- The employees accept the communication as being consistent with the organisation's purposes.
- The employees feel that their actions will be consistent with the needs and desires of the other employees.
- The employees feel that they are mentally and physically able to carry out the order.

Although he was not an academic but a practicing business leader, Barnard wrote a book called **The Functions of the Executive** in **1938**, which Andrea Gabor has described as the century's seminal book on corporate leadership (in **Capitalist philosophers**, Wiley, 2000). Barnard also authored several papers, selections of which were published in **Organisation and management: selected papers** (1948).

4. QUANTITATIVE APPROACH

Major contributors in Quantitative Approach are-

Johan MacDonald

George R. Terry

Andrew Szilagyi

Quantitative Approach	Management Science	Operations Management	Management Information Systems

Management Science

At the beginning of World War II, Great Britain desperately needed to solve a number of new, complex problems in Warfare. With their survival at stake, British formed the first operational research (OR) teams. By pooling the expertise of mathematicians, physicists, and other scientists in OR teams, The British were able to achieve significant and tactical breakthroughs. When the Americans entered the war, they formed what they called operations research teams, based on the successful British model, to solve similar problems. The teams used early computers to perform the thousands of calculations involved in mathematical modeling.

When the war was over, the applicability of operations research to problems in industry gradually became apparent. New industrial technologies were being put into use and transportation and communication were becoming more complicated. These developments brought with them a host of problems that could not be solved easily by conventional means. Increasingly, OR specialists were called on to help managers come up with answers to these new problems. Over the years, OR procedures were formalised into what is now more generally called the management science school.

The management science school gained popularity through two post-war phenomena. First, the development of high speed computers and of communications among computers provided the means for tackling complex and large scale organisational problems. Second, **Robert McNamara** implemented a management science approach at **Ford Motor Company** in the 1950s and 1960s.

Operations Management

Operations management is somewhat less mathematical and statistically sophisticated than management science and can be applied more directly to managerial situations. Operations management is a form of applied management science.

Operations management techniques are generally concerned with helping the organisation produce its products or services more efficiently and can be applied to a wide range of problems. Thus, it will deal with decisions like plant layout, plant location, inventory control and distribution of finished goods. For example, linear programming helps Air Lines plan their flight schedules. Other operations management techniques include queuing theory, breakeven analysis, and simulation. All of these techniques and procedures apply directly to operations, but they are also helpful in such areas as finance, marketing, and human resource management.

Management Information Systems

Management information systems (MIS) is the most recent subfield of the quantitative school. A management information system organises past, present and projected data from both internal and external sources and processes it into usable information, which it then makes available to managers at all organisational levels. The information systems are also able to organise data into usable and accessible formats. As a result, managers can identify alternatives quickly, evaluate alternatives by using a spreadsheet programme, pose a series of "what if" questions, and finally, select the best alternatives based on the answers to these questions. It helps managers design information systems that provide information about events occurring inside the organisation as well as in its external environment, information that is vital for effective decision making.

5. MODERN APPROACHES TO MANAGEMENT

Modern Approach	The Systems Theory	Contingency Theory

The Systems Theory was developed in late 1960s. **Herbert A. Simon** is the father of **system theory**. H. Simon viewed organisation as a complex system of decision-making process.

Its early contributors include **Ludwing Von Bertalanfty, Lawrence J. Henderson, W.G. Scott, Deniel Katz, Robert L. Kahn, W. Buckley** and **J.D. Thompson**.

According to **Cleland and King**, "A system is composed of related and dependent elements which when in interaction from a unity whole".

Systems theory treats an organisation as a system. A system can be either closed or open, but most approaches treat an organisation as an open system. An **open system** interacts with its environment by way of inputs, throughputs, and outputs. A simple example is a living organism, such as an animal. An open system consists of three essential elements. An organisation receives resources such as equipment, natural resources, and the work of employees, referred to as **inputs**. The inputs are transformed, called **throughputs**, and then yield products or services called **outputs**. Outputs are released into the environment.

Feedback loops are also an important feature of open systems. They provide information to the organisation by connecting the outputs to the inputs. A **negative feedback loop** indicates a problem that should be corrected. For example, the failure of product design indicated by the need to recall the product.

A **positive feedback loop** can identify outputs that have worked well. For example, a successful marketing campaign that yields high sales. Thus, feedback loops are a means of confirming success or signaling that corrections to the system need to be made.

A **closed system** is not affected by its environment. For example, a chuck of iron ore is not substantially affected by its environment.

Features of Systems Approach:

1. A system consists of interacting elements. It is set of inter-related and inter-dependent parts arranged in a manner that produces a unified whole.
2. The various sub-systems should be studied in their inter-relationships rather, than in isolation from each other.
3. An organisational system has a boundary that determines which parts are internal and which are external.
4. A system does not exist in a vacuum. It receives information, material and energy from other systems as inputs. These inputs undergo a transformation process within a system and leave the system as output to other systems.
5. An organisation is a dynamic system as it is responsive to its environment. It is vulnerable to change in its environment.

Systems theory is useful to management because it aims at achieving the objectives and it views organisation as an open system. **Chester Barnard** was the **first person** to utilise the systems approach in the field of **management**.

Contingency Approach

Major contributors in the contingency theories are:-

1. G.M. Stalker
2. Joan Woodward
3. Tom Burns
4. Paul R. Lawrence
5. L.W. Lorsch

The contingency approach sometimes called the **situational approach** was developed by managers, consultants, and researchers who tried to apply the concepts of the major schools to the real-life situations. The contingency school of management can be summarised as an **"it all depends"** approach. The appropriate management actions and approaches depend on the situation. Managers with a contingency view use a flexible approach, draw on a variety of theories and experiences, and evaluate many options as they solve problems.

Contingency management recognises that there is no one best way to manage. In the contingency perspective, managers are faced with the task of determining which managerial approach is likely to be most effective in a given situation. For example, the approach used to manage a group of teenagers working in a fastfood restaurant would be very different from the approach used to manage a medical research team trying to find a cure for a disease.

Contingency thinking avoids the classical "one best way" arguments and recognises the need to understand situational differences and respond appropriately to them. It does not apply certain management principles to any situation. Contingency theory is recognition of the extreme importance of individual manager performance in any given situation. The contingency approach is highly dependent on the experience and judgment of the manager in a given organisational environment.

6. EMERGING APPROACHES IN MANAGEMENT THOUGHT

William Ouchi, a management expert, conducted research on both American (Theory X) and Japanese (Theory Y) and outlined a new theory called **Theory Z**. This theory combines the positive aspects of both the theories. The Theory Z approach involves providing job security to employees to ensure their loyalty and long-term association with the company. It also involves job rotation of employees to develop their cross-functional skills. It also advocates the decision-making participation of the employees and emphasises the use of formal control in the organisation along with explicit performance measures. The organisation shows concern to their employees' well-being and lays emphasis on their training and development.

Functions of Management

Management, as defined by **Mary Parker Follett, "The art of getting things done through people".**

Different experts have classified functions of management. According to **George & Jerry**, "There are four fundamental functions of management i.e. planning, organising, actuating and controlling".

According to Henry Fayol, "To manage is to forecast and plan, to organize, to command, and to control". Whereas Luther Gullick has given a keyword **'POSDCORB'** where P stands for Planning, O for Organizing, S for Staffing, D for Directing, Co for Co-ordination, R for reporting and B for Budgeting. **Gulick** is often considered as the **'Dean of Public Administration'**. But the most widely accepted functions of management are given by **Koontz and O'Donnell** i.e. **Planning, Organising, Directing and Controlling.**

PLANNING

It is the basic function of management. It deals with chalking out a future course of action and deciding in advance the most appropriate course of actions for achievement of pre-determined goals. According to Koontz, "Planning is deciding in advance - what to do, when to do and how to do. It bridges the gap from where we are and where we want to be". A plan is a future course of actions. It is an exercise in problem solving and decision making. Planning is determination of courses of action to achieve desired goals. Thus, planning is a systematic thinking about ways and means for accomplishment of pre-determined goals. Planning is necessary to ensure proper utilisation of human and non-human resources. It is all pervasive, it is an intellectual activity and it also helps in avoiding confusion, uncertainties, risks, wastages, etc.

Types of Planning

On the basis of scope, there are mainly three types of planning. These are as follows:

Strategic planning is an organisation's process of defining its strategy, or direction, and making decisions on allocating its resources to pursue this strategy. Generally, strategic planning deals, on the whole business, rather than just an isolated unit, with at least one of following three key questions:

- "What do we do?"
- "For whom do we do it?"
- "How do we excel?"

Tactical planning is short range planning emphasising the current operations of various parts of the organisation. Tactical plans are usually developed in the areas of production, marketing, personnel, finance and plant facilities.

Operational planning is the process of linking strategic goals and objectives to tactical goals. It describes milestones, conditions for success and explains how, or what portion of, a strategic plan will be put into operation during a given operational period.

An operational plan addresses four questions:

- Where are we now?
- Where do we want to be?
- How do we get there?
- How do we measure our progress?

On the basis of **time**, there are mainly three types of planning. These are as follows:

1. Long range plan
2. Intermediate plan
3. Short range plan

Hierarchy of Plans

1. Single plan : **Programmes, Budgets and Projects**
2. Standing plan: **Policies, Procedures and Rules**

Programmes: It is large scale single use plan that co-ordinate a complex set of activities to achieve important non-recruiting goals.

Budgets: It outlines the expected result of a given future period in numerical terms.

Projects: A Project is similar to a programme but is similar in scale and less complex.

Policies: It specifics the broad parameter within which organisation members are expected to operate in accomplishment of organisational goal.

Procedures: Procedures is a chronological sequence of steps to be undertaken to achieve an objective.

Rule: It is a statement that spells out what should or what should not be done in a particular situation.

Steps of Planning

The process of planning includes the determination of objectives and outlining the future actions that are needed to achieve these objectives. Various steps that are followed in the process of planning are:

(i) **Identifying the problem:** It involves the identification of the aim for the fulfillment of formulated plans.

(ii) **Gathering information about the activities involved:** An effective plan needs complete knowledge of the activities involved and their effect on other external and internal activities.

(iii) **Analysis of information:** This information is then analysed minutely and the information related with similar subjects is classified so that similar type of data can be kept together.

(iv) **Determining alternate plans:** There are alternate plans available for the achievement of the objectives and ingenuity and creativeness are required as some plans are also developed at this stage.

(v) **Selecting the plan:** At this stage the plan which is acceptable to the operating personnel is proposed. The adaptability and the cost of the plan are also taken into consideration.

(vi) **Detailed sequence and timing:** Detailed like who will perform which activity under the plan and the time within which the plan should be carried out is determined in this step.

(vii) **Progress check of the plan:** The provisions are made for the follow up of the plan as the success of any plan can be measured by the results only.

Planning Premises

According to H. Weihrich and H. Koontz, "Planning premises are identified as the anticipated environment in which plans are expected to operate."

According to C. B. Gupta, "Planning premises are the critical factors which lay down the boundary for planning".

ORGANISING

It is the process of bringing together physical, financial and human resources and developing productive relationship amongst them for achievement of organisational goals. According to Henry Fayol, "To organise a business is to provide it with everything useful or its functioning i.e. raw material, tools, capital and personnel's". To organise a business involves determining and providing human and non-human resources to the organisational structure. Organising as a process involves:

- Identification of activities.
- Classification of grouping of activities.
- Assignment of duties.
- Delegation of authority and creation of responsibility.
- Coordinating authority and responsibility relationships.

McKinney's 7s Framework

1. Strategy 2. Structure 3. System 4. Style 5. Staff 6. Shared Values 7. Skills

Matrix Structure: A combination of both Horizontal Structure and Vertical Structure

Hybrid Structure: A combination of both Functional and Divisional Structure

SBU: Strategic Business Units. General Electric Company first used this concept.

Staffing

Staffing has assumed greater importance in the recent years due to advancement of technology, increase in size of business, complexity of human behaviour, etc. The main purpose of staffing is to put right man on right job. According to Kootz and O'Donnell, "Managerial function of staffing involves manning the organisation structure through proper and effective selection, appraisal and development of personnel to fill the roles designed in the structure". Staffing involves:

- Manpower Planning
- Recruitment, Selection and Placement
- Training and Development
- Compensation
- Performance Appraisal
- Promotions and Transfer

DIRECTING

It is that part of managerial function which actuates the organisational methods to work efficiently for achievement of organisational purposes. Direction is that inert-personnel aspect of management which deals directly with influencing, guiding, supervising, motivating subordinates for the achievement of organisational goals. Direction has following elements:

- Supervision
- Motivation

- Leadership
- Communication

Supervision- It implies overseeing the work of subordinates by their superiors. It is the act of watching and directing work and workers.

Motivation- It means inspiring, stimulating or encouraging the subordinates with zeal to work. Positive, negative, monetary, non-monetary incentives may be used for this purpose.

Leadership- It may be defined as a process by which manager guides and influences the work of subordinates in desired direction.

Communications- It is the process of passing information, experience, opinion, etc from one person to another. It is a bridge of understanding.

CONTROLLING

It implies measurement of accomplishment against the standards and correction of deviation if any to ensure achievement of organisational goals. The purpose of controlling is to ensure that everything occurs in conformities with the standards. An efficient system of control helps to predict deviations before they actually occur. According to **Theo Haimann**, "Controlling is the process of checking whether or not proper progress is being made towards the objectives and goals and acting if necessary, to correct any deviation". According to Koontz and O'Donnell, "Controlling is the measurement and correction of performed activities of subordinates in order to make sure that the enterprise objectives and plans desired to obtain them as being accomplished". Therefore controlling has the following steps:

1. Determining areas to control
2. Establishing standard
3. Measuring performance
4. Comparing performance against standards
5. Recognising good or positive performance
6. Taking corrective action

Types of Controlling

Control is of three types. These are 1. Feed forward control, 2. Concurrent control and 3. Feedback control.

1. **Feed Forward Control:** Inputs are monitored to ensure that they meet the standards necessary for the transformation process.
2. **Concurrent Control:** It regulates ongoing activities to ensure that they conform to organisational standards.
3. **Feedback Control:** It is exercised after a product or service has been already produced.

On the basis of scope control is of three types

1. Strategic control
2. Tactical control
3. Operational control

Managerial Levels and Control Systems

1. Top level———————— Financial control
2. Middle Level———————Budgetary control/quality control
3. Lower level management————————-Inventory (stock)

Span of Management: V.A. Graicunas developed a particular formula to determine relationship. In his formula, he considered direct relationship, indirect relationship and group relationship.

$$n\,(2^{n-1}+n-1)$$

Where R = relationship

n = number of subordinates

Controlling Techniques

1. **JIT:** It implies just in time. It focuses on having the right part at the right place at the right time. It is also called as "**zero inventory**" or "**stock less production**".

   JIT was introduced first by **Toyota Japan**.

2. **Kan Ban System:** In this system, KAN means **Card** and BAN means **Signal**. It involves the use of cards and containers to move parts or components from one work area to another.
3. PERT: **Project Evaluation Review Technique,** and
4. CPM: **Critical Path Method**.

COORDINATING

The coordinating function of leadership controls all the organising, planning and staffing activities of an organisation and ensures all functions together for the good of an organisation. Coordinating typically takes place in meetings and other planning sessions with the department heads of an organisation to ensure all departments are on the same pace in terms of objectives and goals. Coordinating involves communication, supervision and direction by management.

Managerial Roles

Mintzberg published his **Ten Management Roles** in his book, **"Mintzberg on Management: Inside our Strange World of Organisations,"** in 1990.

Henry Mintzberg's Ten Managerial Roles

Category	***Roles***
Interpersonal	Figurehead, Leader, Liaison
Informational	Monitor, Disseminator, Spokesperson
Decisional	Entrepreneur, Disturbance Handler, Resource Allocator, Negotiator

Skills of Manager: Technical Skills, Human Skills, Conceptual Skills, and Design Skills.

Unit-II

- Functions
- Structure of Personnel Department
- Line and Staff
- Job Analysis
- Manpower Planning
- New Challenges
- Recruitment and Selection
- Placement and Induction
- Wage and Salary Administration
- Job Evaluation
- Methods of Wage Payment
- Linking Wages with Productivity
- Grievance Handling and Disciplinary Action

PERSONNEL MANAGEMENT

Functions

"The personnel function is concerned with the procurement, development, compensation, integration, and maintenance of the personnel of an organisation for the purpose of contributing towards the accomplishment of that organisation's major goals or objectives. Therefore, personnel management is the planning, organising, directing, and controlling of the performance of those operative functions." - **Edwin B. Flippo**, Principles of Personnel Management

Functions of Personnel Management

Functions of human resource management may broadly be classified into two categories, viz ; (1) managerial functions, and (2) operative functions.

Managerial Functions

Managerial functions are common functions to all managers. Like other managers, human resource managers perform the basic functions of planning, organising, directing and controlling.

Planning: A plan is a trap to capture the future. Planning is the process of deciding the goals and formulating policies and programmes to achieve the goals of an organisation. Human resource managers make human resource planning to get right quantity and right quality of people at the right time and at the right place. In the area of human resource management, planning involves deciding personnel goals and implementation of formulated policicies, programmes and practices in order to achieve these goals of an organisation.

Organising: Organising is the process of allocating tasks among the employees, establishing authority-responsibility relationships among them and integrating their activities towards achievement of the common objectives of an organisation.

Directing: Directing is the process of motivating, communicating, leading and supervising people. Human resource management involves proper direction in order to get the maximum potential of employees for attaining organisational goals.

Controlling: It implies the establishment of standards and compares it with actual performance in order to measure deviation and taking remedial measures to minimise the gap. Controlling the management of human resources involves performance appraisal of employees, auditing human resources, analysing the effectiveness of training programme, analysing labour turnover rate and such other means.

Operative Functions

These functions are concerned with specific activities of procurement, development, compensation, integration and maintenance.

Procurement Function: It consists of the following activities:

Job Analysis: It is the process of studying in details the operations and responsibilities involved in a job so as to identify the nature and level of employees required to perform the job effectively.

Human Resource Planning: Through it, management strives to have the right number and the right kind of people at the right places, at the right time, doing things which result in both the organisation, and the individual receiving maximum long-range benefit.

Recruitment: It is the process of searching for required personnel and stimulating them to apply jobs in the organisation.

Selection: It implies the suitability of different candidates for jobs in the organisation and choosing the most appropriate people.

Placement: It means assigning suitable jobs to the selected candidates so as to match employee qualifications with job requirements.

Induction: It involves familiarising the new employees with the company, the work environment and the existing employees so that the new people feel at home and can start work confidently.

Development Function: It consists of the following activities:

Performance Appraisal: It implies systematic evaluation of employees with respect to their performance on the job and their potential for development.

Training: It is the process by which employees learn knowledge, skills and attitudes to further organisational and personal goals.

Executive Development: It is the process of developing managerial talent through appropriate programmes.

Career Planning and Development: It involves planning the career of employees and implementing career plans so as to fulfill the career aspirations of people.

Compensation Function: It consists of the following activities:

Job Evaluation: It is the process of determining the relative worth of a job.

Wage and Salary Administration: It implies developing and operating a suitable wage and salary programme.

Bonus: It involves payment of bonus under the Payment of Bonus Act, 1965 as well as non-statutory bonus and other incentives.

Integration Function: It is the process of reconciling the goals of the organisation with those of its members. It involves motivating employees through various financial and non-financial incentives, providing job satisfaction, collective bargaining, workers' participation in management, conflict resolution, developing sound human relations, employee counseling, improving quality of work life, etc.

Maintenance Function: It is concerned with protecting and promoting the physical and mental health of employees. For this purpose, several types of fringe benefits such as housing, medical aid, educational facilities, conveyance facilities, etc. are provided to employees.

Models of HRM

Warwick Model

This model was developed by the Centre for Strategy and Change at Warwick University in the early 1990s. It emphasises on analytical approach to human resource management. It also recognises the impact of the role of the HR function on the human resource strategy content.

The researchers who developed the model, **Hendry and Pettigrew**, focused their research on mapping the context; identifying an **inner** (organisational) context and an **external** (environmental) context. It takes into account the importance of organisational learning in the formation of strategy and thereby incorporates Mintzberg's model of emergent strategy formation rather than a purely top down rational planned approach.

The five elements of the Warwick model are:

- Outer context (the external environment)
- Inner context (internal factors)
- Business strategy content
- Human resource management context
- Human resource management content.

Guest Model

A second 'soft' HRM model came from **David Guest** in 1987. Guest argued that HRM in the UK should be about designing policies and practices to achieve four main outcomes: strategic integration (planning/implementation); high employee commitment to the organisation; high workforce flexibility and adaptability; and a high-quality workforce. Strategic integration means ensuring that the organisation's business plans are implemented through appropriately designed HR policies and practices. Companies have been criticised for trading HRM and strategy separately, therefore failing to combine HRM with the business strategy.

He proposed that these four HRM outcomes will lead to the desirable organisational outcomes of high job performance, stronger problem solving, greater change consistent with strategic goals and improved cost-effectiveness, while also reducing employee turnover, absences, and grievances. However, Guest warned that these outcomes will be achieved only if an organisation has a coherent strategy of HRM policies fully integrated into the business strategy and supported by all levels of line management.

Harvard Model

Harvard Model of HRM was devised by Beer *et al* (1984). The Harvard Model is based on all management decisions that directly affect the relationship between the organisation and its employees. It also views employees as an asset to the organisation than a burden on the balance sheet.

The model is based upon situational factors and stakeholder interests. Situational factors are not within the organisation's control such as legal, environmental and trade unions. Stakeholder interests are factors which are influenced by any person or body with a vested interest in the organisation. Beer *et al* goes into state 'managers can affect a number of factors by means of the policy choices they make'. The 4 C's of Beer's model are listed below:

- Commitment
- Competence
- Cost effectiveness
- Congruence

Commitment is around the commitment of employees to an organisation based upon the HR policies, more commitment will lead to better loyalty and improved performance; however, poor HR policies could have the opposite effect. Competence is based upon the impact of HR policies have on retaining highly skilled and knowledgeable staff; it also involves the development of employees. Cost effectiveness of the HR policies will include the impact on salaries, benefits, and the reward system. It answers questions such as what does the HR policy say regarding bonuses and pay increments. Congruence is the quality of agreement between the employees and the organisation's goals.

Matching Model

One of the first explicit statements of the HRM concept was made by the **Michigan School** (Fombrun *et al,* 1984). They held that HR systems and the organisation structure should be managed in a way that is congruent with organisational strategy (hence the name 'matching model'). They further explained that there is a human resource cycle which consists of four generic processes or functions that are performed in all organisations. These are:

Selection – matching available human resources to jobs;

Appraisal (performance management);

Rewards – 'the reward system is one of the most under-utilised and mishandled managerial tools for driving organisational performance'; it must reward short- as well as long-term achievements, bearing in mind that 'business must perform in the present to succeed in the future';

Development – developing high-quality employees.

Model by John Sorey (1989) Model

John Storey emerged to be one of the strongest proponents of HRM as a completely different discipline from the preceding disciplines embraced by the TPM approach. He believed that HRM is a holistic approach with a set of interrelated policies with an ideological and philosophical underpinning. Because of these ideological and philosophical aspects, HRM does not only stand distinctively outstanding from TPM but also emerges to be a much more humane approach to employment management.

The model by John Storey is based on four aspects.

1. Beliefs and Assumptions

- The model is premised on the notion that HRM is based on a set of beliefs and assumptions, which makes it a distinctive approach.
- Fundamentally it is believed that it is the human resource among all the other factors of production, which gives the difference.
- Successful organisations are distinguished from the rest by the capabilities and commitment of the people who work for them.
- It is therefore imperative that the human resource ought to be treated with great care and nurtured as valuable assets.

- Finally, it is believed that the employment relationship is based on commitment and not compliance.

2. Strategic Qualities

HRM is further distinguished by the fact that it is strategic in nature and therefore requires the attention of senior management and top executives.

- The above-mentioned assumption stems from the 1st belief that the human resource is the most important source of competitive advantage.
- HR Policies are too important to be a product of prescribed best professional practice only. In fact they must be sensitive to the demands of the competitive business environment, business strategy and the HR strategy.

3. Role of Line Managers

- Line managers have a very important role to play in people management.
- It is clear from the HRM philosophy that people management is too important to be left to operational personnel specialists.
- Fundamentally, the importance of line managers is seen through the strong link that exists between them and their respective subordinates or employees.

4. Key Levers

There is a strong belief that culture management is important than managing procedures and systems. This is primarily important because culture management brings consensus on overall organisational values, beliefs and assumptions. **Culture management** is also believed to be essential in flexibility and commitment.

STRUCTURE OF PERSONNEL DEPARTMENT

Structure of Personnel Department in Small Enterprises

By small enterprise is meant the enterprise which employs less than one thousand employees. In such enterprises personnel department may or may not exist. Services of outsiders who specialise in maintaining accounts and records relating to provident fund, pension and other statutory requirements are retained for a fee.

Earlier, personnel as an activity was seen as a necessary but unimportant part of the organisation. Fortunately, things have changed for the better and the status of the personnel department has improved enormously over the years.

An idea of the organisation of personnel department in a small enterprise can be drawn from the following figure:

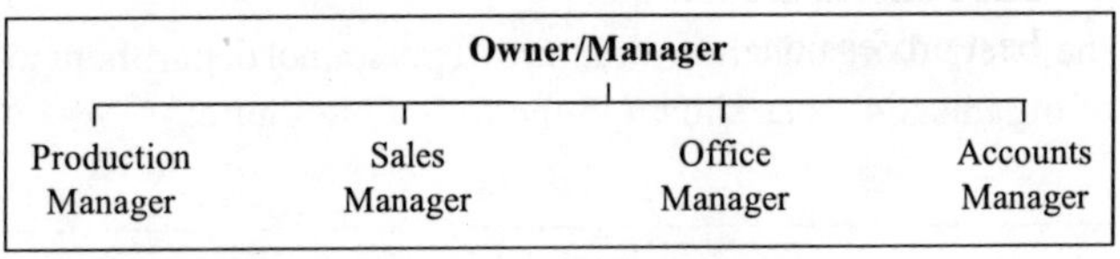

Personnel Department in a Small Enterprise.

Structure of Personnel Department in Large Scale Enterprise

A large scale enterprise will have a manager/director heading the personnel department. His status will be equal to that of any executive. The following figure shows this structure.

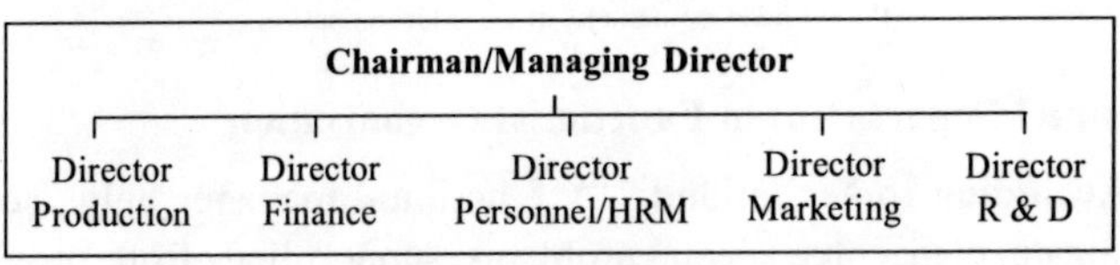

Personnel Department in a Large Scale Unit.

This arrangement holds good when the company has a single unit. Where a company has multiple plants located in different parts of the country, there may be a centralised personnel department at the head office and each plant will have separate personnel departments.

Routine activities relating to each plant are handled by the personnel department attached to the work whereas the broad policies, matters concerning executives, etc. are handled by the central department.

Coming to the composition of the personnel department, it depends on the scale of operations and attitudes of the top management towards its personnel.

Personnel Department in Line Organisation

In line organisations there is uninterrupted line of authority and responsibility running through the management hierarchy. Line relationship generally exists between a superior and a subordinate. Managers identified as line are not subject to command by staff personnel. In case of disagreement between line and staff, line manager has the right to make final operating decisions.

The internal organisation structure of personnel department in line type of organisation's as shown in the following figure:

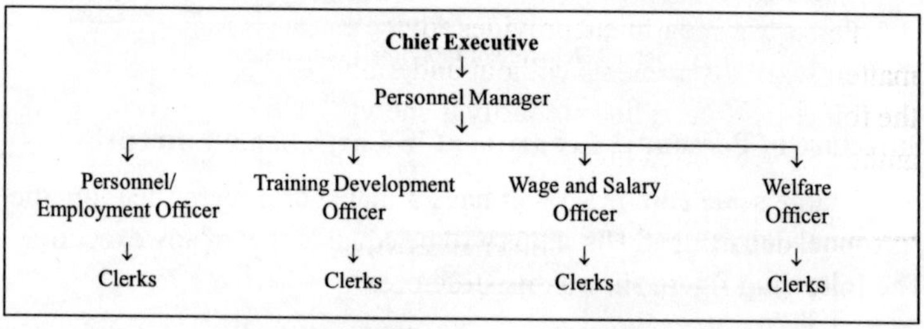

Personnel Department in Line Organisation.

Personnel Department in Functional Organisation

According to McFarland, "A functional manager helps serve, investigate, plan, solve special problems, support line effort, provides ideas and has special expertise."

In functional structure, all activities in the company are grouped according to certain functions like production, marketing, finance, personnel, etc. Each function is put under the charge of a functional specialist. Functional authority is advisory, which means that the functional specialist recommends action or alternative actions to line managers.

Every functional head has functional authority over other departments and every employee reports to several functional heads as shown on the following figure:

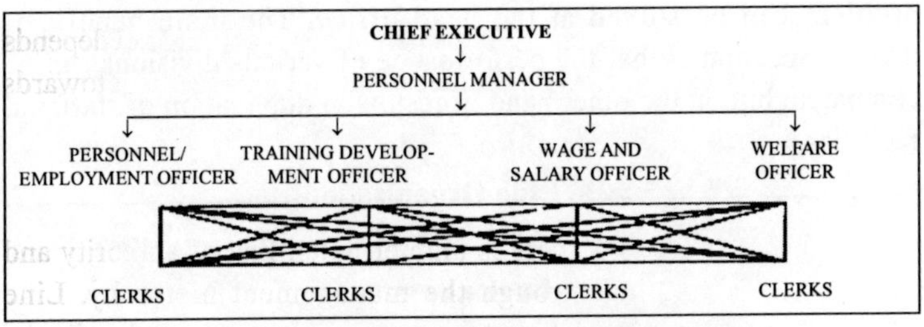

Personnel Department in Functional Organisation.

Personnel Department in Line and Staff Organisation

Large enterprises generally have organisation structures with both line and staff executives. Line and staff structure combines the advantages of both line organisation and functional organisation. Under this system, staff positions are attached to line executives.

Personnel department provides advice and assistance on personnel matters to all departments without undermining unity of command. In the following figure, line authority is shown by a straight line and staff authority by a dotted line.

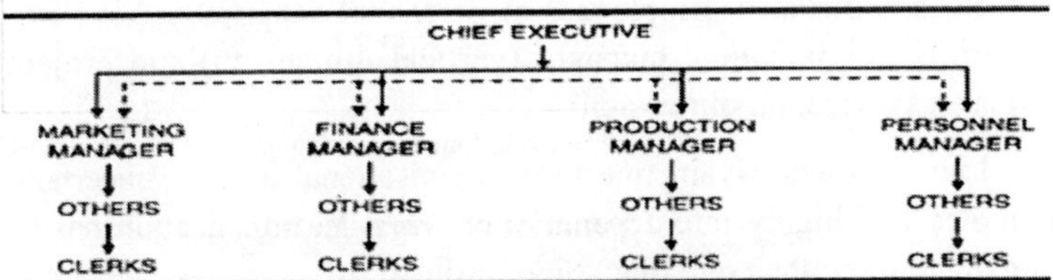

Personnel Department in in Line and Staff Organisation

Personnel Department in a Divisionalised Organisation Structure

The role of a personnel manager attached to the divisional office/ branch office of a decentralised organisation is particularly a difficult one. In a divisional organisation structure, personnel staffs are attached to divisional officers. The personnel officer at divisional level is responsible to the local divisional manager.

He is subordinate to the personnel manager at the head office. In case of rift between personnel officer and divisional manager, the problem can be solved at the head office. The main benefit of divisionalisation is that the performance of various divisions can be compared, but on the other hand, it results in duplication of staff and facilities.

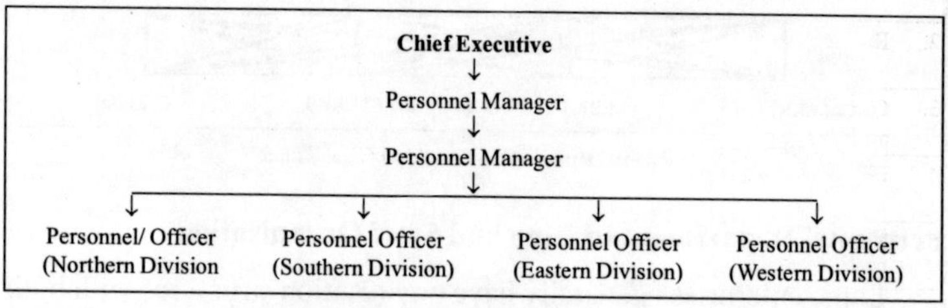

Personnel Department in Divisional Structure.

Personnel Department in a Matrix Organisation Structure

In a matrix organisation structure, every employee has two superiors i.e. they are under dual authority. One chain of command is functional and the other chain of command is a project team. Hence, matrix structure is referred to as a multi command system, both vertical and horizontal dimension.

Thus, the team of employees of personnel department have two superiors i.e. personnel manager (vertical dimension) and project manager (horizontal dimension).

Matrix structure is suitable when organisational tasks are uncertain, complex and highly interdependent or when an organisation has to cope with more than one function or project.

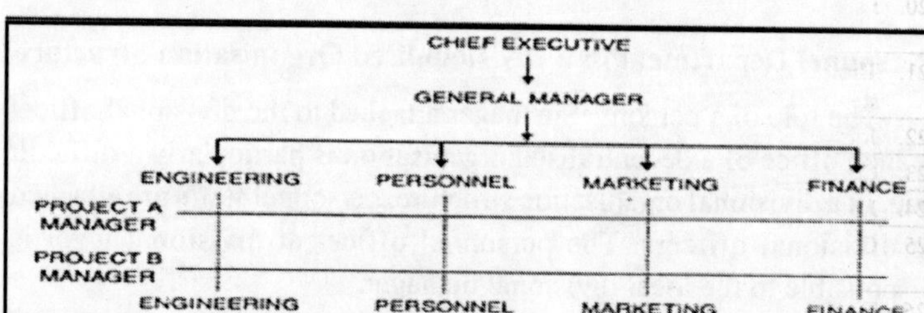

Personnel Department in a Matrix Organisation.

Difference between Personnel and IR and HRM

Dimensions	*Personnel and IR*	*HRM*
	Beliefs and Assumptions	
1. Contract	Careful delineation of written contracts	Aim to go beyond contract
2. Rules	Importance of devising clear rules/mutually	'Can-do'outlook; Impatience with 'rule'
3. Guide to management action	Procedures	Business-need
4. Behaviour referent	Norms/custom and practice	Values/mission
5. Managerial task vis-á-vis labour	Monitoring	Nurturing
6. Nature of relations	Pluralist	Unitarist
7. Conflict	Institutionalised	De-emphasised
	Strategic Aspects	
8. Key relations	Labour management	Customer
9. Initiatives	Piecemeal	Integrated
10. Corporate plan	Marginal	Central
11. Speed of decision	Slow	Fast
	Line Management	
12. Management role	Transactional	Transformational leadership
13. Key managers	Personnel/ IR specialists	General/business/line managers
14. Communication	Indirect	Direct
15. Standardisation	High	Low
16. Prized management skills	Negotiation	Facilitation
	Key Levers	
17. Selection	Separate, marginal task	Integrated, key task
18. Pay	Job evaluation	Performance-related
19. Conditions	Separately negotiated	Harmonisation
20. Labour-management	Collective bargaining contracts	Towards individual contracts
21. Thrust of relations with stewards	Regularised through facilities and training	Marginalised
22. Job categories and grades	Many	Few
23. Communication	Restricted flow	Increased flow
24. Job design	Division of labour	Teamwork
25. Conflict handling	Reach temporary truces	Manage climate and culture
26. Training and development	Controlled access to courses	Learning companies
27. Foci of attention for interventions	Personnel procedures	Wide ranging cultural, structural and personnel strategies

LINE AND STAFF

Personnel administration is a staff function. It provides only the advice to the line authority and assists the line executives in developing the personnel policies and procedures by providing necessary expert advice. It interprets the policies, procedures and programmes to different management levels of to deal effectively with their subordinates. Personnel manager is an advisor and not the executor.

Personnel Administration is a line authority. The administration of personnel is not the responsibility of the personnel manager. He can only advise the line executive and the line executive is responsible for formulating and executing the policies. But within the personnel department itself. Personnel manager has line authority overall the managers under him.

Harold Stieglitz has pinpointed three roles that staff personnel typically perform to assist line personnel:

1. **The Advisory or Counseling Role:** In this role, staff personnel use their professional expertise to solve organisational problems. The staff personnel are, in effect, internal consultants whose relationship with line personnel is similar to that of a professional and a client.
2. **The Service Role:** Staff personnel in this role provide services that can more efficiently and effectively be provided by a single centralised staff group than by many individuals scattered throughout the organisation. This role can probably best be understood if staff personnel are viewed as suppliers and line personnel as customers.
3. **The Control Role:** Staff personnel help establish a mechanism for evaluating the effectiveness of organisational plans.

JOB ANALYSIS

In simple terms, job analysis may be understood as a process of collecting information about a job. The process of job analysis results in two sets of data:

(i) Job description and

(ii) Job specification.

Specifically, job analysis involves the following steps:

1. Collecting and recording job information.
2. Checking the job information for accuracy.
3. Writing job description based on the information.
4. Using the information to determine the skills, abilities and knowledge that are required on the job.
5. Updating the information from time to time.

Job Description

Job description is an important document, which is basically descriptive in nature and contains a statement of job analysis. It provides both organisational information's (like location in structure, authority etc) and functional information (what the work is).

It gives information about the scope of job activities, major responsibilities and positioning of the job in the organisation. This information gives the worker, analyst, and supervisor with a clear idea of what the worker must do to meet the demand of the job.

Contents of Job Description

Following are the main content of a job description. It usually consists of following details or data. A statement containing items such as:

Job Identification or Organisation Position: This includes the job title, alternative title, department, division and plant and code number of the job. The job title identifies and designates the job properly. The department, division, etc., indicate the name of the department where it is situated and the location give the name of the place.

Job Summary: This serves two important purposes. Firstly, it gives additional identification information when a job title is not adequate; and secondly, it gives a summary about that particular job.

Job Duties and Responsibilities: This gives a total listing of duties together with some indication of the frequency of occurrence or percentage of time devoted to each major duty.

Relation to Other Jobs: This gives the particular person to locate job in the organisation by indicating the job immediately below or above in the job hierarchy.

Supervision: This will give an idea the number of person to be supervised along with their job titles and the extent of supervision.

Machine: It gives information about the tool, machines and equipment to be used.

Working Conditions: It gives us information about the environment in which a jobholder must work.

Hazards: It gives us the nature of risks of life and limb, their possibilities of occurrence, etc.

Job Specification

Job specification is a **written statement of qualifications, traits, physical and mental characteristics** that an individual must possess to perform the job duties and discharge responsibilities effectively.

Job Specification Information

The first step in the programme of job specification is to prepare a list of all jobs in the company and where they are located. The second step is to secure and write up information about each of the jobs in a company. Usually this information includes:

1. **Physical Specifications:** Physical specifications include the physical qualifications or physical capacities that vary from job to job. Physical qualifications or capacities include physical features like height, weight, chest, vision, hearing, ability to lift weight, ability to carry weight, health, age, capacity to use or operate machines, tools, equipment, etc.
2. **Mental Specifications:** Mental specifications include ability to perform, arithmetical calculations, to interpret data, information blueprints, to read electrical circuits, ability to plan, reading abilities, scientific abilities, judgment, ability to concentrate, ability to handle variable factors, general intelligence, memory, etc.

3. **Emotional and Social Specifications:** Emotional and social specifications are more important for the post of managers, supervisors, foremen, etc. These include emotional stability, flexibility, social adaptability in human relationships, personal appearance including dress, posture, etc.
4. **Behavioural Specifications:** Behavioural specifications play an important role in selecting the candidates for higher-level jobs in the organisational hierarchy. This specification seeks to describe the acts of managers rather than the traits that cause the acts. These specifications include judgments, research, creativity, teaching ability, maturity trial of conciliation, self-reliance, dominance, etc.

Methods of Job Analysis

Methods of collecting job analysis information include direct observation, work method analysis, critical incident technique, interview and questionnaire method. These are discussed below:

1. **Direct Observation Method:** Direct observation is a method of job analysis to observe and record behaviour / events / activities/tasks/duties when the worker or group engaged in doing the job. Observation method can be effective only when the job analyst is skilled enough to know what is to be observed and how to analyse what is being observed.
2. **Work Method Analysis:** Work methods analysis is used to describe manual and repetitive production jobs, such as factory or assembly-line jobs. Work methods analysis includes **time and motion study** and micro-motion analysis.
3. **Critical Incident Technique:** Critical incident technique is a method of job analysis used to identify work behaviours that classify in good and poor performance. Under this method jobholders are asked to describe critical incidents concerning the job and the incidents so collected are analysed and classified according to the job areas they describe.
4. **Interview Method:** Interview method is a useful tool of job analysis to ask questions to both incumbents and supervisors in either an individual or a group setting. Interview includes

structured interviews, unstructured interview, and open-ended questions.

5. **Questionnaire Method:** It includes six techniques, which are as follows:

   (a) Position Analysis Questionnaire (PAQ Model)

   PAQ model is a questionnaire technique of job analysis. It developed by McCormick, Jeanneret, and Mecham (1972), is a structured instrument of job analysis to measure job characteristics and relate them to human characteristics. It consists of **195 job elements** that describe generic human work behaviours.

   (b) Functional Job Analysis (FJA Model)

   FJA model is a technique of job analysis that was developed by the Employment and Training Administration of the United States Department of Labour. It includes seven scales. Out of seven scales, three worker-function scales: measure percentage of time spent with: data, people, things; one worker-instruction scale; and remaining three scales that measure reasoning, mathematics, and language.

   (c) Work Profiling System (WPS Model)

   WPS model is a questionnaire technique of job analysis. It is a computer-administered system for job analysis, developed by Saville & Holdsworth, Ltd.

   (d) MOSAIC Model

   MOSAIC model is a questionnaire technique of job analysis used to collect information from incumbents and supervisors. It contains 151 job tasks rated in terms of importance for effective job performance and 22 competencies rated in terms of importance, and needed proficiency at entry.

   (e) Common Metric Questionnaire (CMQ Model)

   CMQ model is a technique of job analysis that was developed by Harvey as a "worker-oriented" job analysis instrument designed to have applicability to a broad range of exempt and nonexempt jobs. It includes

41 general questions of background section, 62 questions of contacts with people, 80 items of decision-making, 53 items of physical and mechanical activities, 47 items of work setting.

(f) Fleishman Job Analysis System (FJAS Model)

FJAS model is a technique of job analysis that describes jobs from the point of view of the necessary capacities. It includes 52 cognitive, physical, psycho-motor, and sensory ability; each of the categories consists of two parts – an operational and differential definition and a grading scale.

MANPOWER PLANNING

Concept and Definition of Human Resource Planning

HRP is the process by which an organisation ensures that it has the right number and kinds of people, at the right places, at the right time and that these people are capable of performing their tasks effectively and efficiently. This helps the organisation to achieve its overall objectives.

According to Geisler, "Human resource planning is the process – includes forecasting, developing and controlling by which a firm ensures that it has –the right number of people, the right kind of people, at the right places, at the right time, doing work for which they are economically most useful."

According to Beach, "Human resource planning is a process of determining and assuming that the organisation will have an adequate number of qualified persons, available at the proper times, performing jobs which meet the needs of the enterprise and which provide satisfaction for the individuals involved."

Objectives of Human Resource Planning

Human Resource Planning is the process by which a management determines how an organisation should move from its current manpower position to its desired manpower position. Through it, management strives to have the right number and the right kind of people at the right places at the right time. The main objectives of Human Resource Planning are as follows:

(i) To make an inventory of present manpower resources;

(ii) Manpower planning is needed in order to identify areas of surplus personnel or areas in which there is shortage of personnel;

(iii) To forecast future manpower requirements;

(iv) Planning the necessary programmes of recruitment, selection, training and development to ensure that future manpower requirements are properly met;

(v) Human Resource Planning is essential because of frequent labour turnover that arises from social and economical factors like voluntary quits, marriage, promotions, etc;

(vi) The present workforce has to be changed in relation to the challenging needs of technology and production;

(vii) To facilitate productivity bargaining;

(viii) To meet the needs of expansion and diversification programmes;

(ix) To link human resource planning with organisational planning;

(x) To ensure higher labour productivity.

Levels of Human Resource Planning

Human resource planning may be prepared at the following four levels:

1. National Level

The Central Government makes human resource plans for the country as a whole. National level plan covers factors like population forecast, educational facilities, economic development programme, etc. Government uses population policy, family planning, education policy, etc. to create a match between the demand and supply of human resources.

2. Sectoral Level

Central and State Governments formulate plans for human resources for particular sectors, e.g., agricultural sector, industrial sector, service sector, etc.

3. Industry Level

Human resource plans for specific industries like textiles, iron, cement, etc. are prepared on the basis of projected output of the particular industry.

4. Unit Level

Human resource requirements of a particular enterprise are prepared at this level. These may be estimated department-wise, job category-wise, etc.

Process of Human Resource Planning

Human resource planning is a process consisting of five steps. These are analysing organisational plan, demand forecasting, forecasting supply of human resources, estimating human resource gaps and action planning. These are mentioned below:

1. **Analysing Organisational Plans:** First of all, the objectives of the company are analysed. Plans' relating to production, marketing, finance, mergers and acquisitions give an estimate of man power requirement of future work in an organisation. It is also necessary to decide the time horizon for which human resource planning is to be made. Our manpower planning must be consistent with organisational planning in order to achieve overall organisational objectives.
2. **Demand Forecasting:** The common demand forecasting techniques of manpower planning are managerial judgement, ratio trend analysis, work-study method, work force analysis, Delphi method, etc. These are discussed below:

   (a) **Managerial Judgement:** Managerial judgement technique is very common technique of demand forecasting. This approach is applied by small as well as large scale organisations. This technique involves two types of approaches i.e. 'bottom-up approach' and 'top-down approach'. Under the **'bottom-up approach'**, line managers send their departmental requirement of human resources to top management. Top management ultimately forecasts the human resource requirement for the overall organisation on the basis of proposals of departmental heads. Under the **'Top-down approach'**, top management forecasts the human resource requirement for the entire organisation and various departments. This information is supplied to various departmental heads for their review and approval. However, a combination of both the approaches i.e. **'Participative Approach'** should be applied for demand forecasting. Under this approach, top management and departmental heads meet and decide about the future human resource requirement.

(b) Ratio Trend Analysis: Under this method future ratios are calculated on the basis of calculated past ratio from past data of a company. Then on the basis of past ratios manpower requirement is estimated. The following example illustrates this method:

Example: Produced unit in 2009-10	60000 units
Workers worked 2009-10	60
Past ratio	60:60000 or 1: 1000
Estimated production in 2010-11	80000 units
Estimated number of workers in 2010-11	80000×1/1000=80

(c) Work-Study: In this method, standard time required per unit of work is determined with the help of time and motion study. This technique can be used when it is possible to apply work measurement to calculate the length of operations and the amount of labour required.

Example: Planned output for next year:	50000 units
Standard hours per unit:	2
Planned hours required:	50000×2 = 100000
Productive hours per worker in the year:	2000
Number of workers required =	100000/2000=50

(d) Work Force Analysis: All the employees may not be available throughout the year due to absenteeism and turnover. Therefore, it is very necessary to make some provision for loss of manpower to avoid the unwarranted situation. If from the work load analysis it is estimated that manpower requirement in a year is 1000, then the actual number of workers needed will be 1000 + 1000 ×.10 = 1100. Here 10 per cent has been taken as loss of manpower due to absenteeism and turnover.

(e) **Delphi Method:** It seeks estimates of personnel needs from a group of experts. The HRP experts act as intermediaries, summarise the various responses and report the findings back to the experts. Summaries and surveys are repeated until the experts opinions begin to agree. The agreement reached is the forecast of the personnel needs. There will be no interaction among experts.

(f) **Econometrics Models:** These models are based on mathematical and statistical techniques for estimating future demand. Under these models relationship is established between the dependent variable to be predicted (e.g. manpower/human resources) and the independent variables (e.g., sales, total production, work-load, etc.). Using these models, estimated demand of human resources can be predicted.

3. Supply Forecasting

There are mainly two sources where from organisation can get required number of human resources. These are internal source and external source. If the number of requirements is less then organisation can fulfill the vacant posts through internal source like promotion, transfer, demotion, etc. If the number of requirements is more then organisation can fulfill the vacant posts through external source of recruitment.

4. Estimating Manpower Gaps

Manpower gaps can be identified by comparing demand and supply of manpower after forecast. There may be surplus or deficit of human resources in future. Action plan has to be taken depending upon the situation.

5. Action Planning

Once the manpower gaps have been identified, plans are prepared to bridge these gaps. Plans to meet the surplus manpower may be redeployment, retrenchment, transfer, etc. On the other hand deficit can be checked by selection, promotion, etc.

Problems in HRP

The main problems relating to human resource planning are as follows:

1. Unbalanced Approach

Many human resource people give more emphasis on the quantitative aspects of manpower to ensure that there is adequate flow of people in and out of the organisation. They overlook the qualitative aspects like career planning and development, skills levels, moral, etc.

2. Expensive and Time Consuming

Human resource planning is an expensive and time consuming process. Employers may resist HRP feeling that it will increase the cost of manpower.

3. Management Information System

Effectiveness of human resource planning depends upon the reliability of the information system. In most of the Indian industries, human resource information system has not fully developed.

4. Resistance from Employees

Employees and trade unions resist manpower planning. They feel that this planning increase their overall workload and regulates them through productivity bargaining. They also feel that it would lead to wide spread unemployment.

5. Accuracy of Forecasts

If the forecast are not accurate, planning will not be accurate. Inaccuracy increases when departmental forecasts are merely prepared without critical review.

6. Support of Top Management

It requires full and wholehearted support from the top management.

In the absence of this support and commitment, it would not be possible to ensure the necessary resource and co-operation for the success of the human resource planning.

NEW CHALLENGES OF HRM

With the ongoing changes in Human Resources Management (HRM), it's important that managers, executives and HR employees, specifically, be aware of the challenges that today's HRM team may face. Some challenges are stated below:

1. **Workplace Diversity:** This may consist of issues involving age, education, ethnicity, gender, income, marital status, physical limitations, religion, sexual orientation, or any number of other things. Understanding the challenges that may be faced by the interaction of any of these diverse groups, as well as the required openness of the company toward such groups, will help HR personnel provide assistance in training employees to work with those they may consider "different," accept that such workers may be present in the business, and agree to treat each other respectfully, even if they never come to agree with each other over various issues.
2. **Change Management:** This is another challenge that HR departments are facing. Being able to deal with their own changing roles in corporate society, in addition to the changes to other jobs, the overlapping responsibilities, and more. Understanding that change is required is the first step toward accepting the change.
3. **Compensation and Benefits:** With a slow economy and tightening corporate purse-strings, the issue of compensation and employee benefits is one that almost every business must deal with. The key is to present mandatory changes in such a way that employees can accept, if not necessarily agree with them while providing non-monetary morale boosting incentives whenever possible to make the changes less traumatic.
4. **Recruiting Skilled Employees:** In an era of rising unemployment, it would seem that finding qualified workers would be

easier than ever. But that's seldom the case. Many industries are facing dire needs for employees with acceptable skills and the required training or degree. This applies not only to healthcare, but also to technology and other fields as well, causing many employers to search outside their local marketplace for workers who can do the jobs they need filled.

5. **Training and Development:** This is another challenge that HR managers and personnel must deal with more frequently. With the need to cut training costs, training itself often suffers. Yet the skills an employee needs must still be taught. Many companies are meeting this challenge by providing eLearning opportunities that allow employees to receive the training they need without the expenses associated with travel, on-site trainers, hours away from their jobs and high-priced materials.

RECRUITMENT AND SELECTION

Recruitment

Recruitment is the process of attracting qualified applicants for a specific job. The process begins when applications are brought in and ends when the same is finished. The result is a pool of applicants, from where the appropriate candidate can be selected.

According to Flippo, "Recruitment is the process of searching for prospective employees and stimulating and encouraging them to apply for jobs in an organisation."

In the words of Yoder, "Recruitment is a process to discover the sources of manpower to meet the requirements of the staffing schedule and to employ effective measures for attracting that manpower in adequate numbers to facilitate effective selection of an efficient working force."

Objectives of Recruitment

The objectives of recruitment are given below:

(i) To attract and encourage more candidates to apply in the organisation;

(ii) To create a talent pool of candidates to enable the selection of best candidates for the organisation;

(iii) To determine present and future requirements of the organisation in conjunction with its personnel planning and job analysis activities;

(iv) To link the employers with the employees;

(v) To increase the pool of job candidates at minimum cost;

(vi) To meet the organisation's legal and social obligations regarding the composition of its workforce.

Sources of Recruitment

Various sources of recruitment may be classified into two broad categories, namely internal sources and external sources.

Internal Sources: It is a recruitment which takes place within the concern or organisation. Internal sources consist of the following:

(a) **Transfers:** Employees are transferred from one department to another according to their efficiency and experience.

(b) **Promotions:** The employees are promoted from one department to another with more benefits and greater responsibility based on efficiency and experience.

(c) **Demotion:** Demotion of present employees according to their performance.

(d) **Retired and Retrenched Employee:** Retired and Retrenched employees may also be recruited once again in case of shortage of qualified personnel or increase in load of work.

(e) **Deceased and Disabled Employees:** The dependents and relatives of deceased employees and disabled employees are also done by many companies so that the members of the family do not become dependent on the mercy of others.

External Sources: External sources of recruitment have to be solicited from outside the organisation. External sources consist of the following:

1. **Advertising:** There is a trend toward more selective recruitment in advertising. This can be effected in at least two ways. First, advertisements can be placed in media read only

by particular groups. Secondly, more information about the company, the job, and the job specification can be included in the advertisement to permit some self-screening.

2. **Employment Agencies:** Additional screening can be affected through the utilisation of employment agencies, both public and private. Today, the public employment agencies in several States are well-regarded, particularly in the fields of unskilled, semi-skilled and skilled operative jobs. In the technical and professional areas, however, the private agencies appear to be doing most of the work. Many private agencies tend to specialise in a particular type of worker and job, such as sales, office, executive or engineer.

3. **Employee Referrals:** Friends and relatives of present employees are also a good source from which employees may be drawn. When the labour market is very tight, large employers frequently offer their employees bonus or prizes for any referrals that are hired and stay with the company for a specific length of time. Some companies maintain a register of former employees whose record was good to contact them when there are new job openings for which they are qualified. This method of recruitment, however, suffers from a serious defect that it encourages nepotism, i.e. persons of one's community or caste are employed, who may or may not be fit for the job.

4. **Schools, Colleges and Professional Institutions:** Offer opportunities for recruiting their students. They operate placement services where complete bio-data and other particulars of the students are available. The companies that need employees maintain contact with Guidance Counsellors of Employment Bureaus and teachers of business and vocational subjects. The prospective employers can review credentials and interview candidates for management trainees or probationers. Whether the education sought involves a higher secondary certificate, specific vocational training, or a college background with a bachelor's, masters' or doctoral degree, educational institutions provide an excellent source of potential employees for entry-level positions in

organisations. These general and technical/ professional institutions provide blue-collar applicants, white-collar and managerial personnel.

5. **Labour Unions:** Firms with closed or union shops must look to the union in their recruitment efforts. Disadvantages of a monopolistically controlled labour source are offset, at least particularly, by savings in recruitment costs. With one-fifth of the labour force organised into unions, organised labour constitutes an important source of personnel.
6. **Casual Applicants:** Unsolicited applications, both at the gate and through the mail, constitute a much-used source of personnel. These can be developed through provision of attractive employment office facilities and prompt and courteous replies to unsolicited letters.
7. **Professional Organisations or Recruiting Firms or Executive Recruiters:** These firms are looked upon as 'head hunters', 'raiders' and 'pirates' by organisations which lose personnel through their efforts. However, these same organisations may employ 'executive search firms' to help them find talent. These consulting firms recommend persons of high caliber for managerial, marketing and production engineers' posts.
8. **Indoctrination Seminars for Colleges Professors:** These are arranged to discuss the problem of companies and employees. Professors are invited to take part in these seminars. Visits to plants and banquets are arranged so that the participant professors may be favourably impressed. They may later speak well of a company and help it in getting the required personnel.
9. **Unconsolidated Applications:** For positions in which large numbers of candidates are not available from other sources, the companies may gain keeping files of applications received from candidates who make direct enquiries about possible vacancies on their own, or may send unconsolidated applications. The information may be indexed and filed for future use when there are openings in these jobs.

10. **Nepotism:** The hiring of relatives will be an inevitable component of recruitment programmes in family-owned firms, such a policy does not necessarily coincide with hiring on the basis of merit, but interest and loyalty to the enterprise are offsetting advantages.
11. **Leasing:** To adjust to short-term fluctuations in personnel needs, the possibility of leasing personnel by the hour or day should be considered. This practice has been particularly well-developed in the office administration field. The firm not only obtains well-trained and selected personnel but avoids any obligation in pensions, insurance, and other fringe benefits.
12. **Voluntary Organisations:** Such as private clubs, social organisations might also provide employees – handicaps, widowed or married women, old persons, retired hands, etc., in response to advertisements.
13. **Computer Data Banks:** When a company desires a particular type of employee, job specifications and requirements are fed into a computer, where they are matched against the resume data stored therein. The output is a set of resumes for individuals who meet the requirements. This method is very useful for identifying candidates for hard-to-fill positions which call for an unusual combination of skills.

Methods of Recruitment

Dunn and Stephen have broadly classified methods of recruitment into three categories:

(a) **Direct:** In this method, recruiters visit colleges and technical schools, e.g. Infosys, the Tata Group, Accenture, IBM, Siemens and several other companies maintain continuous relationship with institutions to hire students for responsible positions.

(b) **Indirect:** This involves advertising in newspaper, radio, T.V., journals etc. Advertising can be very effective if its media is properly chosen.

(c) **Third Party Methods:** This include use of commercial or private employment agencies, placement officials of schools, recruitment firms etc. Friends and relatives of present employees are also a good source from which employees may be drawn as part of the 'Buddy Referral' programmes.

Selection

Selection is the process of choosing the best candidate from the numbers of candidate. It is a process of collecting the all necessary information and matching the desired skills with the available skill. It is a process which helps to distinguish best candidate from the normal one. It comes after recruitment.

In the opinion of Koontz *et.al,* "Selection is the process of choosing from among the candidates from within the organisations or from the outside, the most suitable person for the current position or for the future position."

Selection Test

Tests may be classified as follows:

Aptitude Tests: These tests measure the latent ability of a candidate to learn a new job or skill. Such tests are of the following types:

Intelligence Test: This test measures the intellectual capacity of a person. It helps to determine a person's memory, reasoning skill, comprehension, perception, etc.

Mechanical Test: This test measures a person's capacity to learn a particular type of mechanical work. Capacity for spatial visualisation, specialised knowledge of techniques, problem-solving ability, technical vocabulary, etc. are judged in this test.

Psycho-motor Test: This test measures a person's ability to perform a specific job. It helps to determine mental dexterity or motor ability of a person.

Achievement Tests: These tests measure what a person can do. Such tests are of the following types:

Job Knowledge Test: These are used to judge proficiency in typing, shorthand, adding machines, dictating and transcribing machines, etc. Such tests are useful in the selection of typists, stenographers, office workers and the alike.

Work Sample Tests: In this test, a candidate is given a piece of work to perform in order to judge the efficiency of the candidate.

Personality Tests: These are used to judge the psychological make up of a person. These are of three types:

Objective Test: This test measures neurotic tendencies, dominance-submission and self confidence.

Projective Test: In this test, a candidate is asked to project his own interpretation on to a certain stimuli like ambiguous pictures, figures, etc. These ways he responds to these stimuli reflect his own values, motives and personality.

Situation Test: This test measures a candidate's reaction when placed in a peculiar situation. It determines the ability to undergrow stress and his demonstration under pressure.

Interest Test

This test determines a candidate's likes and dislikes in relation to work. This test is used to discover a person's areas of interest and to identify the kind of work that will satisfy him.

Process/Steps in Selection

1. **Preliminary Interview:** The purpose of preliminary interviews is basically to eliminate unqualified applications based on information supplied in application forms. The basic objective is to reject misfits. On the other hands preliminary interviews is often called a courtesy interview and is a good public relations exercise.
2. **Selection Tests:** Jobseekers who past the preliminary interviews are called for tests. There are various types of tests conducted depending upon the jobs and the company. These tests can be Aptitude Tests, Personality Tests, and Ability Tests and are conducted to judge how well an individual can perform tasks related to the job. Besides this there are some other tests also like **Interest Tests (activity preferences)**, **Graphology Test (Handwriting)**, Medical Tests, Psychometric Tests, etc.

3. **Employment Interview:** The next step in selection is employment interview. Here interview is a formal and in-depth conversation between applicant's acceptability. It is considered to be an excellent selection device. Interviews can be One-to-One, Panel Interview, or Sequential Interviews. Besides there can be Structured and Unstructured interviews, Behavioural Interviews, Stress Interviews.
4. **Reference and Background Checks:** Reference checks and background checks are conducted to verify the information provided by the candidates. Reference checks can be done through formal letters, telephone conversations. However, it is merely a formality and selections decisions are seldom affected by it.
5. **Selection Decision:** After obtaining all the information, the most critical step is the selection decision is to be made. The final decision has to be made out of applicants who have passed preliminary interviews, tests, final interviews and reference checks. The views of line managers are considered generally because it is the line manager who is responsible for the performance of the new employee.
6. **Physical Examination:** After the selection decision is made, the candidate is required to undergo a physical fitness test. A job offer is often contingent upon the candidate passing the physical examination.
7. **Job Offer:** The next step in selection process is job offer to those applicants who have crossed all the previous hurdles. It is made by way of letter of appointment.

Difference between Recruitment and Selection

Recruitment	***Selection***
1. Recruitment refers to the process of identifying and encouraging prospective employees to apply for jobs.	1. Selection is concerned with picking up the right candidates from a pool of applicants.
2. Recruitment is said to be **positive** in its approach as it seeks to attract as many candidates as possible.	2. Selection on the other hand is **negative** in its application in as much as it seeks to eliminate as many unqualified applicants as possible in order to identify the right candidates.

Selection Error

The False Positive Error

An organisation that makes a false positive error incurs three types of costs. The first type of costs are those incurred while the person is employed. These can be the result of production or profit losses, damaged public relations or company reputation, accidents due to ineptitude or negligence, absenteeism, etc. The second types of costs are those associated with training, transfer, or terminating the employee. Costs of replacing the employee, the third type of cost, include costs of recruiting, selecting, and training a replacement. Generally, the more important the job, the greater the costs of the selection error.

The False Negative Error

In the case of false negative error, an applicant who would have succeeded is rejected because failure was predicted. Most false negative selection errors go unnoticed, except when the applicant is a member of a protected class and files a discrimination charge. Costs associated with this type of error are generally difficult to estimate.

A situation in which the impact of both false positive and false negative selection errors can be detected and measured, however, is in professional sports such as football and basketball. Here, coaches and scouts analyse game films, physical statistics, scouting reports, and other data and decide whether they wish to draft a particular player. If they draft the player and his performance fails to meet expectations, a false positive selection error has occurred. Suppose, however, a team decides against drafting a player and another team chooses the individual. If the player subsequently turns out to be a star, the first team's rejection represents a false negative selection error.

PLACEMENT AND INDUCTION

Concept of Placement

Placement is a process of assigning a specific job to each of the selected candidates. It involves assigning a specific rank and responsibility to an individual. It implies matching the requirements of a job with the qualifications of the candidate.

In the words of Pigors and Myers, "Placement is the determination of the job to which an accepted candidate is to be assigned, and his assignment to that job. It is a matching of what the supervisor has reason to think he can do with the job demands. It is a matching of what he imposes in strain, working conditions, and what he offers in the form of payroll, companionship with others, promotional possibilities, etc."

Objectives of Placement

The objectives of placement are as follows:

(i) It improves employee morale.

(ii) It helps in reducing employee turnover.

(iii) It helps in reducing absenteeism.

(iv) It helps in reducing accident rates.

(v) It avoids misfit between the candidate and the job.

(vi) It helps the candidate to work as per the predetermined objectives of the organisation.

Concept of Induction

Once an employee is selected and placed on an appropriate job, the process of familiarising him with the job and the organisation is known as induction or orientation.

"Induction is the process of receiving and welcoming an employee when he first joins the company and giving him basic information he needs to settle down quickly and happily and starts work."

Objectives of Induction

An induction programme is designed to achieve the following objectives:

(i) To help the newcomer to overcome his shyness and overcome his nervousness in meeting new people in a new environment.

(ii) To give newcomer necessary information such as location of a café, rest period etc.

(iii) To build new employee's confidence in the organisation.

(iv) It helps in reducing labour turnover and absenteeism.

(v) It reduces confusion and develops healthy relations in the organisation.

(vi) To ensure that the newcomer do not form false impression and negative attitude towards the organisation.

(vii) To develop among the newcomer a sense of belonging and loyalty to the organisation.

WAGE AND SALARY ADMINISTRATION

Concept of Wage and Salary Administration

"One of the biggest factors affecting industrial relations is the salary or wage – the compensation an employee receives for a fair day's work".

Wage and Salary Administration is the group of activities involved in the development, implementation and maintenance of a pay system. It can also be called the ongoing process of managing a wage and salary structure.

Wage: Paid to blue-collar workers-paid daily, weekly or monthly-paid for the jobs which can, to some extent, be measured in terms of money's worth.

Salary: Paid to white collar workers-paid monthly-paid to employees whose contribution cannot be easily measured.

Compensation: A comparative term- includes wage and all other allowances and benefits like allowances, leave facilities, housing, travel and non-cost such as recognition, privileges and symbols of status.

Wage Concepts

The committee on Fair Wages (1948) and the 15th session of The Indian Labour Conference (1957) put forward certain Wage Concepts:

The committee on Fair Wages (1948) defined-

Minimum Wage

Fair Wage

Living Wage

Need-based Minimum Wage

Minimum Wages

It is the amount of remuneration, which is just sufficient to enable an average worker to fulfill all his obligations. It is applicable to workers across the country and is governed by the Minimum Wages Act 1948. The law states that an employer who cannot pay the minimum wage has no right to engage labour and no justification to run a firm. The current minimum wage in India is Rs 66 per day to all the workers in scheduled employment. It is revised every five yrs. The committee on Fair wage has defined minimum wage as " the wage must provide not merely for the bare sustenance of life, but for the preservation of the efficiency of the workers. For this purpose, minimum wage must provide some measures of education, medical requirements and amenities".

Fair Wages

Workers performing work of equal skills, difficulty or unpleasantness should receive equal or fair wages. The basis of fair wage is the minimum wage, within the capacity of the organisation to pay. Fair wage should be related to the productivity of the labour. It should match the prevailing rates of wages in the same or neighbouring localities. It should reflect the level of national income and its distribution. Fair wage, according to the committee on Fair Wage, is the wage which is above the minimum wage but below the living wage. Factors affecting the fair wage are as follows:

While the lower limit of the fair wage obviously is the minimum wage, the upper limit is equally set by what may broadly be called the capacity of industry to pay. Between these two limits the actual wage would depend on:

- The Productivity of Labour;
- The prevailing rates of wages;
- The level of national income and distribution;
- The place of the industry in the economy of the country.

Living Wages

It represents a standard of living which is provided not merely for a bare physical sustenance but decency, protection against ill-health, requirements of essential social needs and some insurance against the more important misfortunes including old age.

Living wages should enable the male earner to provide for himself and his family, not only the bare essentials of food, clothing and shelter, but also a measure of frugal comfort including:

(i) Education for the children;

(ii) Protection against ill-health;

(iii) Requirements of essential social needs;

(iv) A measure of insurance against the more important misfortunes including old age.

Need-based Minimum Wage

The minimum wage should be need-based and "should ensure the minimum human needs of the industrial worker, irrespective of any other consideration."

The basis for calculating need-based minimum wage is as follows:

(a) The standard working-class family taken to consist of three consumption units for one earner; earnings of women, children and adolescents should be disregarded.

(b) Minimum food requirements-net intake of 2700 calories for an average Indian adult.

(c) Clothing requirements- 18 yards per annum (Average worker's family of 4 = 72 yards/annum).

(d) Housing- minimum rent charged by Govt. in any area for houses provided under subsidised industrial housing scheme for low-income group.

(e) Fuel, Lighting and other miscellaneous items- 20 per cent of total minimum wage.

Objectives of Wage and Salary Administration

(i) The basic purpose of wage and salary administration is to establish and maintain an equitable wage and salary structure;

(ii) The secondary objective is to establish and maintenance of equitable labour-cost i.e. an optimal balancing of conflicting personnel interests so that satisfaction of employer and employee is maximised;

(iii) It is concerned with the financial aspects of needs, motivation and rewards. Managers, therefore, analyse and interpret the needs of their employees so that rewards can be individually designed to satisfy these needs;

(iv) To establish a fair and equitable remuneration offering similar pay for similar work;

(v) To attract qualified and competent personnel;

(vi) To retain the present employees by keeping wage levels in tune with competing units;

(vii) To control labour and administrative cost in line with the ability of the organisation to pay;

(viii) To improve motivation and morale of employees and to improve union management relations;

(ix) To project a good image of the company and to comply with legal needs relating to wages and salaries.

Factors Influencing Wage and Salary Structure and Administration

A sound wage policy is to adopt a job evaluation programme in order to establish fair differentials in wages based upon differences in job contents. Beside the basic factors provided by a job description and job evaluation, those that are usually taken into consideration for wage and salary administration are:

(1) **The Organisations Ability to Pay:** Wage increases should be given by those organisations which can afford them. Companies that have good sales and, therefore, high profits tend to pay higher those which running at a loss or earning low profits because of higher cost of production or low sales.

All employers, irrespective of their profits or losses, must pay no less than their competitors and need to pay no more if they wish to attract and keep workers. In the long run, the ability to pay is important.

(2) **Supply and Demand of Labour:** The labour market conditions or supply and demand forces operate at the national, regional and local levels, and determine organisational wage structure and level. If the demand for certain skills is high and supply is low, the result is a rise in the price to be paid to these skills. The other alternative is to pay higher wages if the labour supply is scarce; and lower wages when it is excessive. Similarly, if there is a great demand for labour expertise, wages rise; but if the demand for manpower skill is minimal, the wages will be relatively low. The supply and demand compensation criterion is very closely related to the prevailing pay, comparable wage and ongoing wage concepts since; in essence, all of these remuneration standards are determined by immediate market forces and factors.

(3) **Prevailing Market Rate:** This is known as the 'comparable wage' or 'going wage rate', and is the widely used criterion. An organisation compensation policy generally tends to conform to the wage rate payable by the industry and the community. This is done for several reasons. First, competition demand that competitors adhere to the same relative wage level. Second, various government laws and judicial decisions make the adoption of uniform wage rates as attractive proposition. Third, trade union encourages this practice so that their members can have equal pay, equal work and geographical differences may be eliminated. Fourth, functionally related firms in the same industry require essentially the same quality of employees, with same skill and experience. This results in a considerable uniformity in wage and salary rates. Finally, if the same or about the same general rates of wages are not paid to the employees as are paid by the organisation's competitors, it will not be able to attract and maintain the sufficient quantity and quality of manpower. Some companies pay on a high side of the market

in order to obtain goodwill or to insure an adequate supply of labour, while other organisations pay lower wages because economically they have to or because by lowering hiring requirements they can keep jobs adequately manned.

(4) **The Cost of Living:** The cost of living pay criterion is usually regarded as an automatic minimum equity pay criterion. This criterion calls for pay adjustments based on increases or decreases in an acceptable cost of living index. However, when living costs are stable or decline, the management does not resort to this argument as a reason for wage reductions.

(5) **The Living Wage:** Criterion means that wages paid should be adequate to enable an employee to maintain himself and his family at a reasonable level of existence. However, employers do not generally favour using the concepts of a living wage as a guide to wage determination because they prefer to base the wages of an employee on his contribution rather than on his need.

(6) **Psychological and Social Factors:** These determine in a significant measure how hard a person will work for the compensation received or what pressures he will exert to get his compensation increased. Psychologically, persons perceive the level of wages as a measure of success in life; people may feel secure; have an inferiority complex, seem inadequate or feel the reverse of all these. They may not take pride in their work, or in the wages they get. Therefore, these things should not be overlooked by the management in establishing wage rate. Sociologically and ethically, people feel that "equal work should carry equal wages 'that' wages should be commensurate with their efforts 'that' they are not exploited, and that no distinction is made on the basis of caste, colour, sex or religion. To satisfy the conditions of equity, fairness and justice, a management should take these factors into consideration.

(7) **Skill Levels Available in the Market:** With the rapid growth of industries business trade, there is shortage of skilled resources. The technological development, automation has

been affecting the skill levels at faster rates. Thus, the wage levels of skilled employees are constantly changing and an organisation has to keep its level up to suit the market needs.

Theories of Wage

Subsistence Theory: This theory was propounded by David Ricardo. Ricardo states that "The labourers are paid to enable them to subsist and perpetuate the race without increase or diminution". This theory is also known as "Iron Law of Wages". According to this theory, if the wage fall below the subsistence level, the number of workers would decrease as many of them would die of hunger, disease, malnutrition. This would make the wage rates go up as labour will become scarce. However, if the workers are paid more than the subsistence wages, they would marry and procreate. This would increase their number and bring down the rate of wages.

Wage Fund Theory: This theory was propounded by Adam Smith. According to him, wages are paid out of a pre-determined fund of wealth. If the fund is large, wages would be high; if it is small, wages would be reduced to the subsistence level.

Surplus Value Theory: This theory was propounded by Karl Marx. According to Marx, the price of any product was determined by the labour time needed for producing it. The labour was not paid in proportion to the time spent on work but subsistence wages which is much less and the surplus went to the capitalist.

Residual Claimant Theory: This theory was propounded by Francis A. Walker. According to Walker, there are four factors of production namely, land, labour, capital and organisation. Wages represent the amount of value created in the production which remains after payment of the other three factors of production namely, land, capital and organisation.

Marginal Productivity Theory: This theory was propounded by Henry Wicksteed and John Clark. According to this theory, workers are paid what they are economically worth. As long as each additional worker contributes more to the total value than the cost in wages, the employer will continue to hire workers. The employer will stop hiring when it becomes uneconomical for him to do so.

Bargaining Theory: This theory was propounded by John Davidson. According to this theory, wages are determined by the relative bargaining power of employers and employees. According to this theory, there is an upper limit and a lower limit on wage rates and the actual rates between these limits are determined by the bargaining power of the employers and the workers. The upper limit makes the highest wages the employers would be willing to pay, whereas, the lower limit indicates the minimum wages prescribed under the strength of resistance of the workers at the subsistence wages below which they will not available for work.

Demand and Supply Theory: Alfred Marshall, the chief exponent to this theory, explained the complexity of the economic world tried to provide a less rigid and deterministic theory. According to him, the determination of wages is affected by the whole set of actors which govern demand for and supply of labour. They demand price of labour, however, determined by the marginal productivity of the individual worker.

The Purchasing Power Theory: This theory was propounded by Keynes. According to him, wages are not only the cost of production for an employer but also incomes for the wage earners who constitute a majority in the total working population. A major part of the products of an industry is consumed by the same workers and their families. Hence, if the wage rates are high they will have more purchasing power, which would increase the aggregate demand for goods and the level of output. Conversely, if the wage rates are low, their purchasing power would be less, which would bring about a fail in the aggregate demand.

JOB EVALUATION

Job evaluation is the output given by job analysis. **Job analysis** illustrates the duties of a job, skills required, authority relationship, conditions of work, and extra pertinent information. Job evaluation in contrast, makes use of information in job analysis to assess each job, determining the relative job value and valuing its components.

In other words, it involves an organised and formal assessment of jobs so as to ascertain the value of one job in relation to another, consequently a wage or salary hierarchy results. It is a procedure by which jobs in an organisation are assessed.

When jobs are evaluated, the relative importance of a given set of duties and responsibilities to the organisation is assessed. This process is implemented to assist a management to uphold high levels of employee efficiency and employee contentment. If job values are not accurately studied, it is expected that jobs would not be correctly priced. When employees recognise that this is happening, they become discontented. They may leave the organisation, or trim down their efforts. Thus, in present world, a huge attention is paid to the worth of the job. According to the International Labour Office (ILO), "job evaluation is an attempt to determine and compare the demands which the normal performance of a particular job makes on normal workers, without taking into account the individual abilities or performance of the workers concerned".

In the words of Kimball and Kimball, "Job evaluation is an effort to determine the relative value of every job in a plant to determine what the fair basic wage for such a job should be".

Methods of Job Evaluation

Job evaluation is the systematic process of assessing and determining the value of jobs performed within the organisation and the relative value or worth of the employee's efforts. The four major methods of job evaluations are job ranking, job classification, factor comparison, and the point method.

Job Ranking: The job ranking method is the simplest and easiest job evaluation method; jobs and the employees who perform those jobs are ranked from highest to lowest depending on their quality and value to the organisation.

The variation in payment of salaries depends on the variation of the nature of the job performed by the employees. The ranking method is simple to understand and practice and it is best suited for a small organisation. Its simplicity, however, works to its disadvantage in big organisations because rankings are difficult to develop in a large, complex organisation. Moreover, this kind of ranking is highly subjective in nature and may offend many employees. Therefore, a more scientific and fruitful way of job evaluation is called for.

Job Classification: The job classification method uses job classes or job groups to provide more customisation in the evaluation. This method also uses scales to measure performance rather than comparing and ranking employees.

Factor Comparison: The factor comparison method is more scientific and complex than any other method. Each job is ranked according to a specific set of factors, such as physical effort, mental effort, or responsibility, all of which have predetermined weights indicating their importance to success.

The **steps** involved in factor comparison method may be briefly stated thus:

Select key jobs (say 15 to 20), representing wage/salary levels across the organisation. The selected jobs must represent as many departments as possible.

Find the factors in terms of which the jobs are evaluated (such as skill, mental effort, responsibility, physical effort, working conditions, etc.).

Rank the selected jobs under each factor (by each and every member of the job evaluation committee) independently.

Assign money value to each factor and determine the wage rates for each key job.

The wage rate for a job is apportioned along the identified factors.

All other jobs are compared with the list of key jobs and wage rates are determined.

Point Method: The point method measures performance through scales and job factors rather than focusing on entire job functions and ranking employees against each other. The point method is usually seen as the most reliable and valid evaluation method by employees compared to more subjective methods such as the job ranking method.

Example:

Conversion of Job Grade Points into Money Value

Point range	*Daily wage rate (Rs)*	*Job grades of key bank officials*
500-600	300-400	1. Officer
600-700	400-500	2. Accountant
700-800	500-600	3. Manager I Scale
800-900	600-700	4. Manager II Scale
900-1,000	700-800	5. Manager III Scale

METHODS OF WAGE PAYMENT

Time Rate System: It is one of the simplest and oldest methods of wage payment. Under it, remuneration is based upon the amount of time spent on the work. The wage rate increases with an increase in hours of work done and vice-versa. Here wages are calculated on hourly, daily, weekly, monthly or yearly basis and are usually prescribed in advance.

Piece Rate System: This method takes into consideration the efficiency of the workers. Under it, wages are based upon the amount of work done by the workers. The wage rate rises or falls with increase or decrease in the output of the worker. Here wage rates are prescribed per piece.

Incentive Wage Plan: It is the co-ordinated form of both the above mentioned methods for wage payment. Under it, the workers get additional wages based upon their efficiency in addition to the minimum guaranteed wages. Incentive wage rate rises or falls with increase or decrease in the quantity of production.

LINKING WAGES WITH PRODUCTIVITY

Payment Linked Wage System is a system which establishes a closer link between wages and productivity so as to enhance competitiveness. It ensures that wage increases commensurate with higher productivity increases.

GRIEVANCE HANDLING AND DISCIPLINARY ACTION

Grievance

A grievance is a sign of employee's discontent with job and its nature. The employee has got certain aspirations and expectations which he thinks must be fulfilled by the organisation where he is working. When the organisation fails to satisfy the employee needs, he develops a feeling of discontent or dissatisfaction. Thus, grievance is caused due to the difference between the employee expectation and management practices.

Breach defines grievances as "any dissatisfaction or feeling of injustice in connection with one's employment situation that is brought to the notice of the management".

Methods to Know the Existence of Grievance

Grievances can be uncovered in a number of ways. Gossip and grapevine offer vital clues about employee grievances. Gripe boxes, open door policies, periodic interviews, exit surveys could also be undertaken to cover the mystery surrounding grievances. These methods are discussed below:

Observation: A manager/ supervisor can usually track the behaviours of people working under him. If a particular employee is not getting along with people, spoiling materials due to carelessness or recklessness, showing indifference to commands, reporting late for work or is remaining absent- the signals are fairly obvious. Since the supervisor is close to the scene of action, he can always spot such unusual behaviours and report promptly.

Grievance Procedure: A systematic grievance procedure is best means to highlight employee dissatisfaction at various levels. Management, to this end, must encourage employees to use it whenever they have anything to say. In the absence of such a procedure, grievances pile up and erupt in violent forms at a future date. By that time things might have taken an ugly shape, impairing cordial relations between labour and management. If management fails to induce employees to express their grievances, unions will take over and emerge as powerful bargaining representatives.

Gripe boxes: A gripe box may be kept at prominent locations in the factory for lodging anonymous complaints pertaining to any aspect relating to work. Since the complainant need not reveal his identity, he can express his feelings of injustice or discontent frankly and without any fear of victimisation.

Open door policy: This is a kind of walk-in-meeting with the manager when the employee can express his feelings openly about any work-related grievance. The Manager can cross-check the details of the complaint through various means at his disposal.

Exit interview: Employees usually leave their current jobs due to dissatisfaction or better prospects outside. If the manager tries sincerely through an exit interview, he might be able to find out the real reasons why any employee is leaving the organisation. To elicit valuable information, the manager must encourage the employees to give a correct picture so as to rectify the mistakes promptly. If the employee is not providing fearless answers, he may be given a questionnaire to fill up and post the same after all his dues are cleared from the organisation where he is currently employed.

Opinion Surveys: Surveys may be conducted periodically to elicit the opinions of employees about the organisation and its politics.

Model Grievance Procedure

The Model grievance procedure suggested by the National Commission of Labour involves six successive time bound steps each leading to the next, in case of dissatisfaction. The aggrieved worker in the first instance will approach the foreman and tell him of his grievances orally. The foreman has to redress his grievance and if the worker is not satisfied with this redressal, he can approach the supervisor. The supervisor has to provide an answer within 48 hours. In the event of the supervisor not giving an answer or the answer not being acceptable to the worker, the worker goes to the next step. At this stage, the worker either alone or accompanied with his departmental representative approaches the Head of the Department who has to give an answer within three days. If the Department fails to give answer or if the worker is not satisfied with his answer, the worker may appeal to the Grievance Committee, consisting of the representatives of the employer and the employees. The recommendation of this Committee should be communicated to the Manager within seven days from the date of the grievance reaching it. Unanimous decisions, if any, of the Committee shall be implemented by the Management. If there is no unanimity, the views of the members of the Committee shall be placed before the Manager for decision. The Manager has to take a decision and the worker within three days.

The worker can make an appeal against the manager's decision and such an appeal has to be decided within a week. A Union official may accompany the worker to the manager for discussion and if no decision is arrived at this stage, both the union and management may refer the grievance to voluntary arbitration within a week of receipt of the management's decision. The worker in actual practice may not resort to all the above mentioned steps. For example, if the grievance is piqued because of his dismissal or discharge he can resort to the second step directly and he cán make an appeal against dismissal or discharge.

Discipline and Disciplinary Action

Types of Discipline

Action applied by managers:

1. Positive Discipline
2. Negative Discipline

These are discussed one by one

1. Positive Discipline

This is also called 'self-imposed discipline'. It involves creation of an atmosphere in the organisation through rewards, appreciation, incentive payment, promotion, constructive support etc. to motivate employees to work willingly to accomplish the set goals.

In essence, positive discipline emphasises the concept of self-discipline or self-control. Thus, it reduces the need for personal supervision to make employees conform to organisational rules, regulations, procedures and standards.

According to William R. Spriegel, "Positive discipline does not replace reason but applies reason to the achievement of a common objective. Positive discipline does not restrict the individual but enables him to have a greater freedom in that he enjoys a greater degree of self-expression in striving to achieve the group objective, which he identifies as his own'".

Evidences suggest that self-disciplined person tends to be a better worker than one who is not. Self-discipline, when developed from within, leads to building up morale and esprit de corps that is the desideratum of the time to run organisations successfully.

2. Negative Discipline

It is also called 'enforced discipline'. In case of negative discipline, employees are forced to obey orders and abide by rules and regulations that have been laid down, failing which penalties and punishment would be imposed on them. Thus, the objective of using punitive or coercive discipline is to ensure that employees do not violate rules and regulations formed by the organisation.

In other words, the purpose of negative discipline is to scare other employees and to ensure that they do not indulge in undesirable behaviour. It is worth mentioning here that negative discipline cannot eliminate the undesirable behaviour of the employees, but can merely suppress it.

Punishment is not pleasant. It causes resentment and hostility on the part of employees. That is why this kind of discipline results in only the minimum standards of performance on the part of employees. This is precisely the reason why it is rarely used in the organisations.

Because punitive discipline leads to resentment, it needs to be exercised in a progressive, sequential and chronological manner. A progressive system of discipline generally contains five steps, viz., an oral reprimand, a written reprimand, a second written warning, temporary suspension and dismissal or discharge.

Disciplinary Action

Though there is no rigid and specific procedure for taking a disciplinary action, the disciplinary procedure followed in Indian industries usually consists of the following steps:

Issuing a Letter of Charge: When an employee commits an act of misconduct that requires disciplinary action, the employee concerned should be issued a charge sheet. Charges of misconduct or indiscipline should be clearly and precisely stated in the charge sheet. The charge sheet should also ask for an explanation for the said delinquent act and the employee should be given sufficient time for answering this.

Consideration of Explanation: On getting the answer for the letter of charge served, the explanation furnished is considered and if it is satisfactory, no disciplinary action need be taken. On the contrary when the management is not satisfied with the employee's explanation there is a need for serving a show-cause notice.

Show-cause Notice: Show-cause notice is issued by the manager when he believes that there is sufficient prima-facie evidence of employee's misconduct. However, this gives the employee another chance to account for his misconduct and rebut the charges made against him. Enquiry should also be initiated by first serving him a notice of enquiry indicating clearly the name of the enquiring officer, time, date and place of enquiry, etc.

Holding of a Full-fledge Enquiry: This must be in conformity with the principle of natural justice, i.e. the employee concerned must be given an opportunity, of being heard. When the process of enquiry is over and the findings of the same are recorded, the Enquiry Officer should suggest the nature of disciplinary action to be taken.

Making a Final Order of Punishment: Disciplinary action is to be taken when the misconduct of the employee is proved. While deciding the nature of disciplinary action, the employee's previous record, precedents, effects of disciplinary action on other employees, etc., have to be considered. When the employee feels that the enquiry conducted was not proper and the action taken is unjustified, he must be given a chance to make an appeal.

Follow up: After taking the disciplinary action, a proper follow up action has to be taken and the consequences of the implementation of disciplinary action should be noted and taken care of.

Difference between Show Cause Notice and Charge Sheet

A Show Cause Notice is a statement which informs the delinquent employee of the acts alleged to have been committed by him and seeks his explanation in respect of them. It is a fact finding exercise. However, it does not strictly indict the employee of any misconduct or contain any statement of charges.

A Show Cause Notice enables the Disciplinary Authority to ascertain whether there is any prima facie case for conducting any enquiry into the matter or treat the matter as closed or dispose it with a minor penalty of censure or warning.

Whereas a Charge Sheet is a Statement of Imputations/Allegations and contains clearly spelt out charges quoting penal provisions of standing orders or service rules. The Show Cause Notice may form part of the Charge Sheet. The force of Charge Sheet is higher than the Show Cause Notice.

Hot Stove Rule

The "Hot-Stove Rule" of **Douglas McGregor** gives a good illustration of how to impose disciplinary action without generating resentment. This rule draws an analogy between touching a hot stove, and undergoing discipline. When you touch a hot stove, your discipline is immediate, with warning, consistent, and impersonal.

These four characteristics, according to McGregor, as applied to discipline are as follows:

1. When you touch the hot stove, you burn your hand. The burn was immediate. Will you blame the hot stove for burning your hand? Immediately, you understand the cause and effect of the offense. The discipline was directed against the act not against anybody else. You get angry with yourself, but you know it was your fault. You get angry with the hot stove too, but not for long as you know it was not its fault. You learn your lesson quickly.
2. You had warning as you knew the stove was red hot and you knew what would happen to you if you touched it. You knew the rules and regulations previously issued to you by the

company prescribing the penalty for violation of any particular rule so you cannot claim you were not given a previous warning.

3. **The discipline was consistent.** Every time you touch the hot stove you get burned. Consistency in the administration of disciplinary action is essential. Excessive leniency as well as too much harshness creates not only dissatisfaction but also resentment.
4. **The discipline was impersonal.** Whoever touches the hot stove gets burned, no matter who he is. Furthermore, he gets burned not because of who he is, but because he touched the hot stove. The discipline is directed against the act, not against the person. After disciplinary action has been applied, the supervisor should take the normal attitude toward the employee.

Unit-III

- Importance
- Evolution
- Functions
- Organisation of HRD Function
- Performance Appraisal
- Training and Development
- Quality of Work Life
- Career Planning
- Quality Circles
- Training Programmes for Workers
- Management Development Programmes
- Evaluation of Training

HRD Concept

Human resource development is a newly emerging field of study. HRD can be applied both for the national level and organisational level. HRD is mainly concerned with developing the skill, knowledge and competencies of people that can be acquired and developing the attitude, aptitude, beliefs, values that can be molded.

The concept of HRD was formally introduced by Leonard Nadler in 1969 in a conference organised by the America Society for Training and Development. Leonard Nadler defines HRD as, "those learning experiences which are organised for a specific time and designed to bring about the possibility of behavioral change". The term learning experience refers to purposeful or intentional learning not incidental learning.

Among the Indian authors T. Venkateswara Rao worked extensively on HRD. He defines HRD in organisational context as, "a process by which the employees of an organisation are helped in continuous and planned way to:

(i) Acquire or sharpen capabilities required to perform various functions associated with their present or expected future roles;

(ii) Develop their general capabilities as individuals and discover and exploit their own inner potentials for their own and/or organisational developmental purposes;

(iii) Develop an organisational culture in which superior-subordinate relationship, team work and collaboration among subunits are strong and contribute to the professional well-being, motivation and pride employees."

The analysis of the third definition shows that there are three aspects, viz:

(a) It is a motivational process. Employees of an organisation are helped or motivated;

(b) Acquire, develop and mould various aspects of human resources; and

(c) Contribute to the organisational, group, individual and social goals. It is called contributing factor.

The above three factors are called 'Enabling, helping and contributing factors' of human resource development.

Leonard Nadler introduced the term HRD in 1969. He defined HRD as "those learning expenses which are organised for a specific time and designed to bring about the possibility of behavioural change".

IMPORTANCE

Human resource is needed to be developed as per the change in external environment of the organisation, hence, HRD helps to adapt such changes through the development of existing human resource in terms of skills and knowledge.

The importance or significance of HRD can be explained as follows:

1. HRD Develops Competent HR

HRD develops the skills and knowledge of individual, hence, it helps to provide competent and efficient HR as per the job requirement. To develop employment's skill and competencies, different training and development programmes are launched.

2. HRD Creates Opportunity for Career Development

HRD helps to grasp the career development opportunities through development of human skills and knowledge. Career development consists of personal development efforts through a proper match between training and development opportunities with employee's need.

3. Employ Commitment

Trained and efficient employees are committed towards their jobs which is possible through HRD. If employees are provided with proper training and development opportunities, they will feel committed to the work and the organisation.

4. Job Satisfaction

When people in the organisation are well oriented and developed, they show higher degree of commitment in actual work place.

This inspires them for better performance, which ultimately leads to job satisfaction.

5. Change Management

HRD facilitates planning, and management of change in an organisation. It also manages conflicts through improved labour management relation. It develops organisational health, culture and environment which lead to change management.

6. Opportunities for Training and Development

Training and development programmes are tools of HRD. They provide opportunity for employee's development by matching training needs with organisational requirement. Moreover, HRD facilitates integrated growth of employees through training and development activities.

7. Performance Improvement

HRD develops necessary skills and abilities required to perform organisational activities. As a result of which, employees can contribute for better performance in an organisation. This leads to greater organisational effectiveness.

EVOLUTION OF HRD

In the early seventies two consultants Professor Udai Pareek and Professor T. V. Rao from the IIM were approached by L&T for a review exercise of their performance appraisal system. In 1974, the consultants studied the system and made recommendations for improving it. They felt that a development oriented performance appraisal system may not achieve its objectives unless accompanied by other sub-systems like employee counselling, potential appraisal, career planning and development, training, OD, etc. So, a new HRD system was introduced at L&T in the year 1975.

This was the first of its kind in India. The new system clearly established the linkages between the various personnel related aspects such as performance appraisal, employee counseling, potential appraisal, training, etc.

Today most of larger private and public sector organisations in India are using the techniques and approaches of HRD to develop their workforce for the attainment of organisation goals along with individual satisfaction and growth.

Evolution of HRD in a Chronological Sequence

Concept	*Description*
The Commodity Concept	Human resource was referred as 'a commodity' to be bought and sold. Wages were decided on the basis of demand and supply forces. Government also did not care much about the work force at that time.
The Factor of Production Concept	Labour is treated as any other factor of production, viz; money, material, land, etc.
The Goodwill Concept	Welfare measures like safety, first aid, lunch room, rest room, etc. These measures proved to be a source of boosting up the morale of workers, and enhancing their performance.
The Paternalistic Concept	Management must assume a fatherly and protective attitude towards employers. Paternalism does not mean merely providing benefits but it signifies to satisfy various needs of employees just as parents meet the requirements of the children.
The Humanitarian Concept	To improve the productivity, physical, social and psychological needs of workers must be fulfilled. Elton Mayo and some other along with him stated that money is less a factor in determining output, than group standards, group incentives and security.
	The organisation is a social system that has both economic and social dimensions.
The Human Resource Concept	Employees are the most valuable assets of an organisation. There should be a conscious effort to realise organisational goals by satisfying needs and aspirations of employees.
The Emerging Concept: HRD	Employees should be accepted as partners in the progress of a company. They should have a feeling that the organisation is their own. To this end, managers must offer better quality of working life and provide opportunities to people to exploit their potential fully. There should be opportunities for self-fulfillment in one's work.

Source: Rao, V.S.P. (2005), Excel Books, New Delhi.

FUNCTIONS

The main functions of HRD are:-

1. Training and Development

Training and development is aimed at improving or changing the knowledge, skills and attitudes of the employees. While training involves providing the knowledge and skills required for doing a particular job to the employees, developmental activities focus on preparing the employees for future job responsibilities by increasing the capabilities of an employee which also helps him perform his present job in a better way. These activities start when an employee joins an organisation in the form of orientation and skills training. After the employee becomes proficient, the HR activities focus on the development of the employee through methods like coaching and counselling.

2. Organisation Development

OD is the process of increasing the effectiveness of an organisation along with the well being of its members with the help of planned interventions that use the concepts of behavioural science. Both micro and macro changes are implemented to achieve organisation development. While the macro changes are intended to improve the overall effectiveness of the organisation the micro changes are aimed at individuals of small groups. Employee involvement programmes requiring fundamental changes in work expectation, reporting, procedures and reward systems are aimed at improving the effectiveness of the organisation. The human resource development professional involved in the organisation development intervention acts as an agent of change. He often consults and advising the line manager in strategies that can be adopted to implement the required changes and sometimes becomes directly involve in implementing these strategies.

3. Career Development

It is a continuous process in which individual progresses through different stages of career each having a relatively unique set of issues and tasks. Career development comprises of two distinct processes: Career Planning and career management. Whereas career planning involves activities to be performed by the employee, often with the help of counsellor and others, to assess his capabilities and skills in order to frame realistic career plan. Career management involves the necessary steps that need to be taken to achieve that plan. Career management generally focus more on the steps that an organisation that can take to foster the career development of the employees.

PERFORMANCE APPRAISAL

According to Flippo, a prominent personality in the field of Human resources, "performance appraisal is the systematic, periodic and an impartial rating of an employee's excellence in the matters pertaining to his present job and his potential for a better job." Performance appraisal is a systematic way of reviewing and assessing the performance of an employee during a given period of time and planning for his future.

Process of Performance Appraisal

The steps in the performance appraisal process are discussed below:

1. Establishing Performance Standards

The first step in the process of performance appraisal is the setting up of the standards which will be used to as the base to compare the actual performance of the employees. This step requires setting the criteria to judge the performance of the employees as successful or unsuccessful and the degrees of their contribution to the organisational goals and objectives. The standards set should be clear, easily understandable and in measurable terms. In case the performance of the employee cannot be measured, great care should be taken to describe the standards.

2. Communicating the Standards

Once set, it is the responsibility of the management to communicate the standards to all the employees of the organisation. The employees should be informed and the standards should be clearly explained to them. This will help them to understand their roles and to know what exactly is expected from them. The standards should also be communicated to the appraisers or the evaluators and if required, the standards can also be modified at this stage itself according to the relevant feedback from the employees or the evaluators.

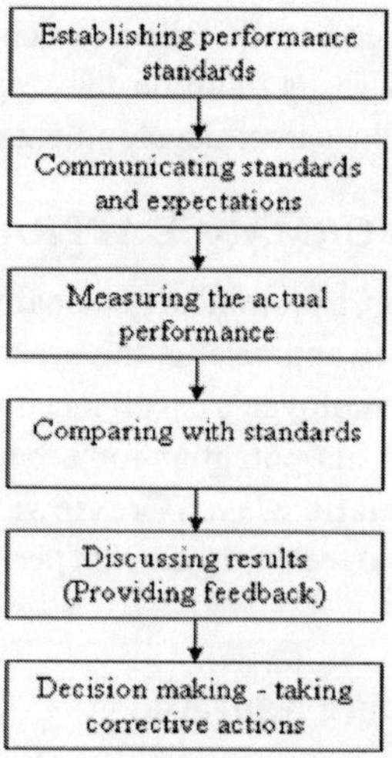

Performance Appraisal Process

3. Measuring the Actual Performance

The most difficult part of the performance appraisal process is measuring the actual performance of the employees that is the work done by the employees during the specified period of time. It is a continuous process which involves monitoring the performance throughout the year. This stage requires the careful selection of the appropriate techniques of measurement, taking care that personal bias does not affect the outcome of the process and providing assistance rather than interfering in an employees work.

4. Comparing the Actual with the Desired Performance

The actual performance is compared with the desired or the standard performance. The comparison tells the deviations in the performance of the employees from the standards set. The result can show the actual performance being more than the desired performance or, the actual performance being less than the desired performance depicting a negative deviation in the organisational performance.

It includes recalling, evaluating and analysis of data related to the employees' performance.

5. Discussing Results

The result of the appraisal is communicated and discussed with the employees on one-to-one basis. The focus of this discussion is on communication and listening. The results, the problems and the possible solutions are discussed with the aim of problem solving and reaching consensus. The feedback should be given with a positive attitude as this can have an effect on the employees' future performance. The purpose of the meeting should be to solve the problems faced and motivate the employees to perform better.

6. Decision Making

The last step of the process is to take decisions which can be taken either to improve the performance of the employees, take the required corrective actions, or the related HR decisions like rewards, promotions, demotions, transfers etc.

Errors in Performance Appraisal

The common errors in performance are as follows:

(i) Central Tendency Error

Some supervisors tend to rank all employees at about average, regardless of an employee's performance. A supervisor who believes in never rating an employee as excellent is demonstrating central tendency error.

(ii) Contrast Error

Supervisors who rate subordinates as they compare against each other rather than how they compare against the performance standards commit contrast error. This error can cause an employee who is performing average against performance standards to rate high because his peers are under performing.

(iii) False Attribution

False attribution is the tendency to attribute bad performance to internal causes and good performance to external causes.

In other words, if an employee performs well, it's because the employee had help, such as a good leader; and if the employee performs badly, it's because the employee did something wrong, such as procrastinate.

(iv) Halo Effect

The halo effect is when a supervisor forms a positive impression of an employee's skill in one area and then gives her high ratings across all rating criteria. Humans tend to view some traits as more important than other traits. When a supervisor rates employees with the traits that he deems more important higher in all rating areas than employees who do not possess those traits, the supervisor is committing the halo effect error.

(v) Leniency Error

Leniency error is the tendency of a supervisor to rate an employee higher than what his performance warrants. Reasons that a supervisor might do this could include avoiding confrontations, or feeling that by giving the employee a high rating, he will work harder to live up to the rating.

(vi) Perceived Meaning

Perceived meaning becomes an issue when appraisers do not agree on the meaning of the rating criteria. For example, one supervisor may perceive an employee's constant reporting of problems as initiative, while another supervisor may feel this behaviour demonstrates dependence on supervisory assistance instead of initiative.

(vii) Recency Error

Recency error happens when a supervisor uses recent events to rate the employee. This usually occurs due to a lack of documentation of the employee's performance over the course of the entire performance appraisal period. An employee who performed highly over the course of the appraisal period may be rated low if the most recent events where negative.

(viii) Severity Error

Severity error is the opposite of leniency error. In severity error, a supervisor tends to rate an employee lower than what her performance warrants. A potential cause of the error could be the use of unrealistic standards of comparison, such as the supervisor rating a new employee against himself. In this scenario, the supervisor forgets that it took time to reach the level of performance he operates at, and a new employee would not have had enough time to develop to that level.

(ix) Stereotyping

Stereotyping is the tendency to apply the same generalisations to all members of specific social groups. One of the more common types of stereotyping that occur in the workplace is gender stereotyping. Research conducted by Madeline Heilman, a Professor of Psychology at NYU, suggests that women are often evaluated more negatively than men, even when both are trained to do a job the same way.

(x) Horn Effect

In this case only the negative qualities of the employee are considered and based on this appraisal is done. This again will not help the organisation because such appraisal may not present a true picture about the employee.

(xi) Spillover Effect

In this case the employee is judged positively or negatively by the boss depending upon the past performance. Therefore, although the employee may have improved performance, he may still not get the benefit.

Methods of Performance Appraisal

As such, there is no single appraisal method accepted and used by all organisations to measure their employees' performance. All the methods of appraisal devised so far have been classified differently by different authors. A more widely used classification of appraisal methods into two categories, viz., traditional methods and modern methods, is given by Strauss and Sayles. The methods of performance appraisal can be classified into two categories: (i) Traditional methods and (ii) Modern methods.

(i) Traditional Methods: Traditional methods of performance appraisal are discussed below:

1. Essay Method

This traditional form of appraisal, also known as "Free Form method" involves a description of the performance of an employee by his superior. The description is an evaluation of the performance of any individual based on the facts and often includes examples and evidences to support the information. A major drawback of the method is the inseparability of the bias of the evaluator.

2. Straight Ranking Method

This is one of the oldest and simplest techniques of performance appraisal. In this method, the appraiser ranks the employees from the best to the poorest on the basis of their overall performance. It is quite useful for a comparative evaluation. The disadvantages of this method are that (i) the task of ranking is difficult when a large number of employees are rated, (ii) it does not tell that how much better or worse one is than another.

3. Paired Comparison Method

A better technique of comparison than the straight ranking method, this method compares each employee with all others in the group, one at a time. After all the comparisons on the basis of the overall comparisons, the employees are given the final rankings. One major disadvantage of this method is that the method can become unwieldy when large numbers of employees are being compared.

4. Critical Incidents Method

In this method of Performance appraisal, the evaluator rates the employee on the basis of critical events and how the employee behaved during those incidents. It includes both negative and positive points. The drawback of this method is that the supervisor has to note down the critical incidents and the employee behaviour as and when they occur.

5. Field Review Method

In this method, a senior member of the HR department or a training officer discusses and interviews the supervisors to evaluate and rate their respective subordinates. A major drawback of this method is that it is a very time consuming method. But this method helps to reduce the superiors' personal bias.

6. Checklist Method

The rater is given a checklist of the descriptions of the behaviour of the employees on job. The checklist contains a list of statements on the basis of which the rater describes the on the job performance of the employees.

7. Graphic Rating Scale

In this method, an employee's quality and quantity of work is assessed in a graphic scale indicating different degrees of a particular trait. The factors taken into consideration include both the personal characteristics and characteristics related to on the job performance of the employees. For example, a trait like Job Knowledge may be judged on the range of average, above average, outstanding or unsatisfactory.

8. Forced Distribution Method

This method was evolved by Tiffen to eliminate the central tendency of rating most of the employees at a higher end of the scale. To eliminate the element of bias from the rater's ratings, the evaluator is asked to distribute the employees in some fixed categories of ratings like on a normal distribution curve. The rater chooses the appropriate fit for the categories on his own discretion.

(ii) Modern Methods: Modern methods of performance appraisal are discussed below:

1. Assessment Centres

An assessment centre typically involves the use of methods like social/informal events, tests and exercises, assignments being given to a group of employees to assess their competencies to take higher responsibilities in the future. Generally, employees are given an assignment similar to the job they would be expected to perform if promoted. The trained evaluators observe and evaluate employees as they perform the assigned jobs and are evaluated on job-related characteristics.

The major competencies that are judged in assessment centres are interpersonal skills, intellectual capability, planning and organising capabilities, motivation, career orientation etc. assessment centres are also an effective way to determine the training and development needs of the targeted employees.

2. Behavioural Anchored Rating Scale

Behaviourally Anchored Rating Scales (BARS) is a relatively new technique which combines the graphic rating scale and critical incidents method. It consists of predetermined critical areas of job performance or sets of behavioural statements describing important job performance qualities as good or bad (for example, the qualities like inter personal relationships, adaptability and reliability, job knowledge etc). These statements are developed from critical incidents.

In this method, an employee's actual job behaviour is judged against the desired behaviour by recording and comparing the behaviour with BARS. Developing and practicing BARS requires expert knowledge.

A behaviourally anchored rating scale is a rating scale that is anchored with specific behavioural examples of good or poor performance. Because of the anchors, which are based on the dimensions of performance illustrated by critical incidents, a BARS combines the benefits of narratives, critical incident, and quantified scales. There are five steps required for developing a BARS. Each step is explained below.

Step 1: Generate critical incidents: In this step, people who know the job are asked to describe specific illustrations of effective and ineffective performance.

Step 2: Develop performance dimensions: The people who know the job are then asked to cluster the incidents into a smaller set of performance dimensions and to define each dimension with a name.

Step 3: Reallocate incidents: Another group of people, who also know the job, should reallocate the original critical incidents. They will receive the cluster definitions and the list of critical incidents. They will then reassign each incident into the cluster they think it fits best. If the assignments made by the first group and second group match well, then that critical incident is retained.

Step 4: Scale the incidents: The second group then rates the behaviour described by the incident as to how effectively or ineffectively it represents performance on the dimension.

Step 5: Develop a final instrument: Six or seven of the incidents as the dimension's behavioural anchors.

3. Human Resource Accounting Method

Human resources are valuable assets for every organisation. Human resource accounting method tries to find the relative worth of these assets in the terms of money. In this method the Performance appraisal of the employees is judged in terms of cost and contribution of the employees. The cost of employees include all the expenses incurred on them like their compensation, recruitment and selection costs, induction and training costs etc whereas their contribution includes the total value added (in monetary terms). The difference between the cost and the contribution will be the performance of the employees. Ideally, the contribution of the employees should be greater than the cost incurred on them.

4. 360° Performance Appraisal Method

360 degree feedback, also known as 'multi-rater feedback', is the most comprehensive appraisal where the feedback about the employees' performance comes from all the sources that come in contact with the employee on his job.

360 degree respondents for an employee can be his/her peers, managers (i.e. superior), subordinates, team members, customers, suppliers/ vendors - anyone who comes into contact with the employee and can provide valuable insights and information or feedback regarding the "on-the-job" performance of the employee.

360 degree appraisal has four integral components:

1. Self appraisal
2. Superior's appraisal

3. Subordinate's appraisal
4. Peer appraisal.

Self appraisal gives a chance to the employee to look at his/her strengths and weaknesses, his achievements, and judge his own performance. Superior's appraisal forms the traditional part of the 360 degree performance appraisal where the employees' responsibilities and actual performance is rated by the superior. Subordinates appraisal gives a chance to judge the employee on the parameters like communication and motivating abilities, superior's ability to delegate the work, leadership qualities etc. Also known as internal customers, the correct feedback given by peers can help to find employees' abilities to work in a team, co-operation and sensitivity towards others.

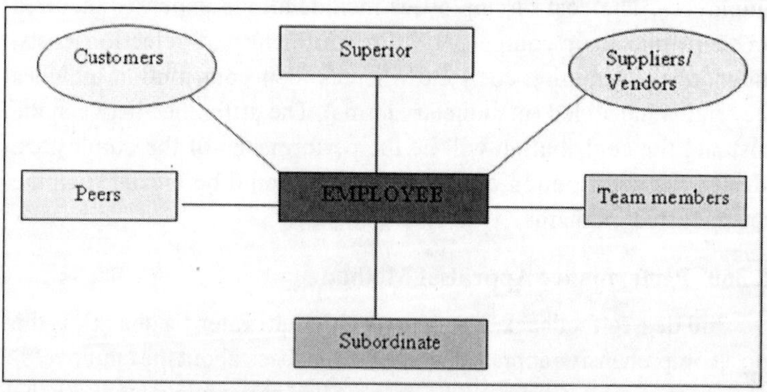

360 degree Performance Appraisal Technique

Self-assessment is an indispensable part of 360 degree appraisals and therefore 360 degree Performance appraisal have high employee involvement and also have the strongest impact on behaviour and performance. It provides a "360-degree review" of the employees' performance and is considered to be one of the most credible performance appraisal methods. 360 degree performance appraisal is also a powerful developmental tool because when conducted at regular intervals (say yearly) it helps to keep a track of the changes others' perceptions about the employees. A 360 degree appraisal is generally found more suitable for the managers as it helps to assess their leadership and managing styles. This technique is being effectively used across the globe for performance appraisals. Some of the organisations following it are Wipro, Infosys, and Reliance Industries etc.

5. Management by Objectives Method

According to George Odiome, MBO is "a process whereby superior and subordinate managers of an Organisation jointly define its common goals, define each individual's major areas of responsibility in terms of results expected of him and use these measures as guides for operating the unit and assessing the contribution of each of its members." According to John Humble, MBO is "a dynamic system which seeks to integrate the company's needs to clarify and achieve its profits and growth goals with the manager's need to contribute and develop himself. It is a demanding and rewarding style of managing a business."

6. 720° Performance Appraisal Method

In this system, we provide a feedback after the original / main 360 degree appraisal. This is only performed in exceptional cases. Some managers feel that doing "one" comprehensive 360 degree is not complete in itself in some cases.

These managers feel that an effective procedure to measure improvements and receive feedback is essential for the success of an appraisal.

This gives a pre- and a post-intervention results. The pre-intervention results set the baseline. The development programme is then carried out to improve the participants' behaviour through training / development/ education.

The post-intervention appraisal then shows the amount of improvement in the participant. This pre- and post-intervention in the performance appraisal system is the 720 degree system.

Training and Development

The major differences between training and development are as under:

1. Training is a learning process for new employees in which they get to know about the key skills required for the job. Development is the training process for the existing employees for their all round development.
2. Training is a short-term process i.e. three to six months, but development is a continuous process, and so it is for the long term.
3. Training focuses on developing skill and knowledge for the current job. Unlike, the development which focuses on the building knowledge, understanding and competencies for overcoming with future challenges.
4. Training has a limited scope; it is specific job oriented. On the other hand, development is career oriented and hence its scope is comparatively wider than training.
5. In training, the trainees get a trainer who instructs them at the time of training. In contrast to development, in which the manager self-directs himself for the future assignments.
6. Many individuals collectively attend the training programme. Development is a self-assessment procedure, and hence, one person himself is responsible for one's development.

QUALITY OF WORK LIFE

According to J. Richard and J. Loy, "QWL is the degree to which members of a work organisation are able to satisfy important personal needs through their experiences in the organisation".

While the task force set in 1979 by the American Society for Training and Development [ASTD] defined QWL as a process of work organisation which enables its members at all levels of to actively participate in shaping the organisation's environments, methods and outcomes. This value-based process is aimed towards meeting the twin goals of enhanced effectiveness of organisation and improved quality of life at work for employees. Quality of work life efforts are systematic efforts made by an organisation to give its employees a greater opportunity to affect the way in which they do their jobs and the contributions they make to the overall effectiveness of their organisation.

Richard E. Walton explains quality of work life in terms of eight broad conditions of employment that constitute desirable quality of work life (QWL). He proposed the same criteria for measuring QWL. Those conditions/criteria include:

1. Adequate and fair compensation.
2. Safe and healthy working condition.
3. Opportunity to use and develop human capacities.
4. Opportunity for career growth.
5. Social integration in the work force.
6. Constitutionalism in the work organisation.
7. Work and quality of life and
8. Special relevance of work.

(i) Adequate and Fair Compensation: There are different opinions about adequate compensation. The committee on Fair Wages defined fair wage as "the wage which is above the minimum wage, but below the living wage."

(ii) Safe and Healthy Working Conditions: Most of the organisations provide safe and healthy working conditions due to humanitarian requirements and/or legal requirements. In fact, these conditions are a matter or enlightened self interest.

(iii) Opportunity to Use and Develop Human Capacities: Contrary to the traditional assumptions, QWL is improved "to the extent that the worker can exercise more control over his or her work, and the degree to which the job embraces and entire meaningful task" but not a part of it. Further, QWL provides for opportunities like autonomy in work and participation in planning in order to use human capabilities.

(iv) Opportunity for Career Growth: Opportunities for promotions are limited in case of all categories of employees either due to educational barriers or due to limited openings at the higher level. QWL provides future opportunity for continued growth and security by expanding one's capabilities, knowledge and qualifications.

(v) Social Integration in the Work Force: Social integration in the work force can be established by creating freedom from prejudice, supporting primary work groups, a sense of community and inter-personnel openness, egalitarianism and upward mobility.

(vi) Constitutionalism in the Work Organisation: QWL provides constitutional protection to the employees only to the level of desirability as it hampers workers. It happens because the management's action is challenged in every action and bureaucratic procedures need to be followed at that level. Constitutional protection is provided to employees on such matters as privacy, free speech, equity and due process.

(vii) Work and Quality of Life: QWL provides for the balanced relationship among work, non-work and family aspects of life. In other words family life and social life should not be strained by working hours including overtime work, work during inconvenient hours, business travel, transfers, vacations etc.

(viii) Social Relevance of Work: QWL is concerned about the establishment of social relevance to work in a socially beneficial manner. The workers' self esteem would be high if his work is useful to the society and the vice versa is also true.

CAREER PLANNING

Career planning is the process by which one selects career goals and the path to these goals. The major focus of career planning is on assisting the employees achieve a better match between personal goals and the opportunities that are realistically available in the organisation.

Career planning seeks to meet the following objectives:

(i) Attract and retain talent by offering careers, not jobs.

(ii) Use human resources effectively and achieve greater productivity.

(iii) Reduce employee turnover.

(iv) Improve employee morale and motivation.

(v) Meet the immediate and future human resource needs of the organisation on a timely basis.

The SODI Career Planning Model

Given the complexity of career development and the fluidity of the world of work, we need to be able to navigate our career paths with purpose and clarity.

Law and Watts (1977) devised a simple model of career education which has stood the test of time. This model has been changed slightly to become a career planning, rather than a career education model and named the **SODI model** where the last element is 'implementation' rather than 'transition learning', and 'decision learning' becomes 'decision making and planning'.

The model encapsulates four concepts which are:

Self-awareness –Individual having knowledge about and understanding of their own personal development. Self-awareness in a careers context involves an understanding of kind of personal resources (both actual and potential) they bring to world.

Opportunity awareness–An understanding of the general structures of the world of work, including career possibilities and alternative pathways.

Decision making and planning–An understanding of how to make career decisions, and being aware of pressures, influences, styles, consequences and goal setting.

Implementing plans–Having the appropriate skill level in a range of areas to be able to translate job and career planning into reality.

QUALITY CIRCLES

Quality circles were first developed in **Japan** in the early **sixties.** A quality circle is a voluntary participatory form. It is small group of employees in the same work area or doing similar type of work who voluntarily meets regularly for about an hour every week to identify, analyse and resolve work related problems not only to improve quality, productivity and the total performance of the organisation but also to enrich the quality of work life of employees. It is constant improvement programme and motivational technique.

The concept behind quality circles is widely believed to have been developed in **Japan in 1962** by **Kaoru Ishikawa** as a method to improve quality, though it is also argued that the practice started with the United States Army soon after 1945, whilst restoring the war torn nation, and the Japanese adopted and adapted the concept and its application.

The concept of quality circle which was originated in the United States and actually proliferated in Japan is of recent origin in India. In India, by now several companies have implemented QC programmes.

Quality Circle concept was first introduced by BHEL, Ramachandrapuram Hyderabad in the year 1981 in India with the initiation of Mr. S.R. Udpa - GM-Operations.

Companies where the QC programmes have been working successfully include BHEL, Kirloskar Oil Engines, Mahindra & Mahindra, Bajaj Auto, HMT, Maruti, Modi Xerox. SBI, Hindustan Aluminum, Modi Rubber, TELCO, LUCAS-TVS, etc.

Problem Solving Tools Used by Quality Circles

- Brainstorming
- Pareto analysis
- Cause and effect diagram (or fish bone diagram or Ishikawa diagram)

Important Terms related to Quality

BPM

Stands for Business Process Management. BPM is a business improvement strategy based on documenting, analysing, and redesigning processes for greater performance.

DMAIC

A Six Sigma quality improvement strategy described by five phases: Define, Measure, Analyse, Improve, and Control.

ERP

Stands for Enterprise Resource Planning.

ISO

ISO organisation as a way to certify the quality control systems of companies across international boundaries.

JIT

Just-in-time is the cornerstone philosophy of Lean Manufacturing and MRP. Using the just-in-time philosophy, raw materials arrive no earlier than they are required to reduce costs and inefficiencies associated with large inventory.

Kaizen

A Japanese quality improvement philosophy named after the phrase "continuous improvement." Kaizen aims to create a quality-oriented culture that permeates all levels of the business from manufacturing to management and aims to improve the organisation in small increments from the ground up.

Lean Manufacturing

A quality methodology focused on eliminating all waste from the manufacturing process.

MRP

Stands for Material Requirements Planning.

QFD

Stands for Quality Function Deployment. The goal of QFD is to prioritise and translate customer needs into technical requirements for engineers, and deliver a quality product or service that aims to satisfy the customer.

Six Sigma

A statistically driven quality management methodology that aims to reduce defects and variation in a business process. In fact, the goal of any Six Sigma initiative is to reduce to the number of defects to

3.4 per one million opportunities thereby increasing customer satisfaction and business profits. Six Sigma was first developed and implemented by Motorola in the 1980s.

There are two main strategies that divide the Six Sigma initiative into five distinct phases: DMAIC and DMADV.

Zero Defects

A practice that aims to reduce defects as a way to directly increase profits. The concept of zero defects lead to the development of Six Sigma in the 1980s.

TQM processes are divided into four sequential categories: plan, do, check, and act (the PDCA cycle). In the planning phase, people define the problem to be addressed, collect relevant data, and ascertain the problem's root cause; in the doing phase, people develop and implement a solution, and decide upon a measurement to gauge its effectiveness; in the checking phase, people confirm the results through before-and-after data comparison; in the acting phase, people document their results, inform others about process changes, and make recommendations for the problem to be addressed in the next PDCA cycle.

W. Edwards Deming, Joseph M. Juran, and Armand V. Feigenbaum jointly developed the concept of total quality management.

TRAINING PROGRAMMES FOR WORKERS

Training is a process of learning a sequence of programmed behaviour. It is the application of knowledge and gives people an awareness of rules and procedures to guide their behaviour. It helps in bringing about positive change in the knowledge, skills and attitudes of employees.

According to Jucious, "training is any process by which the aptitudes, skills and abilities of employees to perform specific jobs are increased".

Training plays a significant role in human resource development. The most widely used methods of training used by organisations are classified into two categories: on the job training and off the job training.

On the Job Training

On the job training methods are those which are given to the employees within the everyday working of a concern. It is a simple and cost-effective training method. The inproficient as well as semi-proficient employees can be well trained by using such training method. The employees are trained in actual working scenario. The motto of such training is "learning by doing." Instances of such on-job training methods are job-rotation, coaching, temporary promotions, etc.

1. Coaching

Coaching is learning by doing. In this, the superior guides his sub-ordinates and gives him/her job instructions. The superior points out the mistakes and gives suggestions for improvement.

2. Job Rotation

In this method, the trainees move from one job to another, so that he/she should be able to perform all types of jobs. For ecample, in banking industry, employees are trained for both back-end and front-end jobs. In case of emergency, (absenteeism or resignation), any employee would be able to perform any type of job.

3. Special Projects

Under this method, a trainee is assigned a project that is closely related to the objectives of his department. The trainee will study the problem and make recommendations upon it.

4. Committee Assignments

Under this method, an adhoc committee is constituted and is assigned a subject to discuss and make recommendations. The committee will make a study of the problem and present its suggestions to the departmental head.

Off the Job Training

Off the job training methods are those in which training is provided away from the actual working condition. It is generally used in case of new employees. Instances of off the job training methods are workshops, seminars, conferences, etc. Such method is costly and is effective if and only if large number of employees have to be trained within a short time period. Off the job training is also called as vestibule training, i.e., the employees are trained in a separate area (may be a hall, entrance, reception area, etc. known as a vestibule) where the actual working conditions are duplicated. These are stated below:

1. Role Playing

It is just like acting out a given role as in a stage play. In this method of training, the trainees are required to enact defined roles on the basis of oral or written description of a particular situation. Role playing is a useful method of developing interpersonal or human relations skills. It helps to bring out desired changes in attitudes and behaviour. Role playing creates an environment similar to real work situation. This is also known as simulation. Two other methods based on simulation are in basket and management games.

2. In Basket Exercise

In this method, the trainee is given a basket or tray of papers related to his functional area. Trainee is expected to give his recommendations after studying all papers. The recommendations of different trainees are compared and conclusions are arrived at.

3. Management Games

Management games are designed to be representative of real life situations. These are classroom exercise in which teams of individuals compete against one another in order to achieve a given objective. In these exercises, the participants play a dynamic role and enrich their skills through involvement and simulated exercise.

4. Sensitivity Training

This method is also called T-Group training. The purpose of this method is to develop interpersonal competence, increase self awareness and sharpen teamwork skills. According to Chris Argyris, "sensitivity training is a group experience designed to provide maximum possible opportunity for the individuals to expose their behaviour, give and receive feedback, experiment with new behaviour and develop awareness of self and of others".

5. Lectures or Conferences

This approach is well adapted to convey specific information, rules, procedures or methods. This method is useful, where the information is to be shared among a large number of trainees. The cost per trainee is low in this method.

6. Case Study Method

It presents an in-depth description of a particular problem an employee might encounter on the job. The employee attempts to find and analyse the problem, evaluate alternative courses of action and decide what course of action would be most satisfactory.

Identifying Training Needs

In order to identify training needs, the gap between the existing and required levels of knowledge, skills, performance and aptitudes should be specified. Training needs can be identified through the following types of analysis.

1. Organisational Analysis

It involves a study of the entire organisation in terms of its objectives, its resources and the utilisation of these resources in order to achieve stated objectives and its interaction pattern with environment. The important elements that are closely examined in this connection are:

(a) Analysis of Objectives

This is a study of short-term and long-term objectives and the strategies followed at various levels to meet these objectives.

(b) Resource Utilisation Analysis

How the various organisational resources are put to use is the main focus of this study. The contributions of various departments are also examined by establishing efficiency indices for each unit. This is done to find out comparative labour cost, whether a unit is under manned or over manned.

(c) Environmental Scanning

Here the economic, political, socio-cultural and technological environment of the organisation is examined.

(d) Organisational Climate Analysis

The climate of an organisation speaks about the attitudes of members towards work, company policies, supervisors, etc. Absenteeism, turnover ratios generally reflect the prevailing employee attitudes.

2. Task Analysis

This is a detailed examination of a job, its components, its various operations and conditions under which it has to be performed. The focus is given on the roles played by an individual and the training needed to perform such roles. The objective is to find out how the various tasks be performed and what kind of skills, knowledge and attitudes are needed to the job needs. Questionnaire, interviews, reports, tests and observation method are generally used to collect job-related information from time to time.

3. Manpower Analysis

Here the focus is on the individual in a given job. There are three issues to be resolved through manpower analysis. First, we try to find whether performances are satisfactory and training is required. Second, whether the employee is capable of being trained and the specific areas in which training is required. Finally, we need to state whether poor performances on the job need to be replaced by those who can do the job. Other options to training such as modifications in the job or processes should also be looked into. Personal observation, performance reviews, supervisory reports, diagnostic tests help in collecting the required information and select particular training options that try to improve the performance of individual workers.

MANAGEMENT DEVELOPMENT PROGRAMMES

Management development: Any attempt to improve current or future management performance by imparting knowledge, changing attitudes, or increasing skills. The ultimate aim is of course, to enhance the future performance of the company itself.

Managerial On-The-Job Training

Job Rotation: A management training technique that involves moving a trainee from department to department to broaden his or her experience and identify strong and weak points. It is a process of moving management trainees from department to department to broaden their understanding of all parts of the business and to test their abilities. The trainee often a recent college graduate may spend several months in each department, but more commonly gets fully involved in its operations. The trainee thus learns the department's business by actually doing it, while discovering what jobs he or she prefers.

Coaching/Understudy approach: Here the trainee works directly with a senior manager or with the person he or she is to replace; the latter is responsible for the trainee's coaching. Normally, the understudy relieves the executive of certain responsibilities, giving the trainee a chance to learn the job.

Action Learning: These programmes give managers and others released time to work full time on projects, analysing and solving problems in departments other than their own. Trainees meet periodically in four or five person's project groups to discuss their findings. Several trainees may work together as a project group, or compare notes and discuss each other's projects.

Off-The-Job Training and Development Techniques

The case study method: As most everyone knows, the case study method presents a trainee with a written description of an organisational problems. Case study is a developmental method in which the manager is presented with a written description of an organisational problem to diagnose and solve. The person then analyses the cause, diagnoses the problem, and presents his or her findings and solutions in a discussion with other trainees. The script of the case study include themes, background stories, detailed personnel histories and role playing instructions.

Management Games: A development technique in which teams of managers compete by making computerised decisions regarding realistic but simulated situations. Here trainees are split into five to ten groups and each should compete with others in a stimulated market place. These things help trainees to develop their problem solving skills, as well as to focus attention on planning rather than just putting out fires.

Outside seminars: Many companies and universities offer web-based and traditional management development seminars and conferences.

Role playing: A training technique in which trainees act out parts in a realistic management situations. Role playing is to create a realistic situation and then have the trainees assume the parts or roles of specific persons in that situation.

Behaviour modeling: A training technique in which trainees are first shown good management techniques in a film, are asked to play roles in a simulated situation, and are then given feedback and praise by their supervisor. These modeling involves (1) showing trainees the right (model) way of doing something (2) letting trainees practice that way and then (3) giving feedback on the trainees on the trainee's performance. The basic behaviour modeling procedure is (a) Modeling (b) Role playing (c) Social reinforcement (d) Transfer of training.

Corporate universities and In-house development centres: Many firms, particularly larger ones, establish in-house development centres. A company based method for exposing prospective managers to realistic exercises to develop improved management skills.

EVALUATION OF TRAINING

The process of examining a training programme is called training evaluation. Training evaluation checks whether training has had the desired effect. Training evaluation ensures that whether candidates are able to implement their learning in their respective workplaces, or to the regular work routines.

The various methods of training evaluation are:

- Observation
- Questionnaire
- Interview
- Self diaries
- Self recording of specific incidents

Types of Evaluation

Evaluating the Training addresses how one determines whether the goals or objectives were met and what impact the training had on actual performance on the job.

Generally there are four kinds of standard training evaluation:

1. Formative
2. Process
3. Outcome
4. Impact

1. **Formative** evaluation provides ongoing feedback to the curriculum designers and developers to ensure that what is being created really meets the needs of the intended audience.
2. **Process** evaluation provides information about what occurs during training. This includes giving and receiving verbal feedback.
3. **Outcome** evaluation determines whether or not the desired results (e.g., what participants are doing) of applying new skills were achieved in the short-term.
4. **Impact** determines how the results of the training affect the strategic goal.

Kirkpatrick's Four-Level Training Evaluation Model

Donald Kirkpatrick, Professor Emeritus at the University of Wisconsin and past president of the American Society for Training and Development (ASTD), first published his Four-Level Training Evaluation Model in 1959, in the US Training and Development Journal.

The model was then updated in 1975, and again in 1994, when he published his best-known work, "Evaluating Training Programs."

The four levels are:

1. Reaction
2. Learning
3. Behaviour
4. Results

Let's look at each level in greater detail.

Level 1: Reaction

This level measures how your trainees (the people being trained), reacted to the training. Obviously, you want them to feel that the training was a valuable experience, and you want them to feel good about the instructor, the topic, the material, its presentation, and the venue.

It's important to measure reaction, because it helps you understand how well the training was received by your audience. It also helps you improve the training for future trainees, including identifying important areas or topics that are missing from the training.

Level 2: Learning

At level 2, you measure what your trainees have learned. How much has their knowledge increased as a result of the training?

When you planned the training session, you hopefully started with a list of specific learning objectives: these should be the starting point for your measurement. Keep in mind that you can measure learning in different ways depending on these objectives, and depending on whether you're interested in changes to knowledge, skills, or attitude.

It's important to measure this, because knowing what your trainees are learning and what they aren't will help you improve future training.

Level 3: Behaviour

At this level, you evaluate how far your trainees have changed their behaviour, based on the training they received. Specifically, this looks at how trainees apply the information.

It's important to realise that behaviour can only change if conditions are favourable. For instance, imagine you have skipped measurement at the first two Kirkpatrick levels and, when looking at your group's behaviour, you determine that no behaviour change has taken place. Therefore, you assume that your trainees have not learned anything and that the training was ineffective.

However, just because behaviour has not changed, it doesn't mean that trainees have not learned anything. Perhaps their boss won't let them apply new knowledge. Or, maybe they have learned everything you taught, but they have no desire to apply the knowledge themselves.

Level 4: Results

At this level, you analyse the final results of your training. This includes outcomes that you or your organisation have determined to be good for business, good for the employees, or good for the bottom line.

UNIT – IV

Concept
Importance
Evolution
Role
Group Dynamics
Motivation
Leadership
Job Satisfaction
Morale, Fatigue and Monotony
Organisational Change and Development
Organisational Effectiveness

ORGANISATIONAL BEHAVIOUR

CONCEPT

Organisational behaviour is the multidisciplinary approach which is an integration of different field of studies like psychology, sociology, social psychology, anthropology, and political science.

OB studies human behaviour at individual level, group level and organisational level. Basically, organisations are made up of peoples, therefore managers in the organisation must know how they behave in an organisation to make organisation productive.

Elements of Organisational Behaviour

1. **People:** People make up the internal social system of the organisation. They consist of individuals and groups. Groups may be formal or informal.
2. **Structure:** Structure defines the formal relationship between people in an organisation.
3. **Technology:** Technology consists of physical objects, activities and process, knowledge, etc through which people accomplish their tasks to achieve organisational objectives.
4. **Environment:** All organisations operate within an external environment. It is part of a larger system that contains thousand of other elements.This includes the suppliers, customers, competitors, governments' agencies, employees, unions, political parties, and economic, political, cultural, technological and social factors in which the organisation embedded.

Keith Davis defined "Organisational Behavior is the study and application of knowledge about how people as individual or as groups act within organisations."

IMPORTANCE

OB is concerned with understanding, applying and controlling of behavioural and structural knowledge of an organisation for organisation's effectiveness. Management function includes Planning, organising, leading and controlling where people are involved in different roles (interpersonal roles, informational roles, and decisional roles) and different capacities. Therefore, for an organisation to succeed, it is very important for it to understand its organisation's culture, people by way of understanding their perception, attitudes, motivation, personality, key personality characteristics relevant to workplace, learning, job satisfaction, etc through theories of motivation, learning, and reinforcement and mould their dissatisfaction to satisfaction, motivate them to achieve desired results, provide them appropriate work culture, growth opportunities, punish their inappropriate behaviour, and infusing learning environment and leadership.

EVOLUTION

In 1776, Adam Smith advocated a new form of organisational structure based on the division of labour. One hundred years later, German Sociologist Max Weber introduced the concept about rational organisations and initiated the concept of charismatic leadership.

Though the origin to the study of Organisational Behaviour can trace its roots back to Max Weber and earlier organisational studies, it is generally considered to have begun as an academic discipline with the advent of scientific management in the 1890's, with Taylorism representing the peak of the movement. Thus, it was Fredrick Winslow Taylor who introduced the systematic use of goal setting and rewards to motivate employees that could be considered as the starting of the academic discipline of Organisational Behaviour.

Proponents of scientific management held that rationalising the organisation with precise sets of instructions and time-motion studies would lead to increased productivity. Studies of different compensation systems were also carried out to motivate workers.

In 1920's Elton Mayo an Australian born Harvard Professor and his colleagues conducted productivity studies at Western Electric's Hawthorne Plant. With this epoch making study the focus of organisational studies shifted to analysis of how human factors and psychology affected organisations. This shift of focus in the study of organisations was called the Hawthorne Effect. The Human Relations Movement focused on teams, motivation, and the actualisation of goals of individuals within organisations. Studies conducted by prominent scholars like Chester Barnard, Henri Fayol, Mary Parker Follett, Frederick Herzberg, Abraham Maslow, David Mc Cellan and Victor Vroom contributed to the growth of Organisational Behaviour as a discipline.

ROLE

There are two roles of organisational behaviour in organisation, i.e. (a) Understanding Human Behaviour, and (b) Influencing the Human Behaviour.

A. Understanding Human Behaviour

Organisations are people and without people there would be no organisations. If the managers are to understand the organisations in which they work, they must first understand the people who make up the organisations. Organisational behaviour is the tool, which helps the managers in understanding human behaviour in all the directions in which the human beings interact.

Human can be studied from the point of view of the following four levels

(i) Individual Behaviour

The main focus of behavioural sciences is on the study of individual behaviour. It tries to analyse why and how an individual behaves in a particular way in a given situation. The behaviour of individuals is affected by a number of psychological, social and cultural factors. The job of organisational behaviourist is to integrate these factors to help in understanding human behaviour.

(ii) Interpersonal Behaviour

Behavioural Sciences also provide means for understanding interpersonal behaviour in the organisations. In organisations, two person relationships are inevitable. Interpersonal interaction represents man's most natural attempt at socialisation. By studying behavioural sciences, the managers can understand themselves and the others better. This will help in improving interpersonal relations also. The techniques, generally, used for studying interpersonal behaviour are study of perception, role analysis, transaction analysis, etc.

(iii) Group Behaviour

Hawthorne studies have proven that an individual behaves differently as an individual and as a member of the group. His behaviour is often modified by group norms. Group behaviour has a synergic impact on the performance. Group formation, behaviour and interactions are studied in the course of the organisational process. Management can use group dynamics for better communication, effective leadership and building high morale.

(iv) Inter Group Behaviour

Organisations consist of a large number of groups, which leads to complexity of relationships. It is very important for the managers to understand the group relationships. The cooperation, coordination and conflicts within groups influence performances. Organisational behaviour helps the managers in achieving cooperative group relationships through interaction, rotation of members among groups, avoidance of win-lose situation and focus on total group objectives.

B. Influencing the Human Behaviour

Managers can influence the behaviour through control and direction.

After understanding the human behaviour in the organisations the next job of the manager is to influence the behaviour so that it conforms to the standards required for achieving the organisational objectives. Organisational behaviour helps the managers in influencing the behaviour in the following ways:

1. Leadership

Leadership helps the management in bringing human behaviour in tune with the organisational requirements. An organisation must have effective leadership for its survival and growth. The leadership theories are perpetually accepted by an organisation for smooth performance of their activities. There are trait, goal and situational approaches for the development of leadership.

An organisation can achieve success only with the right type of leadership. A competent leader uses all the human and physical resources at the maximum levels for achieving the organisational goals. Leadership serves as the link among the individuals, groups and various other aspects of the organisation.

2. Motivation

Motivation in an organisation is essential for ongoing work. Human beings work not only for money but also for getting job satisfaction. The job of a manager in the organisation is to get things done through others. He will be successful in his job when he can motivate his subordinates to work for organisational goals. Organisational behaviour helps the managers in understanding the needs and desires of the subordinates and other factors which affect their motivation. The monetary and non-monetary awards are used as incentives to motivate the subordinates.

3. Communication

People come in contact with each other through communication, thus, communication is known as the building block of the organisation. To achieve organisational effectiveness, the communication must be effective. Behavioural sciences help in improving communication in the organisation. The communication process and how it works in interpersonal dynamics is evaluated by behavioural sciences. Organisational behaviour analyses the factors that affect communication so as to make it more effective.

4. Organisational Change and Development

Organisational development is needed for the change and development of individuals. Organisations have to undergo changes as a result of social, technological, political and other environmental factors. The organisational change and development are successfully handled by the use of behavioural science knowledge. Change can be introduced through group dynamics and proper education of employees through effective communication. The benefits of change should be highlighted and information should be shared with all those likely to be affected by the change.

5. Organisational Climate

Organisational climate is the sum total of all the organisational situations affecting human behaviour. Organisational behaviour views organisational climate in totality rather than merely improving physical working conditions, or increasing employees' satisfaction by changing isolated work process.

Organisational climate is the creation of an atmosphere of effective supervision, the opportunity for the realisation of personal goals, good relations with others at the work place and sense of accomplishment. Organisational climate, thus, takes a systems perspective and affects human behaviour. Organisational behaviour creates an atmosphere of participative leadership, two way communication, adequate compensation and better equipment's for the job.

Models of Organisational Behaviour

There are mainly five models in OB. These are

- Autocratic Model
- Custodial Model
- Supportive Model
- Collegial Model and
- System Model.

Autocratic Model

Autocratic model is the model that depends upon strength, power and formal authority.

In an autocratic organisation, the people (management/owners) who manage the tasks in an organisation have formal authority for controlling the employees who work under them. These lower-level employees have little control over the work function. Their ideas and innovations are not generally welcomed, as the key decisions are made at the top management level.

The guiding principle behind this model is that management/ owners have enormous business expertise, and the average employee has relatively low levels of skill and needs to be fully directed and guided. This type of autocratic management system was common in factories in the industrial revolution era.

One of the more significant problems associated with the autocratic model is that the management team is required to micromanage the staff – where they have to watch all the details and make every single decision.

The autocratic model is also a detractor to job satisfaction and employee morale. This is because employees do not feel valued and part of the overall team. This leads to a low-level of work performance. While the autocratic model might be appropriate for some automated factory situations, it has become outdated for most modern-day organisations.

Custodial Model

The custodial model is based around the concept of providing economic security for employees – through wages and other benefits – that will create employee loyalty and motivation.

In some countries, many professional companies provide health benefits, corporate cars, financial packaging of salary, and so on – these are incentives designed to attract and retain quality staff.

The underlying theory for the organisation is that they will have a greater skilled workforce, more motivated employees, and have a competitive advantage through employee knowledge and expertise.

Supportive Model

Unlike the two earlier approaches, the supportive model is focused around aspiring leadership. It is not based upon control and authority (the autocratic model) or upon incentives (the custodial model), but instead tries to motivate staff through the manager-employee relationship and how employees are treated on a day-to-day basis.

Quite opposite to the autocratic model, this approach states that employees are self-motivated and have value and insight to contribute to the organisation, beyond just their day-to-day role.

The intent of this model is to motivate employees through a positive workplace where their ideas are encouraged and often adapted. Therefore, the employees have some form of "buy-in" to the organisation and its direction.

Collegial Model

The collegial model is based around teamwork – everybody working as colleagues. The overall environment and corporate culture need to be aligned to this model, where everybody is actively participating – is not about status and job titles – everybody is encouraged to work together to build a better organisation.

The role of the manager is to foster this teamwork and create positive and energetic workplaces. In much regard, the manager can be considered to be the "coach" of the team and as coach, the goal is to make the team perform well overall, rather than focus on their own performance, or the performance of key individuals.

System Model

In the system model, the organisation looks at the overall structure and team environment, and considers that individuals have different goals, talents and potential.

The intent of the system model is to try and balance the goals of the individual with the goals of the organisation. Individuals obviously want good remuneration, job security, but also want to work in a positive work environment where the organisation adds value to the community and/or its customers.

The system of model should be an overall partnership of managers and employees with a common goal, and where everybody feels that they have a stake in the organisation.

GROUP DYNAMICS

Kurt Lewin had an impact on a generation of researchers and thinkers concerned with group dynamics. In particular, two key ideas which emerged out of field theory, it is argued are crucial to an appreciation of group processes; they are interdependence of fate and task interdependence.

According to Tuckman's theory, there are five stages of group development: forming, storming, norming, performing, and adjourning. During these stages group members must address several issues and the way in which these issues are resolved determines whether the group will succeed in accomplishing its tasks.

Stages of Group Development

Group Development is a dynamic process. How do groups evolve? There is a process of five stages through which groups pass through. The process includes the five stages: forming, storming, Norming, performing, and adjourning.

Forming: The first stage in the life of a group is concerned with forming a group. This stage is characterised by members seeking either a work assignment (in a formal group) or other benefit, like status, affiliation, power, etc. (in an informal group). Members at this stage either engage in busy type of activity or show apathy.

Storming: The next stage in this group is marked by the formation of dyads and triads. Members seek out familiar or similar individuals and begin a deeper sharing of self. Continued attention to the subgroup creates a differentiation in the group and tensions across the dyads / triads may appear. Pairing is a common phenomenon. There will be conflict about controlling the group.

Norming: The third stage of group development is marked by a more serious concern about task performance. The dyads/triads begin to open up and seek out other members in the group. Efforts are made to establish various norms for task performance. Members begin to take greater responsibility for their own group and relationship while the authority figure becomes relaxed. Once this stage is complete, a clear picture will emerge about hierarchy of leadership. The norming stage is over with the solidification of the group structure and a sense of group identity and camaraderie.

Performing: This is a stage of a fully functional group where members see themselves as a group and get involved in the task. Each person makes a contribution and the authority figure is also seen as a part of the group. Group norms are followed and collective pressure is exerted to ensure the Process of Group effectiveness of the group.The group may redefine its goals Development in the light of information from the outside environment and show an autonomous will to pursue those goals. The long-term viability of the group is established and nurtured.

Adjourning

In the case of temporary groups, like project team, task force, or any other such group, which have a limited task at hand, also have a fifth stage. This is known as adjourning.The group decides to disband. Some members may feel happy over the performance, and some may be unhappy over the stoppage of meeting with group members. Adjourning may also be referred to as mourning, i.e. mourning the adjournment of the group.

Types of Groups

There are two types of groups. These are formal groups and informal groups.

A formal group is a collection of persons, who come together for achieving a specified goal. They are always created with intent to fulfill some official requirement. Formation of the group is done by the management. It possesses a systematic structure, in hierarchical form.

In general, the employees of the organisation are divided into groups and a task is hand over to each group. In this way, the task of the group is accomplished along with the fulfillment of organisational goals. The given are the types of formal groups:

1. **Command groups:** The groups that consist of managers and their subordinates.
2. **Committees:** The group of people who are appointed by an organisation, to resolve the matters, referred to them are known as Committee. For example, Advisory Committee, Standing Committee, etc.
3. **Task Forces:** The group form to carry out a particular task is known as Task Forces.

The various kinds of informal groups are:

1. **Friendship Groups:** Friendship groups are associations of people who like each other and who like to be together. Such groups are formed because members have one or more common characteristics, such as age or ethnic heritage, political beliefs, religious values and other bonds of attraction.
2. **Interest Groups:** Interest groups are composed of individuals who may not be members of the same organisation (command or task groups), but they are united by their interest in a common issue. Example of interest groups may include a group of University Professors. They organise a seminar on Law and Order Problems in the State of West Bengal.
3. **Reference Group:** A reference group is a special type of informal group that people use to evaluate themselves. A reference group may not be an actual one that meets together; it can be an imaginary group.
4. **Cliques:** It consists of colleagues and associates closely intimated to each other. Cliques may be of three types:
   (i) Vertical cliques consist of members working in the same department irrespective of their rank.
   (ii) Horizontal cliques consist of people of similar rank working more or less in the same area.
   (iii) Mixed cliques consist of both vertical and horizontal cliques.
5. **Sub-cliques:** It consists of member of a clique along with outsiders.
6. **Isolates:** Who are not members of any group.

Another classification of informal groups by Sayles from the standpoint of pressure tactics is divided into four groups:

(i) **The Apathetic Group:** Not sincere to their demand and members do not actively engage in union activity.

(ii) **The Erratic Group:** Very sensitive to their demand. Easily inflamed and easily pacified. Engage in union activity.

(iii) **The Strategic Group:** These groups have a well planned strategy for fighting with the management for their grievances. They build continuous pressure.

(iv) **Conservative Group:** Consists of members having critical or scarce skills. Though they have strong position yet are least engaged in union activity.

Theories of Group Formation

1. Propinquity Theory

The most basic theory explaining affiliation is propinquity. This interesting word simply means that individuals affiliate with one another because of spatial or geographical proximity. In an organisation employees who work in the same area of the plant or office or managers with offices close to one another would more probably form into groups than would those who are not physically located together. There is some research evidence to support the propinquity theory and on the surface, it has a great deal of merit for explaining group formation. The drawback of this theory is that it is not analytical and does not begin to explain some of the complexities of group formation. Some more theoretical and practical reasons need to be explored.

2. Homan's Theory

According to George C. Homans, "The more activities persons share, the more numerous will be there interactions and the stronger will be their shared activities and sentiments, and the more sentiments people have for one another, the more will be their shared activities and interactions."

It is a very comprehensive theory and based on activities, interactions and Homan's theory is based on sentiments. These three elements are directly related to each other. The members' activities interactions and of a group share activities and interact with one another not just because of physical proximity but also to accomplish group goals.

The key element is interaction because of which they develop common sentiments for one another. These sentiments gradually get expressed through the formation of informal groups. If any disturbance is caused to any of the three- activities, interactions and sentiments, it is likely to disturb all the others.

Their relationships are shown in the following figure:

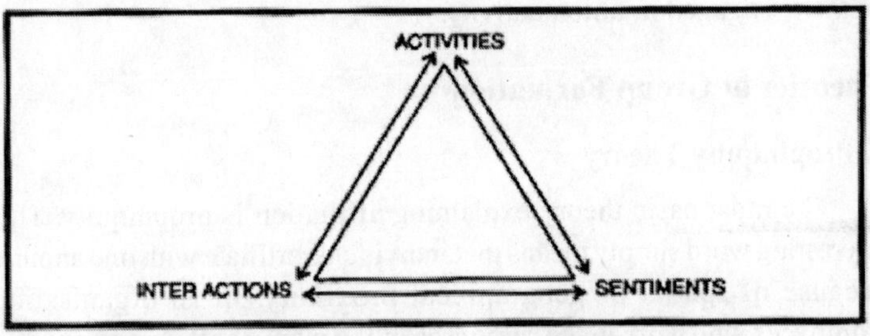

(The Inter-Dependence of Activities, Interaction and Sentiments)

3. Balance Theory

Another very comprehensive theory is a Balance Theory of group formation. This theory as proposed by Theodore Newcomb states that "Persons are attracted to one another on the basis of similar attitudes towards commonly relevant objects and goals. Once a relationship is formed, it strives to maintain a symmetrical balance between the attraction and the common attitudes. If an imbalance occurs, attempts are made to restore the balance. If the balance cannot be restored, the relationship dissolves."

Thus, the balance theory is additive in nature in the sense, that it introduces the factor of balance to the propinquity and interaction factors. There must be a balance in the relationship between the group members for the group to be formed and for its survival. The following figure shows the balance theory.

Individual (A) will interact and form a relationship/group with individual (B) because of common attitudes and values (C). Once this relationship is formed, the participants strive to maintain a symmetrical balance between the attraction and the common attitudes. If an imbalance occurs, an attempt is made to restore the balance. If the balance cannot be restored, the relationship dissolves.

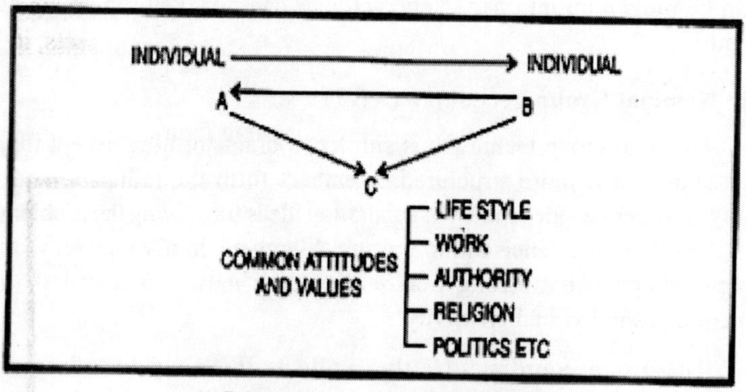

(A Balance Theory of Group Formation)

4. Exchange Theory

This theory is based on reward-cost outcomes of interactions. To be attracted towards a group, a person thinks in terms of what he will get in exchange of interaction with group members. A minimum positive level (rewards greater than costs) of an outcome must exist in order for attraction or affiliation to take place. Rewards from interactions gratify needs while costs incur anxiety, frustrations, embarrassment or fatigue. Propinquity, interaction and common attitudes all have roles in the exchange theory.

Group Decision Making Process

(i) Brainstorming

This technique involves a group of people, usually between five and ten, sitting around a table, generating ideas in the form of free association. The primary focus is on generation of ideas rather than on evaluation of ideas.

If a large number of ideas can be generated, then it is likely that there will be a unique and creative idea among them. All these ideas are written on the black board with a piece of chalk so that everybody can see every idea and try to improve upon such ideas.

Brainstorming technique is very effective when the problem is comparatively specific and can be simply defined. A complex problem can be broken up into parts and each part can be taken separately at a time.

(ii) Nominal Group Technique (NGT)

Nominal group technique is similar to brainstorming except that the approach is more structured. Members form the group in name only and operate independently, generating ideas for solving the problem on their own, in silence and in writing. Members do not interact with each other so that strong personality domination is avoided. It encourages individual creativity.

The group coordinator either collects these written ideas or writes then on a large black board for everyone to see or he asks each member to speak out and then he writes it on the black board as he receives it.

These ideas are then discussed one by one in turn and each participant is encouraged to comment on these ideas for the purpose of clarification and improvement. After all ideas are discussed, they are evaluated for their merits and drawbacks and each participating member is required to vote on each idea and assign it a rank on the basis of priority of each alternative solution. The idea with the highest aggregate ranking is selected as the final solution to the problem.

(iii) Delphi Technique

This technique is the modification of the nominal group technique, except that it involves obtaining the opinions of experts physically separated from each other and unknown to each other. This insulates group members from the undue influence of others. Generally, the types of problems handled by this technique are not specific in nature or related to a particular situation at a given time. For example, the technique could be used to understand the problems that could be created in the event of a war. The steps in the Delphi technique are:

1. The problem is identified and a sample of experts is selected. These experts are asked to provide potential solutions through a series of carefully designed questionnaires.
2. Each expert completes and returns the initial questionnaire.

3. The results of the questionnaire are compiled at a central location and the central coordinator prepares a second questionnaire based on the previous answers.
4. Each member receives a copy of the results along with the second questionnaire.
5. Members are asked to review the results and respond to the second questionnaire. The results typically trigger new solutions or cause changes in the original position.
6. The process is repeated until a consensus is reached.

The process is very time consuming and is primarily useful in illuminating broad range, long-term complex issues such as future effects of energy shortages that might occur.

(iv) Didactic Interaction

This technique is applicable only in certain situations, but is an excellent method when such a situation exists. The type of problem should be such that it results in a yes-no solution. For example, the decision may be to buy or not to buy, to merge or not to merge, to expand or not to expand and so on. Such a decision requires an extensive and exhaustive discussion and investigation since a wrong decision can have serious consequences.

Since, in such a situation, there must be advantages as well as disadvantages of either of the two alternatives, the group required to make the decision is split into two sub-groups, one favouring the "go" decision and the other favouring the "no go" decision.

The first group lists all the "pros" of the problem solution and the second group lists all the "cons". These groups meet and discuss their findings and their reasons. After the exhaustive discussions, the groups switch sides and try to find weaknesses in their own original viewpoints. This interchange of ideas and understanding of opposing viewpoints results in mutual acceptance of the facts as they exist so that a solution can be built around these facts and opinions relating to these facts and thus a final decision is reached.

MOTIVATION THEORIES

Some of the most important theories of motivation are as follows:

1. Maslow's Need Hierarchy Theory
2. Herzberg's Motivation Hygiene Theory
3. McClelland's Need Theory
4. McGregor's Participation Theory
5. Urwick's Theory Z
6. Argyris's Theory
7. Vroom's Expectancy Theory
8. Porter and Lawler's Expectancy Theory
9. ERG Theory
10. Skinner's Theory of Motivation.

From the very beginning, when the human organisations were established, various thinkers have tried to find out the answer to what motivates people to work. Different approaches applied by them have resulted in a number of theories concerning motivation.

These are discussed in brief in that order.

1. Maslow's Need Hierarchy Theory

It is probably safe to say that the most well-known theory of motivation is Maslow's need hierarchy theory. Maslow's theory is based on the human needs. He classified all human needs into a hierarchical manner from the lower to the higher order.

In essence, he believed that once a given level of need is satisfied, it no longer serves to motivate man. Then, the next higher level of need has to be activated in order to motivate the man. Maslow identified five levels in his need hierarchy.

These are now discussed one by one:

(i) Physiological Needs

These needs are basic to human life and, hence, include food, clothing, shelter, air, water and necessities of life. These needs relate to the survival and maintenance of human life. They exert tremendous influence on human behaviour. These needs are to be met first at least partly before higher level needs emerge. Once physiological needs are satisfied, they no longer motivate the man.

(ii) Safety Needs

After satisfying the physiological needs, the next needs felt are called safety and security needs. These needs find expression in such desires as economic security and protection from physical dangers. Meeting these needs requires more money and, hence, the individual is prompted to work more. Like physiological needs, these become inactive once they are satisfied.

(iii) Social Needs

Man is a social being. He is, therefore, interested in social interaction, companionship, belongingness, etc. It is this socialising and belongingness why individuals prefer to work in groups and especially older people go to work.

(iv) Esteem Needs

These needs refer to self-esteem and self-respect. They include such needs which indicate self-confidence, achievement, competence, knowledge and independence. The fulfillment of esteem needs leads to self-confidence, strength and capability of being useful in the organisation. However, inability to fulfill these needs results in feeling like inferiority, weakness and helplessness.

(v) Self-Actualisation Needs

This level represents the culmination of all the lower, intermediate, and higher needs of human beings. In other words, the final step under the need hierarchy model is the need for self-actualisation. This refers to fulfillment.

The term self-actualisation was coined by Kurt Goldstein and means to become actualised in what one is potentially good at. In effect, self-actualisation is the person's motivation to transform perception of self into reality.

According to Maslow, the human needs follow a definite sequence of domination. The second need does not arise until the first is reasonably satisfied, and the third need does not emerge until the first two needs have been reasonably satisfied and it goes on. The other side of the need hierarchy is that human needs are unlimited. However, Maslow's need hierarchy-theory is not without its detractors.

The main criticisms of the theory include the following:

(a) The needs may or may not follow a definite hierarchical order. So, there may be overlapping in need hierarchy. For example, even if safety need is not satisfied, the social need may emerge.

(b) The need priority model may not apply at all times in all places.

(c) Researches show that man's behaviour at any time is mostly guided by multiplicity of behaviour. Hence, Maslow's preposition that one need is satisfied at one time is also of doubtful validity.

(d) In case of some people, the level of motivation may be permanently lower. For example, a person suffering from chronic unemployment may remain satisfied for the rest of his life if only he/she can get enough food.

Notwithstanding, Maslow's need hierarchy theory has received wide recognition, particularly among practicing managers. This can be attributed to the theory's intuitive logic and easy to understand.

2. Herzberg's Motivation Hygiene Theory

The psychologist Frederick Herzberg extended the work of Maslow and proposed a new motivation theory popularly known as Herzberg's Motivation Hygiene (Two-Factor) Theory. Herzberg conducted a widely reported motivational study on 200 accountants and engineers employed by firms in and around Western Pennsylvania.

He asked these people to describe two important incidents at their jobs:

(1) When did you feel particularly good about your job, and

(2) When did you feel exceptionally bad about your job?

The responses when analysed were found quite interesting and fairly consistent. The replies respondents gave when they felt good about their jobs were significantly different from the replies given when they felt bad. Reported good feelings were generally associated with job satisfaction, whereas bad feeling with job dissatisfaction. Herzberg labeled the job satisfiers as motivators, and he called job dissatisfiers as hygiene or maintenance factors.

Herzberg's motivational and hygiene factors have been shown below:

Motivating Factors	***Hygiene Factors***
Achievement	Company policy and administration
Recognition	Supervision
Work itself	Interpersonal relations
Responsibility	Working conditions
Advancement	Salary
Growth	Status
Security	

According to Herzberg, the opposite of satisfaction is not dissatisfaction. The underlying reason, he says, is that removal of dissatisfying characteristics from a job does not necessarily make the job satisfying. According to Herzberg, today's motivators are tomorrow's hygiene because the latter stop influencing the behaviour of persons when they get them. Accordingly, one's hygiene may be the motivator of another.

However, Herzberg's model is labeled with the following criticism also:

(a) People generally tend to take credit themselves when things go well. They blame failure on the external environment.

(b) The theory basically explains job satisfaction, not motivation.

(c) Even job satisfaction is not measured on an overall basis. It is not unlikely that a person may dislike part of his/ her job, still thinks the job acceptable.

(d) This theory neglects situational variable to motivate an individual.

3. McClelland's Need Theory

Another well-known need-based theory of motivation, as opposed to hierarchy of needs of satisfaction-dissatisfaction, is the theory developed by McClelland and his associates'. McClelland developed his theory based on Henry Murray's developed long list of motives and manifest needs used in his early studies of personality. He found that people who acquire a particular need behave differently from those who do not have. His theory focuses on Murray's three needs; achievement, power and affiliation. In the literature, these three needs are abbreviated "n Ach", "n Pow", and "n Aff" respectively.

They are defined as follows:

Need for Achievement

This is the drive to excel, to achieve in relation to a set of standard, and to strive to succeed. In other words, need for achievement is a behaviour directed toward competition with a standard of excellence. McClelland found that people with a high need for achievement perform better than those with a moderate or low need for achievement.

Need for Power

The need for power is concerned with making an impact on others, the desire to influence others, the urge to change people, and the desire to make a difference in life. People with a high need for power are people who like to be in control of people and events. This results in ultimate satisfaction to man.

Need for Affiliation

The need for affiliation is defined as a desire to establish and maintain friendly and warm relations with other people.

4. McGregor's Participation Theory

Douglas McGregor formulated two distinct views of human being based on participation of workers. The first basically negative, labeled Theory X, and the other basically positive, labeled Theory Y.

Theory X is based on the following assumptions:

1. People are by nature indolent. They like to work as little as possible.
2. People lack ambition, dislike responsibility, and prefer to be directed by others.

3. People are inherently self-centered and indifferent to organisational needs and goals.
4. People are generally gullible and not very sharp and bright.

On the contrary,Theory Y assumes that:

1. People are not by nature passive or resistant to organisational goals.
2. They want to assume responsibility.
3. They want their organisation to succeed.
4. People are capable of directing their own behaviour.
5. They have need for achievement.

What McGregor tried to dramatise through his theory X and Y is to outline the extremes to draw the fencing within which the organisational man is usually seen to behave. The fact remains that no organisational man would actually belong either to theory X or theory Y. In reality, he/she shares the traits of both. What actually happens is that man swings from one set or properties to the other with changes in his mood and motives.

5. Urwick's Theory Z

Much after the propositions of theories X and Y by McGregor, the three theorists Urwick, Rangnekar, and Ouchi propounded the third theory labeled as Z theory.

The two propositions in Urwick's theory are that:

(i) Each individual should know the organisational goals precisely and the amount of contribution through his efforts towards these goals.

(ii) Each individual should also know that the relation of organisational goals is going to satisfy his/her needs positively.

In Urwick's view, the above two make people ready to behave positively to accomplish both organisational and individual goals.

However, Ouchi's Theory Z has attracted the lot of attention of management practitioners as well as researchers.

Theory Z is based on the following four postulates:

1. Strong Bond between Organisation and Employees
2. Employee Participation and Involvement
3. No Formal Organisation Structure
4. Human Resource Development

Ouchi's Theory Z represents the adoption of Japanese management practices (group decision-making, social cohesion, job security, holistic concern for employees, etc.) by the American companies. In India, Maruti-Suzuki, Hero-Honda, etc., apply the postulates of theory Z.

6. Argyris's Theory

Argyris has developed his motivation theory based on proposition how management practices affect the individual behaviour and growth. In his view, the seven changes taking place in an individual personality make him/her a mature one.

Immaturity	***Maturity***
Passivity	Activity
Dependence	Independence
Capable of behaving in a few ways	Capable of behaving in many ways
Shallow interest	Deep interest
Short-term perspective	Long-term perspective
Subordinate position	Superordinate position
Lack of self-awarencess	Self-awareness and control

Argyris views that immaturity exists in individuals mainly because of organisational setting and management practices such as task specialisation, chain of command, unity of direction, and span of management. In order to make individuals grow mature, he proposes gradual shift from the existing pyramidal organisation structure to humanistic system; from existing management system to the more flexible and participative management.

He states that such situation will satisfy not only their physiological and safety needs, but also will motivate them to make ready to make more use of their physiological and safety needs. It will motivate them to make ready to make more use of their potential in accomplishing organisational goals.

7. Vroom's Expectancy Theory

One of the most widely accepted explanations of motivation is offered by Victor Vroom in his Expectancy Theory. It is a cognitive process theory of motivation. The theory is founded on the basic notions that people will be motivated to exert a high level of effort when they believe there are relationships between the effort they put forth, the performance they achieve, and the outcomes/ rewards they receive.

The relationships between notions of effort, performance, and reward are depicted below:

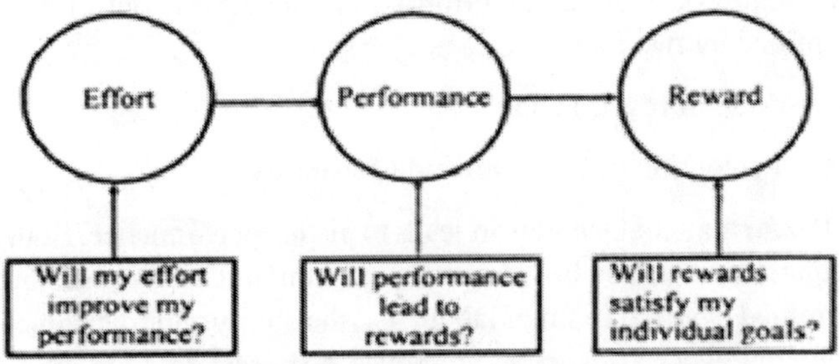

Vroom's Expectancy Model of Motivation

Thus, the key constructs in the expectancy theory of motivation are:

1. **Valence:** It means the value or strength one places on a particular outcome or reward.
2. **Expectancy:** It relates efforts to performance.
3. **Instrumentality:** It means the belief that performance is related to rewards.

Thus, Vroom's motivation can also be expressed in the form of an equation as follows:

$$\text{Motivation} = \text{Valence} \times \text{Expectancy} \times \text{Instrumentality}$$

Being the model multiplicative in nature, all the three variables must have high positive values to imply motivated performance choice.

If any one of the variables approaches to zero level, the possibility of the so motivated performance also touches zero level.

8. Porter and Lawler's Expectancy Theory

In fact, Porter and Lawler's theory is an improvement over Vroom's expectancy theory. They proposed a multivariate model to explain the complex relationship that exists between satisfaction and performance.

There are three main elements in this model. Let us briefly discuss these one by one.

Effort: Effort refers to the amount of energy an employee exerts on a given task. How much effort an employee will put in a task is determined by two factors:

(i) Value of reward and

(ii) Perception of effort-reward probability.

Performance: One's effort leads to his/her performance. Both may be equal or may not be. However, the amount of performance is determined by the amount of labour and the ability and role perception of the employee. Thus, if an employee possesses less ability and/or makes wrong role perception, his/her performance may be low in spite of his putting in great efforts.

Satisfaction: Performance leads to satisfaction. The level of satisfaction depends upon the amount of rewards one achieves. If the amount of actual rewards meet or exceed perceived equitable rewards, the employee will feel satisfied. On the contrary, if actual rewards fall short of perceived ones, he/she will be dissatisfied.

9. ERG Theory

Clayton P. Alderfer's ERG theory from 1969 condenses Maslow's five human needs into three categories: Existence, Relatedness and Growth.

Existence Needs

It includes all material and physiological desires (e.g., food, water, air, clothing, safety, physical love and affection).

Relatedness Needs

It encompasses social and external esteem; relationships with family, friends, co-workers and employers. This also means to be recognised and feel secure as part of a group or family.

Growth Needs

It impels a person to make creative or productive effects on himself and the environment (e.g., to progress toward one's ideal self). This includes desires to be creative and productive, and to complete meaningful tasks.

There are three relationships among the different categories in Alderfer's ERG theory:

Satisfaction-Progression: It means moving up to higher-level needs based on satisfied needs. Individuals move up the need hierarchy as a result of satisfying lower order needs.

Frustration-Regression: If a higher level need remains unfulfilled, a person may regress to lower level needs that appear easier to satisfy. Frustration-Regression suggests that an already satisfied need can become active when a higher need cannot be satisfied.

Satisfaction-Strengthening: Satisfaction-Strengthening indicates that an already satisfied need can maintain satisfaction or strengthen lower level needs iteratively when it fails to gratify high-level needs.

10. Skinner's Theory of Motivation

This theory is linked with reinforcement theory of motivation. Skinner's work is built on the assumption that behaviour is influenced by its consequences. These consequences are referred to as 'operants', and so this theory uses the term "operant conditioning." Behaviour modification is used to describe the learning by reinforcement of an individual.

THEORY OF LEADERSHIP

1. Great Man Theory

The 'great man' theory was originally proposed by Thomas Carlyle.

Assumptions

Leaders are born and not made.

Great leaders will arise when there is a great need.

Description

Early research on leadership was based on the study of people who were already great leaders. These people were often from the aristocracy, as few from lower classes had the opportunity to lead. This contributed to the notion that leadership had something to do with breeding.

2. Trait Theory

Assumptions

People are born with inherited traits.

Some traits are particularly suited to leadership.

People who make good leaders have the right combination of traits.

Stogdill (1974) identified the following traits and skills as critical to leaders.

Traits	*Skills*
• Adaptable to situations	• Clever (intelligent)
• Alert to social environment	• Conceptually skilled
• Ambitious and achievement -orientated	• Creative • Diplomatic and tactful
• Assertive	• Fluent in speaking
• Cooperative	• Knowledgeable about group task
• Decisive	• Organised (administrative ability)
• Dependable	• Persuasive
• Dominant (desire to influence others)	• Socially skilled
• Energetic (high activity level)	
• Persistent	
• Self-confident	
• Tolerant of stress	
• Willing to assume responsibility	

McCall and Lombardo (1983) researched both success and failure identified four primary traits by which leaders could succeed or derail:

- **Emotional Stability and Composure:** Calm, confident and predictable, particularly when under stress.
- **Admitting Error:** Owning up to mistakes, rather than putting energy into covering up.
- **Good Interpersonal Skills:** Able to communicate and persuade others without resort to negative or coercive tactics.
- **Intellectual Breadth:** Able to understand a wide range of areas, rather than having a narrow area of expertise.

3. Behavioural Theory of Leadership

There are two important Behavioural studies. These are discussed below:

(a) Ohio State University (1940s)

As leadership studies that were aimed at identifying the appropriate traits didn't yield any conclusive results, a group of people from Ohio State University developed a list of 150 statements from their generated responses that included 1,800 hundred statements. The list was designed to measure nine different behavioural leadership dimensions. The resulting questionnaire is now well-known as the LBDQ or the Leaders Behaviour Description Questionnaire.

As part of the study, the LBDQ was administered to various groups of individuals ranging from college students and their administrators, private companies including military personnel. One of the primary purposes of the study was to identify common leadership behaviours. After compiling and analysing the results, the study led to the conclusion that there were two groups of behaviours that were strongly correlated. These were defined as Consideration (People Oriented Behavioural Leaders) and Initiating Structure (Task Oriented Leaders).

Task Oriented Leaders

The task concerned leaders are focusing their behaviours on the organisational structure, the operating procedures and they like to keep control. They will favour behaviours that are in line with:

- Initiating
- Organising
- Clarifying
- Information Gathering

People Oriented Leaders

The people oriented leaders are focusing their behaviours on ensuring that the inner needs of the people are satisfied. Thus, they will seek to motivate their staff through emphasising the human relation. People oriented leaders still focus on the task and the results; they just achieve them through different means. They will favour behaviours that are in line with:

- Encouraging
- Observing
- Listening
- Coaching and Mentoring

(b) University of Michigan (1950s)

Dr. Rensis Likert, the leadership studies at the University of Michigan identified three characteristics of effective leadership; two of which were previously observed in studies that had been conducted at Ohio State University. The study showed that task and relationship-oriented behaviours were not of major significance within the world of organisational psychology. However, it was the third observation that introduced a new concept, one of participative leadership.

Blake and Mouton's Managerial Grid

The treatment of task orientation and people orientation as two independent dimensions was a major step in leadership studies. Many of the leadership studies conducted in the 1950s at the University of Michigan and the Ohio State University focused on these two dimensions.

Building on the work of the researchers at these Universities, Robert Blake and Jane Mouton (1960s) proposed a graphic portrayal of leadership styles through a managerial grid. The grid depicted two dimensions of leader behaviour, concern for people on y-axis and concern for production on x-axis, with each dimension ranging from low (1) to high (9), thus, creating 81 different positions in which the leader's style may fall.

The five resulting leadership styles are as follows:

Impoverished Management (1, 1): Managers with this approach are low on both the dimensions and exercise minimum effort to get the work done from subordinates. The leader has low concern for employee satisfaction and work deadlines and as a result disharmony and disorganisation prevail within the organisation. The leaders are termed ineffective wherein their action is merely aimed at preserving job and seniority.

Task Management (9, 1): Here leaders are more concerned about production and have less concern for people. The employees' needs are not taken care of and they are simply a means to an end. The leader believes that efficiency can result only through proper organisation of work systems and through elimination of people wherever possible. Such a style can definitely increase the output of organisation in short run but due to the strict policies and procedures, high labour turnover is inevitable.

Middle-of-the-Road (5, 5): This is basically a compromising style wherein the leader tries to maintain a balance between goals of company and the needs of people. The leader does not push the boundaries of achievement resulting in average performance for organisation. Here neither employee nor production needs are fully met.

Country Club (1, 9): This is a collegial style characterised by low task and high people orientation where the leader gives thoughtful attention to the needs of people thus providing them with a friendly and comfortable environment. The leader feels that such a treatment with employees will lead to self-motivation and will find people working hard on their own. However, a low focus on tasks can hamper production and lead to questionable results.

Team Management (9, 9): Characterised by high people and task focus, the style is based on the theory Y of McGregor and has been termed as most effective style according to Blake and Mouton. The leader feels that empowerment, commitment, trust, and respect are the key elements in creating a team atmosphere which will automatically result in high employee satisfaction and production.

House's Path Goal Theory

The theory was developed by Robert House and has its roots in the expectancy theory of motivation. The theory is based on the premise that an employee's perception of expectancies between his effort and performance is greatly affected by a leader's behaviour. The leaders help group members in attaining rewards by clarifying the paths to goals and removing obstacles to performance. They do so by providing the information, support, and other resources which are required by employees to complete the task.

House's theory advocates servant leadership. As per servant leadership theory, leadership is not viewed as a position of power. Rather, leaders act as coaches and facilitators to their subordinates. According to House's path-goal theory, a leader's effectiveness depends on several employee and environmental contingent factors and certain leadership styles.

Leadership Styles

The four leadership styles are:

Directive: Here the leader provides guidelines, lets subordinates know what is expected of them, sets performance standards for them, and controls behaviour when performance standards are not met. He makes judicious use of rewards and disciplinary action.

Supportive: The leader is friendly towards subordinates and displays personal concern for their needs, welfare, and well-being.

Participative: The leader believes in group decision-making and shares information with subordinates. He consults his subordinates on important decisions related to work, task goals, and paths to resolve goals.

Achievement-oriented: The leader sets challenging goals and encourages employees to reach their peak performance. The leader believes that employees are responsible enough to accomplish challenging goals.

According to the theory, these leadership styles are not mutually exclusive and leaders are capable of selecting more than one kind of a style suited for a particular situation.

Hersey Blanchard Model

According to this model, the leader has to match the leadership style according to the readiness of subordinates which moves in stage and has a cycle. Therefore, this theory is also known as the life-cycle theory of leadership.

The theory, developed by Paul Hersey and Kenneth Blanchard, is based on the 'readiness' level of the people the leader is attempting to influence. Readiness is the extent to which followers have the ability and willingness to accomplish a specific task. Ability is the knowledge, experience, and skill that an individual possesses to do the job and is called job readiness. Willingness is the motivation and commitment required to accomplish a given task. The style of leadership depends on the level of readiness of the followers.

The readiness (R) is divided into a continuum of four levels which are:

R1 - Low Follower Readiness - refers to low ability and low willingnessof followers i.e. those who are unable and insecure.

R2 - Low to Moderate Follower Readiness - refers to low ability and high willingness of followers i.e. those who are unable but confident.

R3 - Moderate to High Follower Readiness - refers to high ability and low willingness of followers i.e. those who are able but insecure.

R4 - High Follower Readiness - refers to high ability and high willingness of followers i.e. those who are both able and confident.

The direction is provided by the leader at the lower levels of readiness. Therefore, the decisions are leader directed. On the other hand, the direction is provided by the followers at the higher levels of readiness. Therefore, the decisions in this case are follower directed. When the followers move from low levels to high levels of readiness, the combinations of task and relationship behaviours appropriate to the situation begin to change.

For each of the four levels of readiness, the leadership style used may be a combination of task and relationship behaviour.

By combining the task and the relationship behaviour, we arrive at the following four different styles of leadership which correspond with the different levels of readiness as shown below.

S1 - Telling: This style is most appropriate for low follower readiness (R1). It emphasises high task behaviour and limited relationship behaviour.

S2 - Selling: This style is most appropriate for low to moderate follower readiness (R2). It emphasises high amounts of both task and relationship behaviour.

S3 - Participating: This style is most appropriate for moderate to high follower readiness (R3). It emphasises high amount of relationship behaviour but low amount of task behaviour.

S4 - Delegating: This style is most appropriate for high follower readiness (R4). It emphasises low levels of both task and relationship behaviour.

Fiedler's Contingency Model

Fred E. Fiedler's contingency theory of leadership effectiveness was based on studies of a wide range of group effectiveness, and concentrated on the relationship between leadership and organisational performance. This is one of the earliest situation-contingent leadership theories given by Fiedler. According to him, if an organisation attempts to achieve group effectiveness through leadership, then there is a need to assess the leader according to an underlying trait, assess the situation faced by the leader, and construct a proper match between the two.

Leader's trait

In order to assess the attitudes of the leader, Fiedler developed the 'least preferred co-worker' (LPC) scale in which the leaders are asked about the person with whom they least like to work. The scale is a questionnaire consisting of 16 items used to reflect a leader's underlying disposition toward others. The items in the LPC scale are pleasant / unpleasant, friendly / unfriendly, rejecting / accepting, unenthusiastic / enthusiastic, tense / relaxed, cold / warm, helpful / frustrating, cooperative / uncooperative, supportive / hostile, quarrelsome / harmonious, efficient / inefficient, gloomy / cheerful, distant / close, boring / interesting, self-assured / hesitant, open / guarded. Each item in the scale is given a single ranking of between one and eight points, with eight points indicating the most favourable rating.

Friendly ________________________________ Unfriendly

8 7 6 5 4 3 2 1

Fiedler states that leaders with high LPC scores are relationship-oriented and the ones with low scores are task-oriented. The high LPC score leaders derived most satisfaction from interpersonal relationships and therefore evaluate their least preferred co-workers in fairly favourable terms. These leaders think about the task accomplishment only after the relationship need is well satisfied. On the other hand, the low LPC score leaders derived satisfaction from performance of the task and attainment of objectives and only after tasks have been accomplished, these leaders work on establishing good social and interpersonal relationships.

Situational Factor

According to Fiedler, a leader's behaviour is dependent upon the favourability of the leadership situation. Three factors work together to determine how favourable a situation is to a leader. These are:

Leader-Member Relations- The degree to which the leaders is trusted and liked by the group members, and the willingness of the group members to follow the leader's guidance.

Task Structure- The degree to which the group's task has been described as structured or unstructured has been clearly defined and the extent to which it can be carried out by detailed instructions.

Position Power- The power of the leader by virtue of the organisational position and the degree to which the leader can exercise authority on group members in order to comply with and accept his direction and leadership.

With the help of these three variables, eight combinations of group-task situations were constructed by Fiedler. These combinations were used to identify the style of the leader.

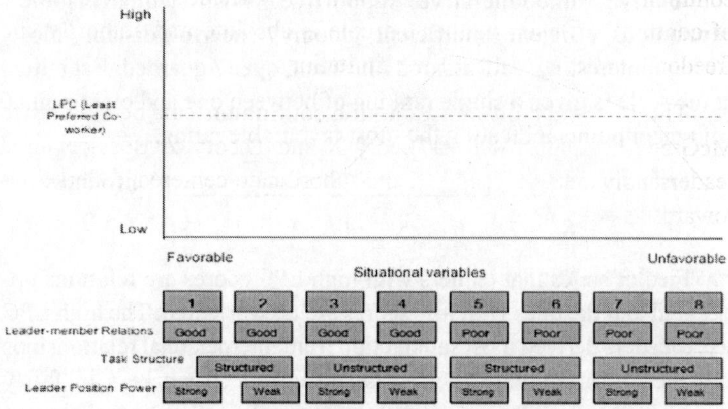

Leader's LPC Scores and Group Effectiveness

Leadership Effectiveness

The leader's effectiveness is determined by the interaction of the leader's style of behaviour and the favourableness of the situational characteristics. The most favourable situation is when leader-member relations are good, the task is highly structured, and the leader has a strong position power.

Research on the contingency model has shown that task-oriented leaders are more effective in highly favorable (1, 2, 3) and highly unfavourable situation (7, 8), whereas relationship-oriented leaders are more effective in situations of intermediate favourableness (4, 5, 6).

Continuum of Leadership Behaviour

The leadership continuum was originally written in 1958 by Tannenbaum and Schmidt and was later updated in the year 1973. Their work suggests a continuum of possible leadership behaviour available to a manager and along which many leadership styles may be placed. The continuum presents a range of action related to the degree of authority used by the manager and to the area of freedom available to non-managers in arriving at decisions. A broad range of leadership styles have been depicted on the continuum between two extremes of autocratic and free rein. The left side shows a style where control is maintained by a manager and the right side shows the release of control. However, neither extreme is absolute and authority and freedom are never without their limitations.

The Tannenbaum and Schmidt continuum can be related to McGregor's supposition of Theory X and Theory Y. Boss-centered leadership is towards Theory X and subordinate-centered leadership is towards Theory Y.

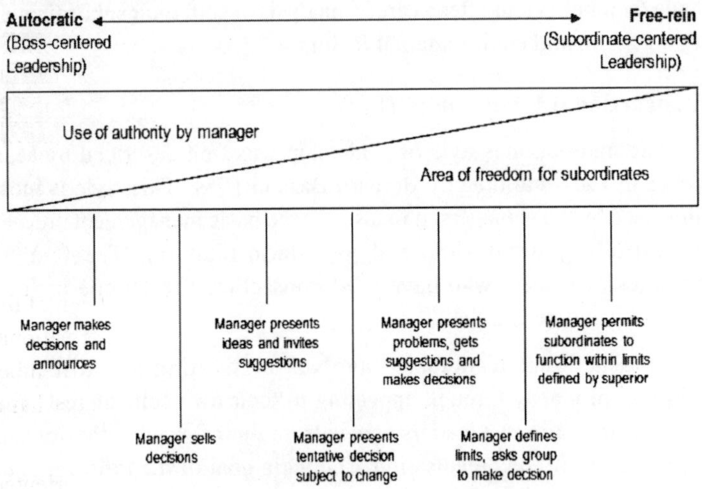

Continuum Leadership Behaviour

A manager is characterised according to degree of control that is maintained by him. According to this approach, four main styles of leadership have been identified:

Tells: The manager identifies a problem, chooses a decision, and announces this to subordinates. The subordinates are not a party to the decision-making process and the manager expects them to implement his decisions as soon as possible.

Sells: The decision is chosen by the manager only but he understands that there will be some amount of resistance from those faced with the decision and therefore makes efforts to persuade them to accept it.

Consults: Though the problem is identified by the manager, he does not take a final decision. The problem is presented to the subordinates and the solutions are suggested by the subordinates.

Joins: The manager defines the limits within which the decision can be taken by the subordinates and then makes the final decision along with the subordinates.

According to Tannenbaum and Schmidt, successful leaders know which behaviour is the most appropriate at a particular time. They shape their behaviour after a careful analysis of self, their subordinates, organisation, and environmental factors.

Transactional Leadership Theory

The transactional style of leadership was first described by Max Weber in 1947 and then by Bernard Bass in 1981. This style is most often used by the managers. It focuses on the basic management process of controlling, organising, and short-term planning. The famous examples of leaders who have used transactional technique include McCarthy and de Gaulle.

Transactional leadership involves motivating and directing followers primarily through appealing to their own self-interest. The power of transactional leaders comes from their formal authority and responsibility in the organisation. The main goal of the follower is to obey the instructions of the leader. The style can also be mentioned as a 'telling style'.

The leader believes in motivating through a system of rewards and punishment. If a subordinate does what is desired, a reward will follow, and if he does not go as per the wishes of the leader, a punishment will follow. Here, the exchange between leader and follower takes place to achieve routine performance goals.

Leadership-Member Exchange (LMX) Theory

Informal observation of leadership behaviour suggests that leader's action is not the same towards all subordinates. The importance of potential differences in this respect is brought into sharp focus by Graen's leader-member exchange model, also known as the vertical dyad linkage theory. The theory views leadership as consisting of a number of dyadic relationships linking the leader with a follower. The quality of the relationship is reflected by the degree of mutual trust, loyalty, support, respect, and obligation.

According to the theory, leaders form different kinds of relationships with various groups of subordinates. One group, referred to as the in-group, is favoured by the leader. Members of in-group receive considerably more attention from the leader and have more access to the organisational resources. By contrast, other subordinates fall into the out-group. These individuals are disfavoured by the leader. As such, they receive fewer valued resources from their leaders.

Leaders distinguish between the in-group and out-group members on the basis of the perceived similarity with respect to personal characteristics, such as age, gender, or personality. A follower may also be granted an in-group status if the leader believes that person to be especially competent at performing his or her job. The relationship between leaders and followers follows two stages:

Role Taking: When a new member joins the organisation, the leader assesses the talent and abilities of the member and offers them opportunities to demonstrate their capabilities.

Role Making: An informal and unstructured negotiation on work-related factors takes place between the leader and the member. A member who is similar to the leader is more likely to succeed. A betrayal by the member at this stage may result in him being relegated to the out-group.

The LMX 7 scale assesses the degree to which leaders and followers have mutual respect for each other's capabilities, feel a deepening sense of mutual trust, and have a sense of strong obligation to one another. Taken together, these dimensions determine the extent to which followers will be part of the leader's in-group or out-group.

Transformational Leadership Theory

Creating high-performance workforce has become increasingly

important and to do so business leaders must be able to inspire organisational members to go beyond their task requirements. As a result, new concepts of leadership have emerged - transformational leadership being one of them.

Transformational leadership may be found at all levels of the organisation: teams, departments, divisions, and organisation as a whole. Such leaders are visionary, inspiring, daring, risk-takers, and thoughtful thinkers. They have a charismatic appeal. But charisma alone is insufficient for changing the way an organisation operates. For bringing major changes, transformational leaders must exhibit the following four factors:

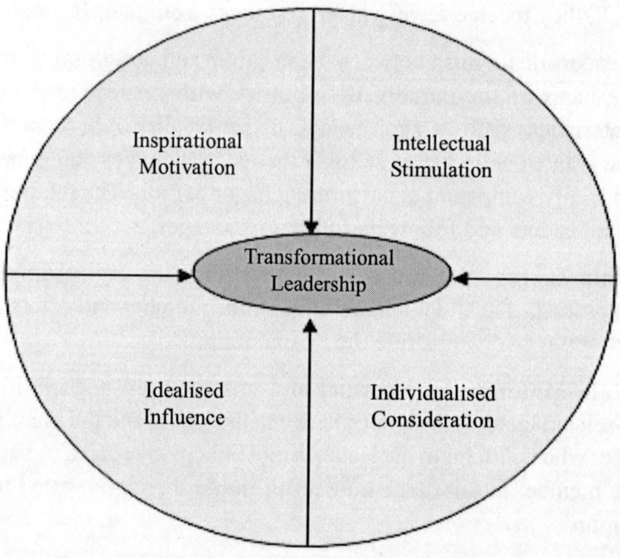

Model of Transformational Leadership

Inspirational Motivation: The foundation of transformational leadership is the promotion of consistent vision, mission, and a set of values to the members. Their vision is so compelling that they know what they want from every interaction. Transformational leaders guide followers by providing them with a sense of meaning and challenge.

They work enthusiastically and optimistically to foster the spirit of teamwork and commitment.

Intellectual Stimulation: Such leaders encourage their followers to be innovative and creative. They encourage new ideas from their followers and never criticise them publicly for the mistakes committed by them. The leaders focus on the "what" in problems and do not focus on the blaming part of it. They have no hesitation in discarding an old practice set by them if it is found ineffective.

Idealised Influence: They believe in the philosophy that a leader can influence followers only when he practices what he preaches. The leaders act as role models that followers seek to emulate. Such leaders always win the trust and respect of their followers through their action. They typically place their followers needs over their own, sacrifice their personal gains for them, and demonstrate high standards of ethical conduct. The use of power by such leaders is aimed at influencing them to strive for the common goals of the organisation.

Individualised Consideration: Leaders act as mentors to their followers and reward them for creativity and innovation. The followers are treated differently according to their talents and knowledge. They are empowered to make decisions and are always provided with the needed support to implement their decisions.

Likert's Management System

Rensis Likert and his associates studied the patterns and styles of managers for three decades at the University of Michigan, USA, and identified a four-fold model of management systems. The model was developed on the basis of a questionnaire administered to managers in over 200 organisations and research into the performance characteristics of different types of organisations. The four systems of management system or the four leadership styles identified by Likert are:

System 1 - Exploitative Authoritative: Responsibility lies in the hands of the people at the upper echelons of the hierarchy. The superior has no trust and confidence in subordinates. The decisions are imposed on subordinates and they do not feel free at all to discuss things about the job with their superior. The teamwork or communication is very little and the motivation is based on threats.

System 2 - Benevolent Authoritative: The responsibility lies at the managerial levels but not at the lower levels of the organisational hierarchy. The superior has condescending confidence and trust in subordinates. Here again, the subordinates do not feel free to discuss things about the job with their superior. The teamwork or communication is very little and motivation is based on a system of rewards.

System 3 - Consultative: Responsibility is spread widely through the organisational hierarchy. The superior has substantial but not complete confidence in subordinates. Some amount of discussion about job-related things takes place between the superior and subordinates. There is a fair amount of teamwork, and communication takes place vertically and horizontally. The motivation is based on rewards and involvement in the job.

System 4 - Participative: Responsibility for achieving the organisational goals is widespread throughout the organisational hierarchy. There is a high level of confidence that the superior has in his subordinates. There is a high level of teamwork, communication, and participation.

JOB SATISFACTION

Job satisfaction is defined as "the extent to which people like (satisfaction) or dislike (dissatisfaction) their jobs".

Job satisfaction is the favourableness or un-favourableness with which the employee views his work. It expresses the amount of agreement between one's expectation of the job and the rewards that the job provides. Job satisfaction is a part of life satisfaction. The nature of one's environment of job is an important part of life as Job Satisfaction influences one's general life satisfaction.

Factors Influencing Job Satisfaction

The major factors influencing job satisfaction are presented below:

Supervision

To a worker, Supervision is equally a strong contributor to the job satisfaction as well as to the job dissatisfaction. The feelings of workers towards his supervisors are usually similar to his feeling towards the company. The role of supervisor is a focal point for attitude formation. Bad supervision results in absenteeism and labour turnover. Good supervision results in higher production and good industrial relations.

Co-Workers

Various studies had traced this factor as a factor of intermediate importance. One's associates with others had frequently been motivated as a factor in job satisfaction. Certainly, this seems reasonable because people like to be near their friends. The workers derive satisfaction when the co-workers are helpful, friendly and co-operative.

Pay

Studies also show that most of the workers felt satisfied when they are paid more adequately to the work performed by them. The relative important of pay would probably changing factor in job satisfaction or dissatisfaction.

Age

Age has also been found to have a direct relationship to level job of satisfaction of employees. In some groups job satisfaction is higher with increasing age, in other groups job satisfaction is lower and in other there is no difference at all.

Marital Status

Marital status has an important role in deciding the job satisfaction. Most of the studies have revealed that the married person finds dissatisfaction in his job than his unmarried counterpart. The reasons stated to be are that wages were insufficient due to increased cost of living, educations to children, etc.

Education

Studies conducted among various workers revealed that most of workers who had not completed their school education showed higher satisfaction level. However, educated workers felt less satisfied in their job.

Working Condition

The result of various studies shows that working condition is an important factor. Good working atmosphere and pleasant surroundings help increasing the production of industry. Working conditions are more important to women workers than men workers.

Job Content

Job content refers to the intrinsic value of the job which depends on the requirement of skills for performing it, and the degree of responsibility and growth it offers. A higher content of these factors provides higher satisfaction. For example, a routine and repetitive lesser satisfaction; the degree of satisfaction progressively increases in job rotation, job enlargement, and job enrichment.

Nature of Job

Higher level jobs provide more satisfaction as compared to lower levels. This happens because high level jobs carry prestige and status in the society which itself becomes source of satisfaction for the job holders. For example, professionals derive more satisfaction as compared to salaried people: factory workers are least satisfied.

MORALE

Morale represents the attitudes of individuals and groups in an organisation towards their work environment. Morale is an indicator of the attitude of employees towards their jobs, superiors and their organisational environment. It is a collection of the employees' attitude, feelings and sentiments.

According to William Spriegel, "morale is the co-operative attitude or mental health of a number of people who are related to each other on some basis".

According to Leighton, "morale is the capacity of a group of people to pull together persistently and consistently in pursuit of a common purpose".

Consequences of Low Morale

Low morale indicates the presence of mental unrest. This mental tension or unrest not only hampers production and productivity but also leads to ill-health of the working people. The other consequences of low morale are the following:

1. High rate of labour turnover;
2. High rate of absenteeism;
3. Excessive complaints and grievances;
4. Resistance to change;
5. Lack of discipline;
6. Antagonism towards the organisation and its management;
7. Low quantity and quality of output.

Low morale can be fatal to the organisation. In order to avoid the evil consequences of low morale, every manager should attempt to build high morale amongst his subordinates.

Steps to Build High Morale

Every manager should attempt to build high morale of his subordinates. Both individual and collective efforts are required to develop and maintain high morale. The following measures are taken to improve the morale of employees in the organisation:

1. A fair system of wage and salary payments should be evolved.
2. A sense of security of job should be ensured.
3. The promotion policy should be sound and should be followed promptly.
4. Competent supervisors should be appointed.
5. The channel of communication should be effective.
6. The employees should be made to feel proud of being employed in the organisation.
7. Employees' welfare schemes like housing, medical benefits, education facilities for children, canteen, credit facilities, and safety measures should be provided as they are very helpful in developing positive attitude among the employees.

8. Workers should be given proper training so that they may perform their jobs without frustration and get job satisfaction.

FATIGUE

Human capacity to work is limited. Every work requires care, attention and concentration. A person cannot work continuously for longer periods. The work output will be more in the morning and it goes on decreasing with passage of time as a worker will feel tried, mentally and physically, in the evening. The decrease in efficiency of working due to longer working periods is known as fatigue.

It is one of the most significant problems before industrial engineers. Fatigue has been defined as a negative appetite for work activity. According to vitals, "The tension, the subjection to specialisation of work and a rhythm uncontrolled by the individual, promote fatigue characterised by decrease in the power to work, a decrease in pressure taken in work, and an increase in the enjoyment of the hours spent away from work".

1. It leads to loss of efficiency.
2. It results in more or less complete loss of responsiveness of tissue.
3. It may be termed as the reduced capacity of work resulting from work itself.
4. It is considered as state of 'lack or interest' in not only work but in other activities too.

Fatigue is related to the mental status of person. One person may not be tired even after long hours of work whereas the other person may feel fatigued or tired even after few hours of work. Some persons may feel fresh after a Shorty relaxation during working periods while others may not regain energy "even after longer rests." A number of factors such as aptitude, interest, nature of job, work environment or working conditions etc., influence the mind of persons on jobs.

Types of Fatigue

Fatigue may be of the following types:

1. Physical Fatigue

Physical fatigue is caused either by continuous work for long periods or the nature of work like the work may be heavy and requiring lot of physical excursion. The physical capacities of workers are limited and they may feel tired after a continuous work for longer periods.

2. Mental Fatigue

A worker utilises his brain for doing a job for a longer period. The doing of same work again and again will result in mental fatigue of the worker.

3. Nervous Fatigue

When work needs the use of mental and physical capabilities for a continuous period, it will result in nervous fatigue.

4. Industrial Fatigue

When a worker continues to work the job for longer periods, his efficiency and productivity will result in nervous fatigue.

Causes of Fatigue

Fatigue may be caused due to the following reasons:

1. Longer hours of continuous work without rest pauses may cause fatigue because muscles will be tired after long work.
2. Unsatisfactory working environment like insufficient light, insanitation, congestion, noise elevated temperatures, etc.
3. Fatigue may also be caused by personal reasons such as family tension, bad health, etc.
4. There may be faulty design of machines and equipment which leads to wastage of energy of workers on them.
5. The complexity or production process may also put more loads on workers resulting into fatigue.
6. The workers may not be properly placed on jobs as per their skill levels.

7. The harsh attitude of supervisor may also result in fatigue of workers.
8. Inconvenient and awkward posture of worker i.e., standing or bending for longer periods may also be the cause of fatigue.

Methods of Reducing Fatigue

A fatigued worker will not be able to work with his original rhythm. Every industrial enterprise is expected to devise ways and means of reducing fatigue so that production does not suffer for longer periods.

Following methods may help in reducing fatigue and providing freshness to workers:

1. Rest Pauses

When workers continue to work for longer periods then they feel tired and need some rest. Rest pauses are of great importance in reducing fatigue as well as monotony. Rest pauses should be provided in such a way that workers feel relieved after working for some hours. A well planned rest pauses schedule will be of great help in reducing fatigue.

2. Less Hours of Work

Longer hours of work are the main cause of fatigue. The hours of work should be reduced to that optimum level where workers are able to keep up their working speed. The Factories Act in India allows only 48 hours a week for adult workers and it should be followed strictly.

3. Proper Lighting

Poor illumination is an important cause of disturbance and fatigue. The work place should be properly lighted so that workers are able to work without burdening their eye sight and brain.

4. Improving Environmental Conditions

The humidity, temperature and ventilation influence workers at work. A proper balance of temperature, humidity should be maintained to make the work place comfortable and worth working so that fatigue is reduced.

5. Reduction of Noise

Undesirable noise will cause fatigue. It may also cause muscular tension. Unnecessary noise should be curbed to its minimum level. Lower noise levels increase productivity of workers by reducing fatigue, removing cause of irritation.

6. Proper Selection of Employees

A wrong selection of employees and their placement may also be a reason for fatigue and monotony. A job may require more physical input than worker has. In such situations, the worker will feel fatigued after short duration of work.

7. Job Rotation

Sometimes workers start feeling bore and tired while working repeatedly on the same job. If job rotation is provided it will avoid boredom and fatigue.

8. Counselling of Employees

Anxieties and worries may be the main cause of fatigue with some workers. There may be job dissatisfaction, domestic problem, etc. The officers of personnel department should counsel the employees and help them in solving their problems.

MONOTONY

Monotony means dull. Monotonous means dry, unvarying, tedious and uninteresting. The terms monotony and boredom are usually used to indicate the undesirable effects of repetitive work. British researchers use the terms tedium and monotony to describe the state of mind caused by repetitive work. Monotony is the first stage which rapidly develops into boredom when a person finds it hard to stand monotonous repetition of the same operations.

Three factors that produce Monotony and Boredom are as follows:

1. The repetitive nature of the task,
2. Intellectual level of the person and
3. The personality characteristic of the individual.

Countering the Effects of Monotony, Boredom and Fatigue

1. Psychological tests are used to locate certain personality factors related with boredom, so that careful selection and placement can solve the problem to a certain extent.
2. Introducing change in the jobs that are highly repetitive.
3. Making job more interesting by attaching some meaning to them.
4. Setting up clear short-term production goals so that the worker is greatly motivated to reach them.
5. Another way of combating monotony is providing social and recreational activities during and outside the working hours.
6. Reducing interruptions of work.
7. Introducing necessary changes in work situations to make workers feel that they have their tasks completed.

ORGANISATION CHANGE AND OD

Organisational Change

Factors such as improvements in technology, the need for business diversification and expansion are all examples of driving forces of change in organisations. These factors contribute to the onset of organisational development by pushing business leaders and managers to take certain actions which will lead to the desired outcome. There are several types of organisational change. Some changes are planned and driven by innovative thinking, while others are unplanned. Sometimes change in an organisation can affect the whole entity, and at other times it can have a direct impact on only one segment of the business structure.

When an organisation experiences change, it re-invents its overall strategy for success, and adds or removes certain components in its current style of operations.

Organisational Development

Business development is defined as "a planned organisation-wide effort to increase an organisation's effectiveness and viability," according to Noetic Outcomes Consulting. One of the most widely known means of implementing organisation development is enterprise master planning. This process allows an organisation to choose the best business solution out of a multitude of alternatives or options. Enterprise master planning involves a thorough analysis of existing business processes and a good understanding of opportunities available for improving those processes. Documentations and resources are used to determine the most appropriate business options, and to qualify and justify the master plan.

The methods used for organisational development will vary, and the steps taken to implement organisational change is contingent on the scale of the project and the sort of results being sought. The timeline for the plan development and integration will therefore depend on the complexity of the enterprise and its starting point in the development stage.

Lewin's Model of OD

Lewin's model is based on premise that before introducing a change, organisation needs to be prepared for change motivated to change and established and integrated the change into behaviours of organisation. A brief description of this model is mentioned below:

Unfreezing: This necessitates unlearning of old things in order to learn new things. It involves encouraging individuals to discard old behaviours by shaking up the equilibrium that maintains status quo. Thus, unfreezing motivates people for change and minimising resistance to change.

Changing: Efforts are made to inject new attitudes, values and behaviours to experimentation with new behaviour. This implies transition from old behaviour to new one.

Refreezing: In this final step, new attitudes, values and behaviours are established. This implies stabilising and integrating the change by reinforcing the new behaviours and integrating them into formal and interpersonal relationships and in one's personality.

ORGANISATIONAL EFFECTIVENESS

Generally speaking, the term of organisational effectiveness describes the degree to which an organisation realises its goals (Etzioni 1964).

Organisational effectiveness has a very broad and often vague definition, so much so that most sources explain the concept by example rather than definition. Basically, the effectiveness of a business constitutes its ability to perform a function with optimal levels of input and output. Companies use organisational effectiveness to measure any number of things, from the relationship between employee performance and company profits to the correlation between manufacturing processes and production volume. No set parameters exist for organisational effectiveness and it follows no definitive mathematical formula - each organisation creates its own method of measuring effectiveness.

UNIT - V

Industrial Relations

Concept

Scope

Approaches

Industrial Relations System

Industrial Disputes

Causes

Effects

Trends

Methods and Machinery for the Settlement of Industrial Disputes

Workers Participation in Management

Code of Discipline

Tripartite Bodies

ILO

Industrial Relations and the New Economic Reforms

CONCEPT OF INDUSTRIAL RELATIONS

Industrial relations is a post-industrial revolution term that replaced the expression "master-servant" used to define the relationship between a worker and an employer.

Industrial relations has become one of the most delicate and complex problems of modern industrial society. Industrial progress is impossible without cooperation of labours and harmonious relationships. Therefore, it is in the interest of all to create and maintain good relations between employees (labour) and employers (management).

By "relations" we mean "the relationships that exist within the boundary wall of the industry between the employer and his workmen. On the other hand, "Industry" refers to any productive activity in which an individual (or a group of individuals) is (are) engaged".

The term industrial relations, is basically the interactions between employers, employees and the government, and the institutions and associations.

The term 'industrial relations' has been variously defined. J.T. Dunlop defines industrial relations as "the complex interrelations among managers, workers and agencies of the governments".

Dale Yoder defines it as a "whole field of relationships that exists because of the necessary collaboration of men and women in the employment process of an industry."

"Industrial relation is an art of living together for the purpose of production" – J. Henry

Industrial relation do not function in a vacuum but multi-dimensional in nature and are conditioned with three determinants (i) Institutional factors, (ii) Economic factors and (iii) Technological factors. Institutional factors are included items such as state policy, labour laws, voluntary codes, collective agreements, worker's unions and employer's organisation, social institution like the community, caste, joint family, creed, system of beliefs, etc, attitudes of work, systems of power status, relative nearness to the centres of power; motivation and influence and industrial relations.

Economic factors are included economic organisation (socialist, capitalist, communist, individual ownership, company ownership, government ownership), power of labour and employers, the nature and composition of the labour force and the sources of supply and demand in the labour market.

Technological factors include the techniques of production, modernisation and rationalisation schemes, capital structures, etc.

Industrial Relations versus Employee Relations

Industrial relations commonly involves three parties: the employee, employer and the union. With employee relations, just the employee and employer are parties to the working relationship.

Objectives of Industrial Relations System

1. To safeguard the interest of labour and management by securing the highest level of mutual understanding and goodwill among all those sections in the industry which participate in the process of production.
2. To avoid industrial conflict or strife and develop harmonious relations, which are an essential factor in the productivity of workers and the industrial progress of a country.
3. To raise productivity to a higher level in an era of full employment by lessening the tendency to high turnover and frequency of absenteeism.
4. To establish and promote the growth of an industrial democracy based on labour partnership in the sharing of profits and of managerial decisions, so that an individual's personality may grow its full stature for the benefit of the industry and of the country as well.
5. To eliminate or minimise the number of strikes, lockouts by providing reasonable wages, improved living and working conditions, fringe benefits, etc.
6. To improve the economic conditions of workers in the existing state of industrial management and political government.

7. Vesting of a proprietary interest of the workers in the industries in which they are employed.

Scope of IRs

The cordial and healthy labour management relations could be brought in- By safeguarding the interest of the workers; By fixing reasonable wages; By providing good working conditions; By providing other social security measures; By maintaining healthy trade unions; By collective bargaining. The industrial peace could be attained – By setting industrial disputes through mutual understanding and agreement; By evolving various legal measure and setting up various machineries such as Works Committee, Boards of Conciliation, Labour Courts, etc. The industrial democracy could be achieved – By allowing workers to take part in management; and By recognition of human rights.

Actors in the IR system

Three main parties are directly involved in industrial relations:

Employers: Employers possess certain rights. They have the right to hire and fire them. Management can also affect workers' interests by exercising their right to relocate, close or merge the factory or to introduce technological changes.

Employees: Workers seek to improve the terms and conditions of their employment. They exchange views with management and voice their grievances. They also want to share decision-making powers of management. Workers generally unite to form unions against the management and get support from these unions.

Government: The central and state government influences and regulates industrial relations through laws, rules, agreements, awards of court and the like.

Approaches to Industrial Relations

The three popular approaches to industrial relations are unitary approach, pluralistic approach and Marxist approach. The details of the approaches are discussed as follows:

1. Unitary Approach: In unitary approach, the organisation is taken as an integrated and harmonious system. A core assumption of unitary approach is that management and workers, and all members of the organisation share the same objectives, interests and purposes; thus, working together, hand-in-hand, towards the shared mutual goals. In this approach the union co-operates with the management and works for a common goal. The assumption of this approach is that everyone benefits when the focus is on a common interest.

2. Pluralistic Approach: Pluralistic approach is opposite to unitary approach. In pluralism approach, the organisation is divided into sub-groups - management and trade unions. In this approach, the conflict between the managers and the workers over the distribution of profits is unavoidable. Union plays an important role in this approach. Employees join union to protect their interest and influence the decision-making by the management. Trade unions are viewed as legitimate representatives of employees. Conflict is dealt by collective bargaining and industrial tribunals, conciliation and arbitration.

3. Marxist Approach: According to Marxist approach, the conflict in an organisation arises not because of the employees and the employer. The conflict takes place due to the division in the society between the capital (i.e. with those who own resources) and labour (i.e. who has only labour to offer). Conflict is therefore seen as inevitable and trade unions are a natural response of workers to their exploitation by capital.

Other Approaches

4. Psychological Approach: The problems of IR have their origin in the perceptions of the management, unions and the workers. The conflicts between labour and management occur because every group negatively perceives the behaviour of the other i.e. even the honest intention of the other party so looked at with suspicion. The problem is further aggravated by various factors like the income, level of education, communication, values, beliefs, customs, goals of persons and groups, prestige, power, status, recognition, security, etc. Industrial peace is a result of proper attitudes and perception of the two parties.

5. Sociological Approach: Industry is a social world in miniature. The management goals, workers' attitudes, perception of change in industry, are all, in turn, decided by broad social factors like the culture of the institutions, customs, structural changes, status-symbols, rationality, acceptance or resistance to change, tolerance, etc. Industry is, thus, inseparable from the society in which it functions. Through the main function of an industry is economic, its social consequences are also important such as urbanisation, social mobility, housing and transport problem in industrial areas, disintegration of family structure, stress and strain, etc. As industries develop, a new industrial-cum-social pattern emerges, which provides general new relationships, institutions and behavioural pattern and new techniques of handling human resources. These do influence the development of industrial relations.

6. Human Relations Approach: Human resources are made up of living human beings. They want freedom of speech, thought of expression, movement, etc. When employers treat them as inanimate objects, encroach on their expectations, throat-cuts, conflicts and tensions arise. In fact major problems in industrial relations arise out of a tension which is created because of the employer's pressures and workers' reactions, protests and resistance to these pressures through protective mechanisms in the form of workers' organisation, associations and trade unions.

In resolving conflicts, understanding of human behaviour – both individual and groups – is a pre-requisite for the employers, the union leaders and the government. Conflicts cannot be resolved unless the management must learn and know what the basic needs of men are and how they can be motivated to work effectively.

7. The System Approach: The system approach was developed by J. T. Dunlop of Harvard University in 1958. According to this approach, individuals are part of an ongoing but independent social system. The behaviour, actions and role of the individuals are shaped by the cultures of the society. The three elements of the system approach are input, process and output. Society provides the cue (signal) to the individuals about how one should act in a situation. The institutions, the value system and other characteristics of the society influence the process and determine the outcome or response of the individuals. The basis of this theory is that group cohesiveness is provided by the common ideology shaped by the societal factors.

According to Dunlop, the industrial relations system comprises certain actors, certain contexts, and an ideology, which binds them together and a body of rules created to govern the actors at the workplace and work community. The actors in the system are the managers, the workers and their representatives, and the government agencies. The rules in the system are classified into two categories: Substantive rules and Procedural rules.

The **substantive rules** determine the conditions under which people are employed. Such rules are normally derived from the implied terms and conditions of employment, legislations, agreements, practices and managerial policies and directives.

The **procedural rules** govern how substantive rules are to be made and understood. Ultimately, the introduction of new rules and regulations and revisions of the existing rules for improving the industrial relations are the major outputs of the industrial relations system. These may be substantive rules as well as procedural rules. The context in the system approach refers to the environment of the system which is normally determined by the technological nature of the organisation, the financial and other constraints that restrict the actors of industrial relations, and the nature of power sharing in the macro environment, namely, the society.

8. Gandhian Trusteeship Approach: Gandhi's views on industrial relations are based on his fundamental principles of truth, non-violence and non-possession. Out of these principles evolved the concept of trusteeship on which his philosophy of industrial relations rests. This philosophy presumes the peaceful co-existence of capital and labour, which calls for the resolution of conflict by non-violent, non-cooperation (i.e., Satyagraha), which actually amounts to peaceful strikes in ordinary parlance. Gandhi accepted the workers' right to strike, but cautioned that this right is to be exercised in a just cause, and in a peaceful and non-violent manner; and it should be resorted to only after employers fail to respond to their moral appeals.

9. Weber's Social Action Approach: The social action approach of Weber has laid considerable importance to the question of control in the context of increasing rationalisation and bureaucratisation.

Closely related to Weber's concern related to control in organisations was his concern with "power of control and dispersal". Thus, a trade union in the Weber's scheme of things has both economic purposes as well as the goal of involvement in political and power struggles. Some of the major orientations in the Weberian approach have been to analyse the impact of techno-economic and politico-organisational changes on trade union structure and processes to analyse the subjective interpretation of workers' approaches to trade unionism and finally to analyse the power of various components of the industrial relations environment – Government, employers, trade unions and political parties. Thus, the Weberian approach gives the theoretical and operational importance to "control" as well as to the power struggle to control work organisations – a power struggle in which all the actors in the industrial relations drama are caught up.

10. The Oxford Approach: According to this approach, the industrial relations system is a study of institutions of job regulations and the stress is on the substantive and procedural rules as in Dunlop's model. Flanders, the exponent of this approach, considers every business enterprise as a social system of production and distribution, which has a structured pattern of relationship. The "institution of job regulation" is categorised by him as internal and external-the former being an internal part of the industrial relations system such as code of work rules, wage structure, internal procedure of joint consultation, and grievance procedure. He views trade unions as an external organisation and excludes collective agreements from the sphere of internal regulation. According to him, collective bargaining is central to the industrial relations system.

Causes of Poor Industrial Relations

The main causes of industrial disputes are:

(i) Wages: Low wages of industrial workers constitute a major cause of industrial disputes in the country. Wages have not been rising in proportion to the rise in prices. This has forced the labourers to demand higher wages, consequently leading to disputes.

(ii) Bonus: The demand for bonus or increase in bonus has been the second major cause of industrial disputes. The workers feel that they should have a greater share in the profits of the industrial concern. Non-acceptance of this fact by the employers has been a source of friction among the employers and the workers.

(iii) Working Conditions: The demand for improvement in working conditions such as lesser working hours, security of job, better safety measures in the factory, leave, canteen, gratuity facilities, etc., are also responsible for many industrial disputes.

(iv) Other Causes: Among other causes that lead to disputes are failure of employers to recognise trade unions, conflict between rival unions for representation, insult to trade union leadership by the employer, introduction of rationalisation in the factory, the fear of retrenchment of workers, sympathetic strikes with fellow employees in other establishments, general discontent and sense of frustration among labourers, political issues, etc.

Effects of Poor Industrial Relations

Industrial relations are of great importance in industrial life. These relations have great bearing on the economic, social and political spheres of our society. If in an organisation, relations between labour and management are cordial, there will be industrial peace and interests of both the parties will be automatically safeguarded. However, organisations where industrial relations are strained, the organisations have to face lot of problems. The atmosphere of such organisations is always surcharged with industrial unrest leading either to strikes or lockouts. Organisations which ignore the importance of industrial relations face high cost of production. Adverse effect on efficiency, low-grade production, negligence in the execution of work, absenteeism among the workers, high rate of labour turnover, etc. are the evils that result from poor industrial relations.

Lack of cordiality in industrial relations not only adversely affects the interests of the labourers and employers but also cause harm to different sections of society. They are faced with lot of difficulties and problems.

Demerits of poor industrial relations can be expressed as under:

Effect on Workers: (i) Loss of wages, (ii) Physical injury or death on account of violence during labour unrest, (iii) Excesses by employers, (iv) Economic losses, (v) Bitterness in relations, (vi) Adverse affect on career.

Effect on Employers / Industrialists: (i) Less production, (ii) Less Profit, (iii) Bad affect on organisation, (iv) Bad effect on human relations, (v) Damage to machines and equipments, (vi) Adverse effect on development of companies, (vii) Burden of fixed expenses.

Effect on Government: (i) Loss of revenue (less recovery of income tax, sales tax, etc.), (ii) Lack of order in society, (iii) Blame by different parties.

Effect on Consumers: (i) Rise in prices, (ii) Scarcity of goods, (iii) Bad affect on quality of goods.

Other Effects: (i) Adverse affect on International Trade (Fall in exports and rise in imports), (ii) Hindrance in Economic Development of the country, (iii) Uncertainty in economy.

TRENDS OF INDUSTRIAL DISPUTES

During the last 20 years, on an average, about ten industrial disputes involving more than 12,52,225 workers and resulting in loss of more than 13,365 man days per year were reported in India. In 1992, 1,714 total strikes and lockout were recorded. As a result, 31,259 workdays were lost. More than 12,52,225 workers were involved in these labour disputes. The number and seriousness of strikes and lockouts have varied from year to year. There were 91 labour disputes in 2011, resulting in the loss of 621 man-days, while the number of workers involved stood at 48,156. Year 1992, recorded highest industrial dispute year and also recorded as highest man days lost year. Year 2011 recorded as less strikes and lockouts, less man-days lost, less worker involved in industrial disputes in India. This continuous decline in strikes and lockouts and extraordinary growth of trade union indicates that the industrial relations in India are improving.

Methods and Machinery for the Settlement of Industrial Disputes

Some of the major industrial dispute settlement machinery are as follows: 1. Conciliation 2. Court of Inquiry 3. Voluntary Arbitration 4. Adjudication.

This machinery has been provided under the Industrial Disputes Act, 1947. It, in fact, provides a legalistic way of setting the disputes. As said above, the goal of preventive machinery is to create an environment where the disputes do not arise at all.

1. Conciliation

Conciliation, is a form of mediation. Mediation is the act of making active effort to bring two conflicting parties to compromise. Mediation, however, differs from conciliation in that whereas conciliator plays only a passive and indirect role, and the scope of his functions is provided under the law, the mediator takes active part and the scope of his activities are not subject to any statutory provisions.

Conciliation is the "practice by which the services of a neutral party are used in a dispute as a means of helping the disputing parties to reduce the extent of their differences and to arrive at an amicable settlement of agreed solution."

The Industrial Disputes Act, 1947 provides for conciliation, and can be utilised either by appointing conciliation officers (permanently or for a limited period) or by constituting a board of conciliation. This conciliation machinery can take a note of a dispute or apprehend dispute either on its own or when approached by either party.

With a view to expediting conciliation proceeding, time-limits have been prescribed—14 days in the case of conciliation officers and two months in the case of a board of conciliation, settlement arrived at in the course of conciliation is binding for such period as may be agreed upon between the parties or for a period of six months and with continue to be binding until revoked by either party. The Act prohibits strike and lock-out during the pendency of conciliation proceedings before a Board and for seven days after the conclusion of such proceedings.

Conciliation Officer

The law provides for the appointment of Conciliation Officer by the Government to conciliate between the parties to the industrial dispute. The Conciliation Officer is given the powers of a civil court, whereby he is authorised to call the witness the parties on oath. It should be remembered, however, whereas civil court cannot go beyond interpreting the laws, the conciliation officer can go behind the facts and make judgment which will be binding upon the parties.

On receiving information about a dispute, the conciliation officer should give formal intimation in writing to the parties concerned of his intention to commence conciliation proceedings from a specified date. He should then start doing all such things as he thinks fit for the purpose of persuading the parties to come to fair and amicable settlement of the dispute.

Conciliation is an art where the skill, tact, imagination and even personal influence of the conciliation officer affect his success. The Industrial Disputes Act, therefore, does not prescribe any procedure to the followed by him.

The conciliation officer is required to submit his report to the appropriate government along with the copy of the settlement arrived at in relation to the dispute or in case conciliation has failed, he has to send a detailed report giving out the reasons for failure of conciliation.

The report in either case must be submitted within 14 days of the commencement of conciliation proceedings or earlier. But the time for submission of the report may be extended by an agreement in writing of all the parties to the dispute subject to the approval of the conciliation officer.

If an agreement is reached (called the memorandum of settlement), it remains binding for such period as is agreed upon by the parties, and if no such period is agreed upon, for a period of six months from the date on which the memorandum of settlement is signed by the parties to the dispute, and continues to be binding on the parties after the expiry of the period aforesaid, until the expiry of two months from the date on which a notice in writing of an intention to terminate the settlement is given by one of the party or parties to the settlement.

Board of Conciliation

In case Conciliation Officer fails to resolve the differences between the parties, the government has the discretion to appoint a Board of Conciliation. The Board is tripartite and ad hoc body. It consists of a chairman and two or four other members.

The chairman is to be an independent person and other members are nominated in equal number by the parties to the dispute. Conciliation proceedings before a Board are similar to those that take place before the Conciliation Officer. The government has yet another option of referring the dispute to the Court of Inquiry instead of the Board of Conciliation.

The machinery of the Board is set in motion when a dispute is referred to it. In other words, the Board does not hold the conciliation proceedings of its own accord. On the dispute being referred to the Board, it is the duty of the Board to do all things as it thinks fit for the purpose of inducing the parties to come to a fair and amicable settlement. The Board must submit its report to the government within two months of the date on which the dispute was referred to it. This period can be further extended by the government by two months.

2. Court of Inquiry

In case of the failure of the conciliation proceedings to settle a dispute, the government can appoint a Court of Inquiry to enquire into any matter connected with or relevant to industrial dispute. The court is expected to submit its report within six months. The court of enquiry may consist of one or more persons to be decided by the appropriate government.

The court of enquiry is required to submit its report within a period of six months from the commencement of enquiry. This report is subsequently published by the government within 30 days of its receipt. Unlike during the period of conciliation, workers' right to strike, employers' right to lockout, and employers' right to dismiss workmen, etc. remain unaffected during the proceedings in a court to enquiry.

A court of enquiry is different from a Board of Conciliation. The former aims at inquiring into and revealing the causes of an industrial dispute. On the other hand, the latter's basic objective is to promote the settlement of an industrial dispute. Thus, a court of enquiry is primarily fact-finding machinery.

3. Voluntary Arbitration

On failure of conciliation proceedings, the conciliation officer may persuade the parties to refer the dispute to a voluntary arbitrator. Voluntary arbitration refers to getting the disputes settled through an independent person chosen by the parties involved mutually and voluntarily.

In other words, arbitration offers an opportunity for a solution of the dispute through an arbitrator jointly appointed by the parties to the dispute. The process of arbitration saves time and money of both the parties which is usually wasted in case of adjudication.

Voluntary arbitration became popular as a method a settling differences between workers and management with the advocacy of Mahatma Gandhi, who had applied it very successfully in the Textile industry of Ahmedabad. However, voluntary arbitration was lent legal identity only in 1956 when Industrial Disputes Act, 1947 was amended to include a provision relating to it.

The provision for voluntary arbitration was made because of the lengthy legal proceedings and formalities and resulting delays involved in adjudication. It may, however, be noted that arbitrator is not vested with any judicial powers.

He derives his powers to settle the dispute from the agreement that parties have made between themselves regarding the reference of dispute to the arbitrator. The arbitrator should submit his award to the government. The government will then publish it within 30 days of such submission. The award would become enforceable on the expiry of 30 days of its publication.

Voluntary arbitration is one of the democratic ways for settling industrial disputes. It is the best method for resolving industrial conflicts and is a close' supplement to collective bargaining. It not only provides a voluntary method of settling industrial disputes, but is also a quicker way of settling them.

4. Adjudication

The ultimate remedy for the settlement of an industrial dispute is its reference to adjudication by labour court or tribunals when conciliation machinery fails to bring about a settlement. Adjudication consists of settling disputes through intervention by the third party appointed by the government. The law provides the adjudication to be conducted by the Labour Court, Industrial Tribunal or National Tribunal.

A dispute can also be referred to adjudication by the government even if there is no consent of the parties in which case it is called 'compulsory adjudication'. As mentioned above, the dispute can be referred to three types of tribunals depending on the nature and facts of dispute in questions.

These include:

(a) Labour courts,

(b) Industrial tribunals, and

(c) National tribunals.

The procedure, powers, and provisions regarding commencement of award and period of operation of award of these three bodies are similar. The first two bodies can be set up either by State or Central Government but the national tribunal can be constituted by the Central Government only, when it thinks that the adjudication of a dispute is of national importance. These three bodies are into hierarchical in nature. It is the government's prerogative to refer a dispute to any of these bodies depending on the nature of dispute.

(a) Labour Court

A labour court consists of one person only, who is normally a sitting or an ex-judge of a High Court. It may be constituted by the appropriate government for adjudication of disputes which are mentioned in the second schedule of the Act.

The issues referred to a labour court may include:

(i) The propriety or legality of an order passed by an employer under the Standing Orders.

(ii) The application and interpretation of Standing Orders.

(iii) Discharge and dismissal of workmen and grant of relief to them.

(iv) Withdrawal of any statutory concession or privilege.

(v) Illegality or otherwise of any strike or lockout.

(vi) All matters not specified in the third schedule of Industrial Disputes Act, 1947.

(b) Industrial Tribunal

Like a labour court, an industrial tribunal is also a one-man body. The matters which fall within the jurisdiction of industrial tribunals are as mentioned in the second schedule or the third schedule of the Act. Obviously, industrial tribunals have wider jurisdiction than the labour courts.

Moreover an industrial tribunal, in addition to the presiding officer, can have two assessors to advise him in the proceedings; the appropriate government is empowered to appoint the assessors.

The Industrial Tribunal may be referred the following issues:

1. Wages including the period and mode of payment.
2. Compensatory and other allowances.
3. Hours of work and rest intervals.
4. Leave with wages and holidays.
5. Bonus, profit sharing, provident fund and gratuity.
6. Shift working otherwise than in accordance with the standing orders.
7. Rule of discipline.
8. Rationalisation.
9. Retrenchment.
10. Any other matter that may be prescribed.

(c) National Tribunal

The Central Government may constitute a national tribunal for adjudication of disputes as mentioned in the second and third schedules of the Act or any other matter not mentioned therein provided in its opinion the industrial dispute involves "questions of national importance" or "the industrial dispute is of such a nature that undertakings established in more than one state are likely to be affected by such a dispute".

The Central Government may appoint two assessors to assist the national tribunal. The award of the tribunal is to be submitted to the Central Government which has the power to modify or reject it if it considers it necessary in public interest.

It should be noted that every award of a Labour Court, Industrial Tribunal or National Tribunal must be published by the appropriate government within 30 days from the date of its receipt. Unless declared otherwise by the appropriate government, every award shall come into force on the expiry of 30 days from the date of its publication and shall remain in operation for a period of one year thereafter.

Prevention of Industrial Disputes

The consequences of an Industrial dispute will be harmful to the owners of industries, workers, economy and the nation as a whole, which results in loss of productivity, profits, market share and even closure of the plant. Hence, Industrial disputes need to be averted by all means. Prevention of Industrial disputes is a pro-active approach in which an organisation undertakes various actions through which the occurrence of Industrial disputes is prevented. Like the old saying goes, "prevention is better than cures".

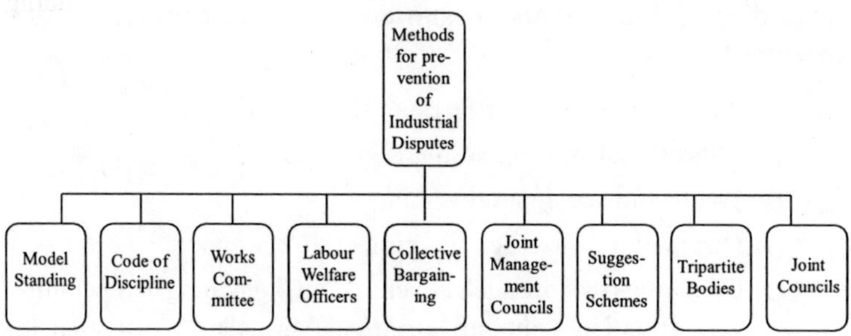

Methods for Prevention of Industrial Disputes

1. Model Standing Orders: Standing orders define and regulate terms and conditions of employment and bring about uniformity in them. They also specify the duties and responsibilities of both employers and employees thereby regulating standards of their behaviour. Therefore, standing orders can be a good basis for maintaining harmonious relations between employees and employers.

Under Industrial Dispute Act, 1947, every factory employing 100 workers or more is required to frame standing orders in consultation with the workers. These orders must be certified and displayed properly by the employer for the information of the workers.

2. Code of Industrial Discipline: The code of Industrial discipline defines duties and responsibilities of employers and workers. The objectives of the code are:

(i) To secure settlement of disputes by negotiation, conciliation and voluntary arbitration.

(ii) To eliminate all forms of coercion, intimidation and violence.

(iii) To maintain discipline in the industry.

(iv) To avoid work stoppage.

(v) To promote constructive co-operation between the parties concerned at all levels.

3. Works Committee: Every industrial undertaking employing 100 or more workers is under an obligation to set up a works committee consisting equal number of representatives of employer and employees. The main purpose of such committees is to promote industrial relations. According to Indian Labour Conference, work committees are concerned with:-

(i) Administration of welfare and fine funds

(ii) Educational and recreational activities

(iii) Safety and accident prevention

(iv) Occupational diseases and protective equipment

(v) Conditions of work such as ventilation, lightening, temperature and sanitation including latrines and urinals

(vi) Amenities such as drinking water, canteen, dining rooms, medical and health services.

The following items are excluded from the preview of the work committees:

(i) Wages and allowances
(ii) Profit sharing and bonus
(iii) Programmes of planning and development
(iv) Retirement benefits
(v) PF and gratuity
(vi) Housing and transport schemes
(vii) Incentive schemes
(viii) Retirement and layoff

The objectives of works committees are to:

1. Remove the causes of friction in the day-to-day work situation.

2. Foster amity and harmonious relationship between the parties.

3. Create an atmosphere for voluntary settlement of disputes and frictions.

In India, TISCO was the first to set up works committee way back in 1920. By 1952, 2075 works committees came into existence in the country.

4. Labour Welfare Officer: The Factories Act, 1948 provides for the appointment of a labour welfare officer in every factory employing 500 or more workers. The officer looks after all facilities in the factory provided for the health, safety and welfare of workers. He maintains liaison with both the employer and the workers, thereby serving as a communication link and contributing towards healthy industrial relations through proper administration of standing orders, grievance procedure, etc.

5. Collective Bargaining: Collective bargaining is a process in which the representatives of the employer and of the employees meet and attempt to negotiate a contract governing the employer-employee-union relationships. Collective bargaining involves discussion and negotiation between two groups as to the terms and conditions of employment.

6. Joint Management Council: In India, the Joint Management Council (JMC) came into existence due to the provisions in this regard made by the Industrial Policy Resolution, 1956. These councils were set up to enable workers to participate in management and infuse a spirit of co-operation between the workers and the management. Joint Councils are set up for the whole unit and deals with matters relating to optimum production and efficiency and the fixation of productivity norms for man and machine as a whole. In every industrial unit employing 500 and more workers; there should be a Joint Council for the whole unit.

The salient features of the JMCs are as follows:

(i) The scheme is a voluntary one.

(ii) The minimum and maximum number of its members are 6 and 12 respectively consisting of equal number of representatives of workers and employers.

(iii) The JMCs deal with matters like information sharing, consultative, and administrative.

(iv) The decisions taken by the JMC should be unanimous ones.

(v) The JMCs can be set up in the units employing 500 or more persons and having strong trade unions.

In India, industrial units like Hindustan Insecticides, HMT, Indian Airlines, Air India, in the public sector and TISCO, Arvind Mills, Modi Spinners and Weaving Mills, in the private sector, have been pioneers to introduce the JMC scheme. Past experience indicates that whenever the JMC schemes have been setup, there have been better industrial relations, more satisfied work force, increase in productivity, better profits, etc.

Functions

(i) Optimum use of raw materials and quality of finished products.

(ii) Optimum production, efficiency and function of productivity norms of man and machine as a whole.

(iii) Preparation of schedules of working hours and of holidays.

(iv) Adequate facilities for training.

(v) Rewards for valuable and creative suggestions received from workers.

7. Suggestion Schemes: Under this system, workers are invited to offer valuable suggestions for improving the working of the enterprise. A suggestion box is installed at an appropriate place. Any worker can put his suggestion into the suggestion box. A committee will evaluate all the suggestions and the best suggestion will be accepted for implementation and the concerned worker will be rewarded.

8. Tripartite Bodies: Several tripartite bodies have been constituted at central, national and state levels. The India labour conference, standing labour committees, Wage Boards and Industries Committees operate at the Central level. At the State level, State Labour Advisory Boards have been set up. All these bodies play an important role in reaching agreements on various labour-related issues. The recommendations given by these bodies are however advisory in nature and not statutory.

WORKERS PARTICIPATION IN MANAGEMENT

Workers' participation in management is an essential ingredient of Industrial democracy. The concept of workers' participation in management is based on Human Relations approach to Management which brought about a new set of values to labour and management. Traditionally the concept of Workers' Participation in Management (WPM) refers to participation of non-managerial employees in the decision-making process of the organisation. Workers' participation is also known as 'labour participation' or 'employee participation' in management. In Germany, it is known as co-determination while in Yugoslavia it is known as self-management. The International Labour Organisation has been encouraging member nations to promote the scheme of Workers' Participation in Management.

Workers' participation in management implies mental and emotional involvement of workers in the management of Enterprise. According to Keith Davis, Participation refers to the mental and emotional involvement of a person in a group situation which encourages him to contribute to group goals and share the responsibility of achievement. It is considered as a mechanism where workers have a say in the decision.

The philosophy underlying workers' participation stresses:

(1) democratic participation in decision-making;
(2) maximum employer-employee collaboration;
(3) minimum state intervention;
(4) realisation of a greater measure of social justice;
(5) greater industrial efficiency; and
(6) higher level of organisational health and effectiveness.

Objectives of Workers Participation in Management

The objectives of workers' participation in management are as follows:

- To raise level of motivation of workers by closer involvement.
- To provide opportunity for expression and to provide a sense of importance to workers.
- To develop ties of understanding leading to better effort and harmony.
- To act on a device to counter-balance powers of managers.
- To act on a panacea for solving industrial relation problems.

Forms of Participation

Different forms of participation are discussed below:

Collective Bargaining: Collective bargaining results in collective agreements which lay down certain rules and conditions of service in an establishment. Such agreements are normally binding on the parties. Theoretically, collective bargaining is based on the principle of balance of power, but, in actual practice, each party tries to outbid the other and get maximum advantage by using, if necessary, threats and counter-threats like; strikes, lockouts and other direct actions. Joint consultation, on the other hand, is a particular technique which is intended to achieve a greater degree of harmony and cooperation by emphasising matters of common interest. Workers prefer to use the instrument of collective bargaining rather than ask for a share in management. Workers' participation in the USA has been ensured almost exclusively by means of collective agreements and their application and interpretation rather than by way of labour representation in management.

Works Councils: These are exclusive bodies of employees, assigned with different functions in the management of an enterprise. In West Germany, the works councils have various decision-making functions. In some countries, their role is limited only to receiving information about the enterprise. In Yugoslavia, these councils have wider decision-making powers in an enterprise like; appointment, promotion, salary fixation and also major investment decisions.

Joint Management Councils and Committees: Mainly these bodies are consultative and advisory, with decision-making being left to the top management. This system of participation is prevalent in many countries, including Britain and India. As they are consultative and advisory, neither the managements nor the workers take them seriously.

Board Representation: The role of a worker representative in the board of directors is essentially one of negotiating the worker's interest with the other members of the board. At times, this may result in tension and friction inside the board room. The effectiveness of workers' representative at the board depend upon his ability to participate in decision-making, his knowledge of the company affairs, his educational background, his level of understanding and also on the number of worker representatives in the Board.

Workers Ownership of Enterprise: Social self-management in Yugoslavia is an example of complete control of management by workers through an elected board and workers council. Even in such a system, there exist two distinct managerial and operative functions with different sets of persons to perform them. Though workers have the option to influence all the decisions taken at the top level, in actual practice, the board and the top management team assume a fairly independent role in taking major policy decisions for the enterprises, especially in economic matters.

Levels of Participation

Workers' participation is possible at all levels of management;

the only difference is that of degree and nature of application. For instance, it may be vigorous at lower level and faint at top level. Broadly speaking there is following five levels of participation:

1. **Information Participation:** It ensures that employees are able to receive information and express their views pertaining to the matters of general economic importance.
2. **Consultative Participation:** Here works are consulted on the matters of employee welfare such as work, safety and health. However, final decision always rests at the option of management and employees' views are only of advisory nature.
3. **Associative Participation:** It is extension of consultative participation as management here is under moral obligation to accept and implement the unanimous decisions of employees.
4. **Administrative Participation:** It ensure greater share of works in discharge of managerial functions. Here, decision already taken by the management come to employees, preferably with alternatives for administration and employees have to select the best from those for implementation.
5. **Decisive Participation:** Highest level of participation where decisions are jointly taken on the matters relation to production, welfare, etc. is called decisive participation.

CODE OF DISCIPLINE

The Code of Discipline is a set of self-imposed mutually agreed voluntary principles of discipline and relations between the management and workers in the industry. In view of growing industrial conflict, the Fifteenth Indian Labour Conference agreed that there should be a set of general principles of discipline, which should be adopted by labour and management voluntarily. To evolve such a set of principles, a tripartite sub-committee was set up. The resulting draft was discussed at Standing Labour Committee meeting in October 1957. At the Sixteenth Indian Labour Conference held in 1958, the final form of the Code of Discipline was approved.

As of now please understand that there are three sets of principles in the Code of Discipline. The first set of principles is for the management and the union. The second set is for the Management and the third one is for the union.

TRIPARTITE BODIES

Industrial relations in India have been shaped largely by principles and policies evolved through tripartite consultative machinery at industry and national levels. The aim of the consultative machinery is "to bring the parties together for mutual settlement of differences in a spirit of cooperation and goodwill".

Thus, these bodies play the role of consultants. Indian Labour Conference (ILC) and Standing Labour Committee (SLC) have been constituted to suggest ways and means to prevent disputes. The representatives of the workers and employers are nominated to these bodies by the Central Government in consultation with the All-India organisations of workers and employers.

The Labour Ministry settles the agenda for ILC/SLC meetings after taking into consideration the suggestions sent to it by member organisations. These two bodies work with minimum procedural rules to facilitate free and fuller discussions among the members. Please note that the ILC meets once a year, whereas the SLC meets as and when necessary.

The functions of ILC are:

(a) To promote uniformity in labour legislation;

(b) To lay down a procedure for the settlement of industrial disputes;

(c) To discuss matters of All-India importance as between employers and employees.

The ILC advises the government on any matter referred to it for advice, taking into account suggestions made by the States and representatives of the organisations of workers and employers. The Standing Labour Committee's main function is to consider and determine such questions as may be referred to it by the Plenary

Conference or the Central Government and to render advice, taking into account the suggestions made by various governments, workers and employers.

INTERNATIONAL LABOUR ORGANISATION (ILO)

The International Labour Organisation (ILO) has the following mission:

To promote opportunities for men and women to obtain decent and productive work, in conditions of freedom, equity, security and human dignity, which is summed up by the expression "Decent work as a global goal".

The International Labour Organisation (ILO) is a specialised agency of the United Nations system which seeks the promotion of social justice and internationally recognised human and labour rights. The ILO formulates international labour standards. These standards take the form of Conventions and Recommendations, which set minimum standards in the field of fundamental labour rights:

Freedom of association,

The right to organise,

The right to collective bargaining,

The abolition of forced labour,

Equality of opportunity and treatment,

as well as other standards addressing conditions spanning across the entire spectrum of work-related issues.

The ILO provides technical assistance, mainly in the following fields:

- Vocational training and vocational rehabilitation;
- Employment policy;
- Labour administration;
- Labour law and industrial relations;
- Conditions of work;
- Management development;

- Cooperatives;
- Social security;
- Labour statistics, and occupational safety and health.

The ILO was created in response to the consciousness that followed the First World War at the Peace Conference, which convened first in Paris and then in Versailles. The ILO is the only major surviving outcome of the Treaty of Versailles. The International Labour Organisation (ILO) was founded, along with the League of Nations, by the Treaty of Versailles on 11 April 1919.

The ILO adopted the Declaration of Philadelphia to reflect its philosophy and fundamental principles, as well as to broaden its aims and purposes. The Declaration was adopted by the ILO in 1944 and is the equivalent of what an organisation commonly refers to as its mission. In 1946, the ILO became the first specialised agency associated with the newly formed United Nations, following the dissolution of the League of Nations. On its 50th anniversary in 1969, the ILO was awarded the Nobel Peace Prize.

Declaration of Philadelphia (1944): The General Conference of the International Labour Organisation, meeting in its Twenty-sixth Session in Philadelphia, hereby adopts, this tenth day of May in the year nineteen hundred and forty-four, the present Declaration of the aims and purposes of the International Labour Organisation and of the principles which should inspire the policy of its Members. The Conference reaffirms the fundamental principles on which the Organisation is based and, in particular, that labour is not a commodity; freedom of expression and of association are essential to sustained progress; poverty anywhere constitutes a danger to prosperity everywhere; the war against want requires to be carried on with unrelenting vigour within each nation with a view to the promotion of the common welfare.

ILO Comprises: ILO comprises of International Labour Conference, Governing Body and International Labour Office.

International Labour Conference (ILC) meets in June every year, in Geneva, and is the highest authority of the ILO. It sets minimum international labour standards and defines the broad policies of the

Organisation. Every two years, the Conference adopts the ILO's biennial work programme and budget, which is financed by member States. The ILC also provides an international forum for the discussion of world labour and social problems. The ILC elects the Governing Body of the ILO which consists of one Employer representative, two Government representatives and one Worker representative. Each member State has four representatives in International Labour Conference.

The Governing Body is the executive council of the ILO which establishes the strategic objectives and policies. The Governing Body meets three times a year in Geneva and makes decisions on ILO policy and establishes the programme and budget, which it subsequently submits to the Conference for adoption. The Governing Body also elects the Director-General for a five-year renewable term.

The ten States of chief industrial importance have permanent seats on the Governing Body, while the other members are elected at the Conference every three years from representatives of the other member countries, taking into account geographical distribution. Employers and workers elect their own representatives independently of one another. Governing Body consists of 14 Employer representatives, 28 Government representatives and 14 Worker representatives.

The ILO has a tripartite structure unique in the United Nations system, in which employers' and workers' representatives – the "social partners" – have an equal voice with those of governments in shaping its policies and programmes.

International labour standards are legal instruments drawn up by the ILO's constituents (governments, employers and workers) which set out basic principles and rights at work. In many cases, a Convention lays down the basic principles to be implemented by ratifying countries, while a related Recommendation supplements the Convention by providing more detailed guidelines on its implementation.

Conventions

These are legally binding international treaties that are subject to ratification by member States.

Recommendations

These serve as non-binding guidelines. They can also be autonomous, namely not linked a Convention. ILS are divided into: ILO's fundamental Conventions and Priority Conventions.

The ILO's Fundamental Conventions

These cover subjects considered to be fundamental principles and rights at work:

Freedom of Association and Protection of the Right to Organise Convention, 1948 (No. 87);

Right to Organise and Collective Bargaining Convention, 1949 (No. 98);

Forced Labour Convention, 1930 (No. 29);

Abolition of Forced Labour Convention, 1957 (No. 105);

Minimum Age Convention, 1973 (No. 138);

Worst Forms of Child Labour Convention, 1999 (No. 182);

Equal Remuneration Convention, 1951 (No. 100); and

Discrimination (Employment and Occupation) Convention, 1958 (No. 111);

Priority Conventions

The ILO's Governing Body has also designated another four Conventions as "priority" instruments, thereby encouraging member States to ratify them because of their importance for the functioning of the international labour standards system.

Labour Inspection Convention, 1947 (No. 81);

Labour Inspection (Agriculture) Convention, 1969 (No. 129);

Tripartite Consultation (International Labour Standards) Convention, 1976 (No. 144); and

Employment Policy Convention, 1964 (No. 122).

Juan Somavia was elected to serve as the ninth Director-General of the International Labour Office by the Governing Body on 23 March

1998. His five-year term of office began on 4 March 1999, when he became the first representative from the Southern hemisphere to head the Organisation. In March 2003, Mr. Somavia was re-elected for a second five-year term.

NEW ECONOMIC POLICY AND IR IN INDIA

The former Finance Minister Dr. Manmohan Singh under the stalwardship of then Prime Minister Shri. Narasimha Rao initiated the New Economic Policy in 1991, through Liberalisation, Privatisation and Globalisation to integrate the Indian economy with the Global market. The major factors that are contributing to the changing scenario of industrial relations are as follows:

Emergence of Knowledge Workers: The new employees are better educated, more career oriented and they do not feel satisfied only with wage but they value the quality of work life. This has led to a paradigm shift in their relationship with the management.

Dwindling Trade Union Leadership: Of late, modern or knowledge workers are very much interested in order to increase the living standard and believe in quality of work life. Workers are dissociating themselves from trade unions. The number of strikes has been declined noticeably. Workers are not ready to sacrifice their wages or loose jobs by calling strike. Modern workers are becoming more and more conscious.

INDUSTRIAL TRUCE RESOLUTION, 1962

In view of the National Emergency proclaimed in 1962 in the wake of Chinese aggression a joint meeting of the central organisations of employers and workers adopted the Industrial Truce Resolution in 1962.

It laid down that there would be no interruption, or slowing down of production; and the production would be maximised and defence efforts promoted in all possible ways. It has been merged with the Central Implementation and Evaluation Committee since 1963.

UNIT-VI

Trade Unions

Meaning

Objectives

Functions

Theories

Structure of Trade Unions

Trade Union Movement in India

Leadership

Finance

Union Politics

Inter Union Rivalry

MEANING

The Trade Union Act 1926 defines a trade union as a combination, whether temporary or permanent, formed primarily for the purpose of regulating the relations between workmen and employers or between workmen and workmen, or between employers and employers, or for imposing restrictive condition on the conduct of any trade or business, and includes any federation of two or more trade unions.

OBJECTIVES

Trade unions are formed to protect and promote the interests of their members. Their primary function is to protect the interests of workers against discrimination and unfair labour practices. Trade unions are formed to achieve the following objectives:

1. **Representation:** Trade unions represent individual workers when they have a problem at work. If an employee feels he is being unfairly treated, he can ask the union representative to sort out the difficulty with the manager or employer. Unions also offer their members legal representation. Normally this is to help people to get financial compensation for work-related injuries or to assist people who have to take their employer to court.
2. **Negotiation:** Negotiation is where union representatives, discuss with management, the issues which affect people working in an organisation. There may be a difference of opinion between management and union members. Trade unions negotiate with the employers to find out a solution to these differences. Pay, working hours, holidays and changes to working practices are the sorts of issues that are negotiated. In many workplaces there is a formal agreement between the union and the company which states that the union has the right to negotiate with the employer. In these organisations, unions are said to be recognised for collective bargaining purposes.
3. **Voice in Decisions Affecting Workers:** The economic security of employees is determined not only by the level of wages and duration of their employment, but also by the

management's personal policies which include selection of employees for layoffs, retrenchment, promotion and transfer. These policies directly affect workers. The evaluation criteria for such decisions may not be fair. So, the intervention of unions in such decision-making is a way through which workers can have their say in the decision-making to safeguard their interests.

4. **Member Services:** During the last few years, trade unions have increased the range of services they offer their members. These include:

   (a) **Education and Training:** Most unions run training courses for their members on employment rights, health and safety and other issues. Some unions also help members who have left school with little education by offering courses on basic skills and courses leading to professional qualifications.

   (b) **Legal Assistance:** As well as offering legal advice on employment issues, some unions give help with personal matters, like housing, wills and debt.

   (c) **Financial Discounts:** People can get discounts on mortgages, insurance and loans from unions.

   (d) **Welfare benefits:** One of the earliest functions of trade unions was to look after members who hit hard times. Some of the older unions offer financial help to their members when they are sick or unemployed.

FUNCTIONS

Trade unions perform a number of functions in order to achieve the objectives. These functions can be broadly classified into three categories:

1. Militant Functions and 2. Fraternal Functions.

1. Militant Functions

One set of activities performed by trade unions leads to the betterment of the position of their members in relation to their employment. The aim of such activities is to ensure adequate wages, secure better conditions of work and employment get better treatment from employers, etc. When the unions fail to accomplish these aims by the method of collective bargaining and negotiations, they adopt an approach and put up a fight with the management in the form of go-slow tactics, strike, boycott, gheraos, etc. Hence, these functions of the trade unions are known as militant or fighting functions. Thus, the militant functions of trade unions can be summed up as:

(i) To achieve higher wages and better working conditions;
(ii) To raise the status of workers as a part of industry;
(iii) To protect labours against victimisation and injustice.

2. Fraternal Functions

Another set of activities performed by trade unions aims at rendering help to its members in times of need, and improving their efficiency. Trade unions try to foster a spirit of co-operation and promote friendly industrial relations and diffuse education and culture among their members. They take up welfare measures for improving the morale of workers and generate self confidence among them. They also arrange for legal assistance to its members, if necessary. Besides these, they undertake many welfare measures for their members, e.g., school for the education of children, library, reading-rooms, in-door and out-door games, and other recreational facilities. Some trade unions even undertake publication of some magazine or journal. These activities, which may be called fraternal functions, depend on the availability of funds, which the unions raise by subscription from members and donations from outsiders, and also on their competent and enlightened leadership. Thus, the fraternal functions of trade unions can be summed up as:

(i) To take up welfare measures for improving the morale of workers;
(ii) To generate self confidence among workers;
(iii) To encourage sincerity and discipline among workers;
(iv) To provide opportunities for promotion and growth;
(v) To protect women workers against discrimination.

THEORIES

The growth and development of trade union movement depends on social, economic and political conditions of a country. The various theories of trade unions are as follows:

1. **Revolutionary Theory:** The Revolutionary Theory was propounded by Marx. According to Marx, trade union took the challenging role to streamline the forces of working classes to struggle against the capitalist. Trade unions took revolutionary programme in order to abolish the capitalist. This theory is also known as "the theory of class war and dialectical materialism".
2. **Evolutionary Theory:** This theory is also popular as "theory of industrial democracy". The theory was propounded by Sydney and Beatrice Webbs. According to Webbs, trade unionism is not an instrument to abolish the capitalism, but a means to establish the industrial democracy in the industry. Trade unions must raise their voice to overcome the managerial dictatorship.
3. **Rebellion Theory:** Frank Rebellion is the pioneer of this theory. According to him, trade unionism is the result of rapid mechanisation. He believes that the use of machines leads to exploitation of workers. So, machine is the cause and trade unionism is the result. Therefore the basic objective of rebellion approach is to protect the interest of workers against mechanisation.
4. **Gandhian Approach:** The Gandhian approach is based on "class collaboration rather than class conflict and struggle". Gandhi emphasised that the aim of trade unionism is eternal reform and also evolution of internal strength. According to Gandhi, self-consciousness among workers led to the emergence of trade unionism.
5. **Theory of Industrial Jurisprudence:** The propounder of this theory is S.H. Slithers. According to him, an individual worker is not able to protect his interest alone, and so they form trade unionism in order to protect their common interest through

collective bargaining with employers. This system is known as "a system of industrial jurisprudence".

STRUCTURE OF TRADE UNIONS

The structure of trade unions in India varies from organisation to organisation. The structure can be classified into four types. These are: (1) Craft Union, (2) General Union, (3) Industrial Union and (4) Federations.

1. **Craft Unions:** If the workers of the same craft or category of the job form into a union, that union is called craft union. These unions are called as horizontal unions. The basic logic behind the formation of such unions is that the workers belonging to the same craft do face similar problems. Mostly non-managerial personnel form such unions. Examples of craft unions are Driver's Associations.
2. **General Unions:** If the workers of any industry, any region and of any job or occupation form into one union in order to protect the overall interests of the workers, such unions are called general unions. The Jamshedpur Labour Union is one example. In India there are several industry-cum-region unions due to concentration of some industries in particular regions.
3. **Industrial Unions:** An industrial union is organised upon an industry-wise rather than a craft-wise basis. Its members belong to different crafts within the same industry. Ahmedabad Textile Labour Association, Giri Kamgar Union are examples of industrial unions in India. These unions are vertical in nature because they consist of all types of workers in an industry. Industrial unions are more powerful because they consist of both skilled and unskilled workers. It is easier for the employer to bargain with one union to cover all workers of a particular industry.
4. **Federations:** These are national level bodies to which plant level unions, craft unions, industrial unions and general unions are affiliated. Federations are the apex organisations of workers. They act as coordinating agencies. These are also

called central trade unions e.g. INTUC, AITUC, CITU, BMS, HMS etc.

TRADE UNION MOVEMENT IN INDIA

The trade unionism in India developed quite slowly as compared to the western nations. Indian trade union movement can be divided into three phases:

1. The First Phase (1850 to 1900)

During this phase the inception of trade unions took place. During this period, the working and living conditions of the labour were poor and their working hours were long. Capitalists were only interested in their productivity and profitability. In addition, the wages were also low and general economic conditions were poor in industries. In order to regulate the working hours and other service conditions of the Indian textile workers, the Indian Factories Act was enacted in 1881. As a result, employment of child labour was prohibited.

The growth of trade union movement was slow in this phase and later on the Indian Factories Act of 1881 was amended in 1891. Many strikes took place in the two decades following 1880 in all industrial cities. These strikes taught workers to understand the power of united action even though there was no union in real terms. Small associations like Bombay Mill-Hands Association came up by this time.

2. The Second Phase (1900 to 1946)

This phase was characterised by the development of organised trade unions and political movements of the working class. Between 1918 and 1923, many unions came into existence in the country. At Ahmedabad, under the guidance of Mahatma Gandhi, occupational unions like spinners' unions and weavers' unions were formed. A strike was launched by these unions under the leadership of Mahatma Gandhi who turned it into a satyagrah. These unions federated into industrial union known as Textile Labour Association in 1920. In 1920, the First National Trade Union Organisation (The All India Trade Union Congress (AITUC)) was established. Many of the leaders of this organisation were leaders of the national movement. In 1926, trade union law came up with the efforts of Mr. N. N. Joshi that became operative from 1927. During 1928, All India Trade Union Federation (AITUF) was formed.

3. The Third Phase (1946 onwards)

The third phase began with the emergence of Independent India (in 1947). The partition of country affected the trade union movement particularly Bengal and Punjab. By 1949, four central trade union organisations were functioning in the country:

1. The All India Trade Union Congress,
2. The Indian National Trade Union Congress,
3. The Hindu Mazdoor Sangh, and
4. The United Trade Union Congress.

The working class movement was also politicised along the lines of political parties. For instance, Indian National Trade Union Congress (INTUC) is the trade union arm of the Congress Party. The AITUC is the trade union arm of the Communist Party of India. Besides workers, white-collar employees, supervisors and managers are also organised by the trade unions, as for example in the Banking, Insurance and Petroleum industries.

Trade Unions in India

The Indian workforce consists of 430 million workers, growing two per cent annually. The Indian labour markets consist of three sectors:

1. The rural workers, who constitute about 60 per cent of the workforce.
2. Organised sector, which employs eight per cent of workforce, and
3. The urban informal sector (which includes the growing software industry and other services, not included in the formal sector) which constitutes the rest 32 per cent of the workforce.

At present there are twelve Central Trade Union Organisations in India:

All India Trade Union Congress (AITUC)-1920

Bharatiya Mazdoor Sangh (BMS) - 1955

Centre of Indian Trade Unions (CITU) - 1970

Hind Mazdoor Kisan Panchayat (HMKP)-1962

Hind Mazdoor Sabha (HMS) - 1948

Indian Federation of Free Trade Unions (IFFTU)-

Indian National Trade Union Congress (INTUC) - 1947

National Front of Indian Trade Unions (NFITU) -1967

National Labour Organisation (NLO) -

Trade Unions Co-ordination Centre (TUCC)-

United Trade Union Congress (UTUC) and -

United Trade Union Congress - Lenin Sarani (UTUC - LS)-

Classification based on Agreement

Another basis on which labour agreements are sometimes distinguished is on the basis of the type of agreement involved, based on the degree to which membership in the union is a condition of employment. These are:

(a) Closed Shop: Where management and union agree that the union would have sole responsibility and authority for the recruitment of workers, it is called a Closed Shop agreement. The worker joins the union to become an employee of the shop. The Taft-Hartley Act of 1947 bans closed shop agreements in the USA, although they still exist in the construction and printing trades. Sometimes, the closed shop is also called the 'Hiring Hall.'

(b) Union Shop: Where there is an agreement that all new recruits must join the union within a fixed period after employment it is called a union shop. In the USA where some states are declared to be 'right-to-work'.

(c) Preferential Shop: When a Union member is given preference in filling a vacancy, such an agreement is called Preferential Shop.

(d) Maintenance Shop: In this type of arrangement no compulsory membership in the union before or after recruitment exists. However, if the employee chooses to become a member after recruitment, his membership remains compulsory right throughout his tenure of employment with that particular employer. This is called maintenance of membership shop or maintenance shop.

(e) **Agency Shop:** In terms of the agreement between management and the union a non-union member has to pay the union a sum equivalent to a member's subscription in order to continue employment with the employer. This is called an agency shop.

(f) **Open Shop:** Membership in a union is in no way compulsory or obligatory either before or after recruitment. In such organisations, sometimes there is no union at all. This is least desirable form for unions. This is referred to as an open shop.

The above classifications are more usual in the West than on the Indian sub-continent.

LEADERSHIP

The trade union movement in India goes back to the year 1875 under, the leadership of Sorabji Shaparji.

Bombay Mills Hands Association in 1890 by Mr. M.M. Lokhande, a workman who organised a meeting of 10,000 workers as a result of which several demands were accepted by the mill owners in Bombay Textile Mills. He started a newspaper called Dinabandhu so as to educate the workmen.

In 1897, the Amalgama Society of Railway Servants of India was established and registered under the Companies Act, which is followed by the Printers' Union Calcutta (1907), Postal Union (1907), Kamgar Hitwardhak Sabha (1909) and the Social Service League (1910). However, these organisations could not make the real start in the Labour Movement till World War I.

The first systematic attempt in this direction was made by B.P. Wadia who established the Madras Labour Union in 1918. The Madras Labour Union was the first organised Trade Union in India followed by a large number of trade unions in the Indian industrial centres.

In 1947, the Indian National Trade Union Congress (INTUC) was formed as a labour wing of Indian National Congress.

In 1948, Praja Socialist Party started another trade union known as Hind Mazdoor Panchayat. Indian Federation of Labour and Hind Mazdoor Panchayat were amalgamated and formed Hind Mazdoor Sabha (HMS) in 1948.

In 1949, ITUC was affiliated to the International Confederation of Free Trade Unions. The United Trade Union Congress was established in 1949 by some radicalists. In 1954, another central trade union was formed in the name of Bharatiya Mazdoor Sangh (BMS). All these unions have been working for the betterment of workers.

In 1920, the All India Trade Union Congress (AITUC) was set up. In 1926, the Trade Unions Act was passed which gave a legal status to the registered trade unions.

With independence and partition, the country was plunged into growing unemployment. A series of strikes occurred, in the country. The All India Trade Union Congress was split up as a result of which the Indian National Trade Union Congress (INTUC) was formed in 1947 under the control of Congress party. The Hind Mazdoor Sabha (HMS) was formed by the Socialist Party in 1948, and United Trade Union Congress (UTUC) was formed in 1949. Recently, Centre of Indian Trade Unions (CITU) has been formed by the Communist Party (Marxists).

FINANCE

Small size of unions has its direct bearing on its financial health. Total income and total expenditure of 9,073 trade unions with a membership of 57.4 lakhs were Rs 3,238 lakhs and Rs 2,532 lakhs respectively in 1992. The per member income and expenditure, thus, come to Rs 56.4 and Rs 44.1 respectively". These are, by all means, very low. It is the small size of trade unions accompanied by small subscriptions; the trade unions cannot undertake welfare activities.

Sound financial position is an essential ingredient for the effective functioning of trade unions, because in the process of rendering services or fulfilling their goals, trade unions have to perform a variety of functions and organise programmes which require enormous financial commitments. Hence, it is imperative on the part of a trade union to strengthen its financial position.

But it is felt that the income and expenditure of trade unions in India over the years is such, with few exceptions, that the financial position of the union is generally weak, affecting their functioning. It is opined that, "trade unions could be more effective, if they paid more attention to strengthening their organisations and achieving higher attention of financial solvency."

The primary source of income to the unions is membership subscription. Their other sources of union finances are donations, sale of periodicals, etc. The items of expenditure include: allowances to office bearers, salaries to office, annual convention/meeting expenses, rents, stationery, printing, postage, telegrams, etc.

Most of the trade unions in India suffer from inadequate funds. This unsound financial position is mostly due to low membership and low rate of membership fee. Trade Union Act, 1926, prescribed the membership fee at 25 paisa per member per month. But the National Commission on Labour recommended the increase of rate of membership subscription from 25 paisa to Re 1 in the year 1990. But the government did not accept this recommendation.

As the National Commission on Labour observes, "an important factor limiting the effective functioning of unions in our country has been their financial weakness. In most unions, poor finances are the result of inadequate membership strength. This in turn, can be traced to the small size of units. In a majority of unions, the rate of contributions required of members is also small. With a relatively low rate of unionisation, total funds collected are small. The general picture of finances of unions is disappointing."

UNION RIVALRY

The formal basis for Trade Union Organisation is provided by the Indian Trade Union Act, 1926. The relevant article reads as follows: "Any seven or more members of a trade union may be subscribing their name to the roles of the trade union and by otherwise complying with the provisions of this act with respect to the registration, apply for registration of the trade union under this Act."

This provision has led to the formation of multiple unions and resulted in inter-union rivalry in different industries. But the inter-union rivalry breaks the very purpose of the trade unions by weakening the strength of collective bargaining. On the other hand, the existence of a single, strong union not only protects the employee interests more effectively but also halts the various unproductive activities of the unions and forces the leaders to concentrate on the strategic issues. Further, it helps to bring about congenial industrial relations by bringing about a system of orderliness in dealing with the employees and by facilitating expeditious settlement of disputes.

Inter-and intra-union rivalries have been a potent cause of industrial disputes in the country. They are responsible for weak bargaining power of trade unions in collective bargaining. These rivalries are responsible for slow growth of trade union movement in the country.

UNION POLITICS

Most popular trade unions in India are affiliated to certain political parties. These political parties are only keen on making every grievance of the working class a political issue to attain political gains. As a result the problem only gets wide publicity and remains unsolved.

Most unions today are run by rival political parties. These political parties have nothing constructive to offer, instead, use unions to spread their political agenda. Furthermore, decisions related to unions are made by politicians.

UNIT-VII

Labour Legislation

Objectives

Principles

Classification

Evolution of Labour Legislation in India

Impact of ILO

Labour Legislation and Indian Constitution

Factories Act, 1948

Employees State Insurance Act, 1948

Workmen's Compensation Act, 1923

Maternity Benefit Act, 1961

LABOUR LEGISLATION

The term 'Labour legislation' is used to cover all the laws which have been enacted to deal with employment and non-employment, wages, working conditions, industrial relations, social security and welfare of persons employed in industries.

OBJECTIVES

The objectives of labour legislation are as follows:

(i) To make statutory provision for the regular trainings of a certain number of apprentices indifferent trades.

(ii) To improve and regulate the working conditions of workers employed in different factories and establishments.

(iii) To ensure that the service conditions should be clearly spelt out by the employer to the employee.

(iv) To protect the workers from profit seeking exploiters.

(v) To maintain the dignity of employees in the organisations.

(vi) To protect the interests of women and children working in the factories.

(vii) To preserve the health, safety and welfare of workers.

(viii) To promote industrial relations and industrial peace between employers and employees.

(ix) To ensure that the employees are paid their wages on fixed dates and there should be no deduction made from the wages.

PRINCIPLES

Labour legislations are based upon the following principles:

(1) Social Justice

(2) Social Equality/ Welfare

(3) National Economy

(4) International Uniformity

(1) Social Justice: The first step in establishing social justice is to protect those who can't protect themselves. Labour laws provide social justice to the workers by ensuring suitable distribution of profits and benefits between the employer and employees. It also provides better working conditions in industry.

(2) Social Equality/Welfare: Another objective of labour laws is to ensure social welfare of workers. These laws help the employees to improve their social status i.e. material and morale of the workers by providing adequate wages and safety measures, ensuring appropriate working hours and health facilities.

(3) National Economy: National economy is another guiding principle of labour legislation. It ensures normal growth of industry for the development of nation. It increases the efficiency of workers and satisfies their needs. Thus, efficient industry finally contributes a lot to improve national economy.

(4) International Uniformity: In attaining international uniformity, International Labour Organisation (ILO) has played an important role. It aims at securing minimum standard on uniform basis in respect of all labour matters. Uniformity of standards can be maintained only by enforcing various labour laws.

CLASSIFICATION

We may classify labour legislations into the following four categories:

1. Protective Labour Legislation
2. Regulative Labour Legislation
3. Social Security Legislations
4. Welfare Legislations.

1. Protective Labour Legislations: The legislations whose primary purpose is to protect minimum labour standards and improve working conditions are protective labour legislations. Legislations laying down the minimum labour standards in the areas of work, safety, employment of children and women and also the manner of wage payment come under this category. The Indian labour laws under this category are: (i) The Factories Act, 1948, (ii) The Mines Act, 1952, (iii) The Plantation Labour Act, 1951.

2. Regulative Legislations: The legislations whose primary purpose is to regulate the relations between employers and employees and to provide for methods and manners for settling industrial disputes are Regulative Legislations. These laws also regulate the relationships between workers and trade unions, the rights and obligations of employers and workers, as well as their mutual relationships. The laws under this category are: (i) The Trade Unions Act, 1926, (ii) The Industrial Disputes Act, 1947, and (iii) The Industrial Employment (Standing Orders) Act, 1946.

3. Social Security Legislations: The Legislations which intend to provide social security benefits to the workmen during certain contingencies of life are Social Security Legislations. Their primary goal is to protect the workers. The laws under this category are: (i) The Workmen's Compensation Act, 1923, (ii) The Employees State Insurance Act, 1948, (iii) The Coal Mines Provident Fund and Miscellaneous Provisions Act, 1948, (iv) The Employees Provident Funds and Miscellaneous Provisions Act, 1952, (v) The Maternity Benefit Act, 1961, and (vi) The Payment of Gratuity Act, 1972.

4. Welfare Legislations: The legislations which aim at promoting the general welfare of the workers and improve their living conditions are Welfare legislations. Such laws carry the term "Welfare" in their titles. The Laws under this category are: i) Mica Mines Labour Welfare Fund Act, 1946, (ii) Iron Ore Mines, Manganese Ore Mines and Chrome Ore Mines Labour Welfare Fund Act, 1976 and (iii) Beedi Workers Welfare Fund Act, 1976. All of these laws provide for the funds which are spent on improving the general welfare of workers including housing, medical, educational and recreational facilities, etc.

EVOLUTION OF LABOUR LEGISLATION IN INDIA

Labour legislation in India grew with the growth of industry. In the eighteenth century, India was not only a great agricultural country but a great manufacturing country too. Asian and European markets were mainly fed by the looms supplied by India but British government in India as a matter of policy discouraged Indian manufacturers in order to encourage the rising manufacturers of England. Their policy was to make Indian people grow only raw materials. The British oppression in India continued for some time, which led to the growth of Indian nationalism. In twentieth century, the national movement took a new turn and there was a common demand for Indian goods.

IMPACT OF ILO

Labour class is indeed one of the classes most vulnerable to exploitation. Most of the labour legislations in India are pre-constitutional. The concept of fundamental rights was introduced in the constitution. The success of these labour legislations must be attributing to the ILO, as the guidelines issued by the ILO formed the principle on which these legislations were drawn. The ILO did have a great impact on the labour laws in India. Many new laws were enacted to incorporate the guidelines of the ILO.

The following conventions have been ratified by India:

Worst Forms of Child Labour Convention (No.182);

Minimum Age Convention (No. 138);

Right to Organise and Collective Bargaining Convention (No. 98);

Freedom of Association and Protection of Right to Organised Convention (No. 87);

Discrimination (Employment Occupation) Convention (No.111);

Equal Remuneration Convention (No. 100);

Abolition of Forced Labour Convention (No.105);

Forced Labour Convention (No. 29).

LABOUR LEGISLATION AND INDIAN CONSTITUTION

The relevance of the dignity of human labour and the need for protecting and safeguarding the interest of labour as human beings has been enshrined in Chapter-III (Articles 16, 19, 23 and 24) and Chapter IV (Articles 39, 41, 42, 43, 43A and 54) of the Constitution of India keeping in line with Fundamental Rights and Directive Principles of State Policy.

Labour is a concurrent subject in the Constitution of India implying that both the Union and the State governments are competent to legislate on labour matters and administer the same.

The legislations can be categorised as follows:

1. Labour laws enacted by the Central Government, where the Central Government has the sole responsibility for enforcement.
2. Labour laws enacted by Central Government and enforced both by Central and State Governments.
3. Labour laws enacted by Central Government and enforced by the State Governments.
4. Labour laws enacted and enforced by the various State Governments which apply to respective States.

THE FACTORIES ACT, 1948

Objective and Applicability

The Factories Act, 1948 has been enacted to consolidate and amend the law regulating the workers working in the factories. It extends to whole of India and applies to every factory wherein 20 or more workers are ordinary employed. Since the aim and object of the Act is to safeguard the interest of workers and protect them from exploitation, the Act prescribes certain standards with regard to safety, welfare and working hours of workers, apart from other provisions.

Factory

Means any premises including the precincts thereof where ten or more persons are working in any manufacturing process being carried on with aid of power and where twenty or more workers are working without the aid of power.

Employee Health

- Every factory should be kept clean and free from effluvia arising from any drain, privy or other nuisance. {Section 11}
- Effective arrangements should be made in every factory for the treatment and effluents due to the manufacturing process

carried on therein, so as to render them innocuous, and for their disposal. {Section 12}

- Effective and suitable provisions should be made in every factory for securing and maintaining in every workroom; adequate ventilation by the circulation of fresh air; and such a temperature will secure to workers therein reasonable conditions of comfort and prevent injury to health. {Section 13}
- Effective measures should be taken to prevent inhalation of dust to prevent inhalation of dust and fume that may produce in the course of manufacturing process. {Section 14}
- In any factory where the humidity of air is artificially increased, the State Government may make rules prescribing standards of humidification; regulating the methods used for artificially increasing humidity of the air; and directing prescribed test for determining the humidity of the air to be correctly carried out and recorded; and prescribing methods to be adopted for securing adequate ventilation and cooling of the air in the workrooms. {Section 15}
- No room in any factory should lie overcrowded to an extent injurious to the health of the workers employed therein. {Section 16}
- In every part of a factory where workers are working or passing, there should be provided and maintained sufficient and suitable lighting, natural or artificial, or both. {Section 17}
- In every factory effective arrangements should be made to provide and maintain at suitable points conveniently situated for all workers employed therein a sufficient supply of wholesome drinking water. {Section 18}
- In every factory sufficient latrine and urinal accommodation of prescribed types should be provided conveniently situated and accessible to workers, separately for male and female workers, at all times while they are at the factory. {Section 19}

- In every factory there should be provided a sufficient number of spittoons in convenient places and they shall be maintained in a clean and hygienic condition. {Section 20}

Employee Safety

- The machinery in every factory should be properly fenced. {Section 21}
- Only the trained adult male worker, wearing tight fitting clothing which should be supplied by the Occupier, should be allowed to work near the machinery in motion. {Section 22}
- No young person shall be employed on dangerous machinery, unless he is fully instructed as to the danger arising in connection with the machine and the precautions to be observed and he has received sufficient training in work at the machine. {Section 23}
- Suitable arrangements should be made to provide striking gear and devices for cutting off power in case of emergencies. {Section 24}
- Sufficient precautions should be taken with regard to self-acting machines to avoid accidents. {Section 25}
- To prevent danger, all machinery driven by power should be encased and effectively guarded. {Section 26}
- Woman worker and children should not be employed in any part of the factory for pressing cotton in which a cotton-opener is at work. {Section 27}
- Hoists and Lifts in a factory should be periodically inspected by the Competent Person. {Section 28}
- Lifting Machines, Chains, Ropes and Lifting Tackles in a factory should be periodically inspected by the Competent Person. {Section 29}
- Where process of grinding is carried on, a notice indicating the maximum safe working peripheral speed of every grind-stone or abrasive wheel etc., should be fixed to the revolving machinery. {Section 30}
- Where any plant or machinery or any part thereof is operated at a pressure above atmospheric pressure, effective measures

should be taken to ensure that the safe working pressure of such plant of machinery or part is not exceeded.{Section 31}

- Floors, stairs and means of access should be soundly constructed and properly maintained. {Section 32}
- Pits, sumps opening in floor etc., should be either securely covered or fenced. {Section 33}
- No workman shall be employed in any factory to lift, carry or move any load so heavy as to be likely to cause him injury. {Section 34}
- Necessary protective equipment should be provided to protect the eyes of the workman, where the working involves risk of injury to the eyes. {Section 35}

Employee Welfare

- Adequate and suitable washing facilities should be provided in every factory. {Section 42}
- Provision should be made to provide suitable places for keeping clothing not worn during working hours and for the drying of wet clothing.{Section 43}
- In every factory, suitable arrangements for sitting should be provided and maintained for all workers obliged to work in a standing position, in order that they may take advantage of any opportunities for rest which may occur in the course of their work.{Section 44}
- First-Aid Boxes with the prescribed contents should be provided and maintained so as to be readily accessible during all working hours at the rate of at least one Box for every 150 workmen. {Section 45}
- In every factory wherein more than 500 workers are employed there should be provided and maintained an Ambulance containing the prescribed equipment and in the charge of such medical and nursing staff. {Section 45(4)}
- The Occupier should provide a canteen for the use of workers in every factory, where the number of workmen employed is more than 250.{Section 46}

- In every factory wherein more than 150 workers are employed adequate and suitable shelters or rest rooms and a suitable lunch room, with provision for drinking water, where workers can eat meals brought by them, should be provided and maintained for the use of the workers. {Section 47}
- In every factory wherein more than 30 women workers are ordinarily employed there should be provided and maintained a suitable room for the use of children under the age of six years of such women. {Section 48}
- In every factory wherein 500 or more workers are employed, the Occupier should employ in the factory such number of Welfare Officers as may be prescribed. {Section 49}

Working Hours of Adult Workers

(i) Ordinarily, a worker should not be allowed to work in a factory for more than 48 hours in any week. {Section 51}

(ii) The workman should have one holiday for a whole day in a week. Where he was asked to work on his scheduled weekly holiday, he should be given compensatory holiday within three days of his scheduled weekly holiday. {Section 52}

(iii) Subject to the provisions of Section 51 no worker should be allowed to work more than nine hours in a day. {Section 54}

(iv) The timings of work should be fixed in such a way that no worker should be required to work continuously for more than five hours; and he should be allowed to avail an interval for rest of at least half-an-hour during his work in a day. {Section 55}

(v) The period of work of a workman should be so arranged that inclusive of his interval for rest under Section 55 should not spread over more than ten and a half hours in any day. {Section 56}

(vi) Worker works in a factory for more than nine hours in any day or for more than forty-eight hours in any week, he shall, in respect of overtime work, be entitled to wages at the rate of twice his ordinary rate of wages.

(vii) Women is not allowed to work during the night hours from between 10 P.M. and 5 A.M. Factories Act 1948, shall allow women to work in between the hours of 6 A.M. and 7 P.M. only. {Section 66}

THE EMPLOYEE STATE INSURANCE ACT, 1948

Objectives of the Act

The Employees State Insurance Act (ESI Act) was enacted with the object of introducing a scheme of health insurance for industrial workers. The scheme envisaged by it is one of compulsory State Insurance providing for certain benefits in the event of sickness, maternity and employment injury to workmen employed in or in connection with the work in factories other than seasonal factories.

Establishment of Employees' State Insurance Corporation [Section 3]

Central government establishes the Corporation to be known as the Employees' State Insurance Corporation. This corporation will be having following characteristics:

- Separate corporate body.
- Having perpetual succession.
- Have a common seal.
- Employees' State Insurance Corporation can sue. (file a suit in court on other)

The Corporation Shall Consist of the Following Members [Section 4]

(a) Chairman, Vice-Chairman to be appointed by the Central Government;

(b) Not more than five persons to be appointed by the Central Government;

(c) One person each representing each of the States in which this Act is in force to be appointed by the State Government concerned;

(d) One person to be appointed by the Central Government to represent the three Union Territories;

(e) Ten persons representing employers to be appointed by the Central Government in consultation with such organisations of employers.

(f) Ten persons representing employees to be appointed by the Central Government in consultation with such organisations of employees.

(g) Two persons representing the medical profession to be appointed by the Central Government in consultation with such organisation of medical practitioners.

(h) Three members of Parliament of whom two shall be members of the House of the People (Lok Sabha) and one shall be a member of the Council of States (Rajya Sabha) elected respectively by the members of the House of the People and the members of the Council of States; and

(i) The Director-General of the Corporation ex-officio.

Term of Office of Members of the Corporation [Section 5]

Members referred to in clauses (f), (g), (h) shall be four years, commencing from the date on which their appointment or election. The members of the Corporation referred to in clauses (a), (b), (c) and (e) of Section 4 shall hold office during the pleasure of the government appointing them.

Constitution of Standing Committee [Section 8]

Standing Committee of the Corporation shall be constituted from among its members, consisting of

(a) A Chairman, appointed by the Central Government;

(b) Three members of the Corporation appointed by the Central Government;

(bb) Three members of the Corporation representing such three State Governments thereon as the Central Government may, by notification Gazette, specify from time to time;

(c) Eight members elected by the Corporation as follows-

  (i) Three members from among the members of the Corporation representing employers;

(ii) Three members from among the members of the Corporation representing employees;

(iii) One member from among the members of the Corporation representing the medical profession; and

(iv) One member from among the members of the Corporation elected by Parliament;

(d) The Director General of the Corporation, ex officio.

Term of Office of Members of Standing Committee [Section 9]

A member of the Standing Committee shall cease to hold office when he ceases to be a member of the Corporation.

The term of office of a member of the Standing Committee, other than a member referred to in clause (a) or clause (b) or clause (bb) of Section 8, shall be two years from the date on which his election.

A member of the Standing Committee referred to in clause (a) or clause (b) or clause (bb) of Section 8 shall hold office during the pleasure of the Central Government.

Medical Benefit Council [Section 10] (2010 Amendment)

(a) The Director General, the Employees' State Insurance Corporation, ex officio as Chairman;

(b) The Director General, Health Services, ex officio as Co-chairman;

(c) One member each representing each of the States;

(d) Three members representing employers to be appointed by the Central Government in consultation with such organisations of employers;

(e) Three members representing employees to be appointed by the Central Government in consultation with such organisations of employees;

(f) Three members, of whom not less than one shall be a woman, representing the medical profession, to be appointed by the Central Government.

Duties of Medical Benefit Council [Section 22]

1. Advise the Corporation and the Standing Committee on matters relating to the administration of medical benefit, the certification for purposes of the grant of benefits and other connected matters;
2. Have such powers and duties of investigation as may be prescribed in relation to complaints against medical practitioners in connection with medical treatment and attendance; and
3. Perform such other duties in connection with medical treatment and attendance.

Cessation of Membership [Section 12]

Three members of Parliament of whom two shall be members of the House of the People (Lok Sabha) and one shall be a member of the Council of States (Rajya Sabha) shall cease to be a member of the Corporation when he ceases to be a Member of Parliament.

Other members Membership of Employees' State Insurance Corporation, Standing Committee or the Medical Benefit Council will be ended when that person ends representing such employers, employees, or the medical profession.

Disqualification [Section 13]

A person shall be disqualified for being chosen as or for being a member of the Corporation, the Standing Committee or the Medical Benefit Council-

- If he is declared to be of unsound mind by a competent court; or
- If he is an undischarged insolvent; or
- If he a shareholder or a partner of company;
- If he has been convicted of an offence involving moral turpitude.

Contributions

All Employees to be Insured [Section 38]

Factory or establishment having more than 10 employees should be insured under the Employee State Insurance Act.

Contribution [Section 39]

(i) Employer and employee are liable for payment of the contribution to the Employee State Insurance Corporation.

(ii) The rate of contribution paid by employer and employee will be decided by the Central Government.

(iii) Currently, the employee's contribution rate (w.e.f. 1.1.97) is 1.75 per cent of the wages and that of employer's is 4.75 per cent of the wages paid/payable in respect of the employees in every wage period.

(iv) If wage is received every month by employee, the Contribution to the ESI Corporation should be made by employer and employee every month without fail.

(v) @ 12 per cent of interest per year should be paid if employer delays in payment of the contribution to ESI Corporation.

Principal Employer to Pay Contributions in the First Instance [Section 40]

- Employer should pay the contribution to ESI Corporation of behalf of his employee.
- Employer may deduct employee contribution from employee wage for payment of contribution to ESI Corporation.
- Employer may recover the employee contribution paid from the wage of the employee which should not exceed the amount equivalent to employer contribution.
- Employer will become responsible for the payment to the ESI contribution after deduction of the employee contribution from the employee wage.
- Employer should bear the expenses occurred in payment of contributions to the Corporation.

General Provisions as to Payment of Contributions [Section 42]

- No employee' contribution shall be payable by or on behalf of an employee whose average daily wages during a wage period are below such wages as may be prescribed by the Central Government.
- The average daily wages of an employee shall be calculated in such manner as may be prescribed by the Central Government.

Benefits

The following benefits will be paid to insured persons or to their dependents. [Section 46]

(i) Periodical payments to any insured person in case of his sickness certified by a duly appointed medical practitioner.

(ii) Periodical payments to an insured woman in case of confinement or miscarriage or sickness arising out of pregnancy, confinement, premature birth of child or miscarriage, such woman being certified to be eligible for such payments.

(iii) Periodical payments to an insured person suffering from disablement as a result of an employment injury.

(iv) Periodical payments to such dependants of an insured person who dies as a result of an employment injury.

(v) Medical benefits.

Funeral Benefit [Section 46]

As prescribed by the Central Government, an amount of Rs 5000 is payable to the dependents or to the person who performs last rites from day one of entering insurable employment.

Sickness Benefit [Section 49]

As prescribed by the Central Government, Sickness Benefit represents periodical cash payments made to an Insured Person during the period of certified sickness occurring in a benefit period when Insured Person requires medical treatment and attendance with abstention from work on medical grounds. Sickness benefit is roughly 60 per cent of the average daily wages and is payable for 91 days during two consecutive benefit periods.

Qualifying Conditions

(i) To become eligible to Sickness Benefit, an Insured Person should have paid contribution for not less than 78 days during the corresponding contribution period.

(ii) A person who has entered into insurable employment for the first time has to wait for nearly nine months before becoming eligible to sickness benefit, because his corresponding benefit period starts only after that interval.

Extended Sickness Benefit (ESB)

Insured Persons suffering from long-term diseases was experiencing great hardship on expiry of 91 days Sickness benefit. Often they, though not fit for duty, pressed for a Final certificate. Hence, a provision for paying Sickness Benefit for an extended period (Extended Sickness Benefit) of upto two years in a ESB period of three years.

An Insured Person suffering from certain long-term diseases is entitled to ESB, only after exhausting Sickness Benefit to which he may be eligible. A common list of these long-term diseases for which ESB is payable, is reviewed by the Corporation from time to time. The list was last reviewed on 5.12.99 and revised provisions of ESB became effective from 1.1.2000 and at present this list includes 34 diseases which are grouped in 11 groups as per International Classification of diseases.

To be entitled to the Extended Sickness Benefit an Insured Persons should have been in continuous employment for two years or more at the beginning of a spell of sickness in which the disease is diagnosed and should also satisfy other contributory conditions.

Maternity Benefit

As prescribed by the Central Government, Maternity Benefit is payable to an Insured Woman in the following cases subject to contributory conditions:

(i) Confinement- payable for a period of 12 weeks (84 days).

(ii) Miscarriage or Medical Termination of Pregnancy (MTP) - payable for six weeks (42 days) from the date following miscarriage.

(iii) Sickness arising out of Pregnancy, Confinement, Premature birth - payable for a period not exceeding one month.

(iv) In the event of the death of the Insured Woman during confinement leaving behind a child, Maternity Benefit is payable to her nominee.

(v) Maternity benefit rate is double the Standard Benefit Rate, or roughly equal to the average daily wage.

Disablement Benefit

Temporary Disablement Benefit (TDB)

Eligibility for TDB

- The benefit is not subject to any contributory conditions. An Insured Person is eligible from the day he joins the insurable employment.
- TDB Rate is 40 per cent over and above the normal sickness benefit rate. This works out to nearly 85 per cent of the average daily wages.

Duration of TDB

There is no prescribed limit for the duration of TDB. This is payable as long as temporary disablement lasts and significant improvement by treatment is possible. If a Temporary Disablement spell lasts for less than three days (excluding day of accident), Insured Person will be paid sickness benefit, if otherwise eligible.

Permanent Disablement Benefit (PDB)

PDB is payable to an Insured Person who suffers permanent residual disablement as a result of Employment Injury (including Occupational Diseases) and results in loss of earning capacity. The PDB rate is calculated as percentage of loss of earning capacity as assessed by the Medical Board.

Employer will be liable for the accidents caused to his employer in the following circumstance:

(i) Accident caused to an employee even if he obeyed the safety instruction of his employer. [Section 51B]

(ii) Accident caused to employee while travelling in employer's transportation vehicles. [Section 51C]

(iii) At the time of employment the accident caused to the employee while protection or rescuing other employee from occurring accident. [Section 51D]

(iv) An accident occurring to an employee while commuting from his residence to the place of employment for duty or from the place of employment to his residence after performing duty, shall be deemed to have arisen out of and in the course of employment. [Section 51E] (2010 amendment)

Dependants' Benefit [Section 52]

As prescribed by the Central Government, the dependants' benefit is payable to the dependants in cases where an Insured Person dies as a result of Employment Injury. The minimum rate of dependants' benefit w.e.f. 1.1.90 is ₹ 14 per day and these rates of the dependants' benefit are increased from time to time. The latest enhancement is with effect from 01.08.2002.

Medical Benefit [Section 56]

As prescribed by the Central Government, Employer or his family members are entitled to the medical benefit. In case of the retirement of the employer his spouse shall be eligible to receive medical benefit subject to payment of contribution. In case of permanent disablement, he can get medical benefit till the date of his retirement. Maximum age for the retirement is 60 years.

Benefits Not to be Combined [Section 65]

(1) An insured person shall not be entitled to receive for the same period-

(a) Both sickness benefit and maternity benefit;

(b) Both sickness benefit and disablement benefit for temporary disablement; or

(c) Both maternity benefit and disablement benefit for temporary disablement.

(2) Where a person is entitled to more than one of the benefits mentioned in sub-Section (1), he shall be entitled to choose which benefit he shall receive.

WORKMEN'S COMPENSATION ACT, 1923

The main objective of the Act is to impose an obligation upon the employers to pay compensation to workers for accidents arising out of and in course of employment.

The Act, however, does not apply to members serving in the Armed Forces of Indian Union, and employees covered under the provisions of the Employees' State Insurance Act 1923 as disablement and dependents' benefit is available under this Act.

'Dependent' means any of the following relatives of a deceased (dead) workman, namely:-

(i) A widow, a minor legitimate or adopted son, and unmarried legitimate or adopted daughter, or a widowed mother; and

(ii) If wholly dependent on the earnings of the workman at the time of his death, a son or a daughter who has attained the age of 18 years and who is infirm;

(iii) If wholly or in part dependent on the earnings of the workman at the time of his death,

  (a) A widower,

  (b) A parent other than a widowed mother,

  (c) A minor illegitimate son, an unmarried illegitimate daughter or a daughter legitimate or illegitimate or adopted if married and a minor or if widowed and a minor,

  (d) A minor brother or an unmarried sister or a widowed sister if a minor,

  (e) A widowed daughter-in-law,

  (f) A minor child of a pre-deceased son,

(g) A minor child of a pre-deceased daughter where no parent of the child is alive, or

(h) A paternal grandparent if no parent of the workman is alive.

'Partial disablement' means, where the disablement is of a temporary nature, such disablement as reduces the earning capacity of a workman in any employment in which he was engaged at the time of the accident resulting in the disablement, and, where the disablement is of a permanent nature, such disablement as reduces his earning capacity in every employment which he was capable of undertaking at that time.

Every injury specified in Part II of Schedule I shall be deemed to result in permanent partial disablement.

'Total disablement' means such disablement, whether of a temporary or permanent nature, as incapacitates a workman for all work which he was capable of performing at the time of the accident resulting in such disablement.

Permanent total disablement shall be deemed to result from every injury specified in Part I of Schedule I, mentioned below:

Employer's Liability for Compensation [Sec 3]

(1) If personal injury is caused to a workman by accident arising out of and in the course of his employment, his employer shall be liable to pay compensation in accordance with the provisions of this Act.

The Employer Shall Not Be So Liable in Following Cases [Sec 3 (1)]

(a) Any injury which does not result in the total or partial disablement of the workman for a period exceeding three days, employer is not liable to pay the compensation.

(b) Accidents caused due to,

(i) The workman having been at the time thereof under the influence of drink or drugs, (alcohol) or

(ii) The willful disobedience of the workman to an order expressly given, or to a rule expressly framed, for the purpose of securing the safety of workmen, or

(iii) The willful removal or disregard by the workman of any safety guard or other device which he knew to have been provided for the purpose of securing the safety of workmen.

Schedule 3: Lists of Occupational Diseases

An occupational disease is any chronic ailment that occurs as a result of work or occupational activity. It is an aspect of occupational safety and health.

The worker/employee must have minimum six months period of service in particular employment under employer to claim the compensation for occupational disease mention in Part B of Schedule III for which he was effected.

Compensation in Case of Death [Sec 4(1) (a)]

While calculating the compensation of the workman, age of the workman and relevant factor is taken in to account.

Fifty per cent of monthly wages of the deceased workman × relevant factor with reference to the age of injured workman or 1,20,000 rupees of compensation. Whichever is more.

Example: A worker aged 35 meets with an accident and dies while at work (i.e. in the course of employment). At the time he drew a monthly wage of ₹ 2,500. As per Schedule IV of the Act the relevant factor applicable to his case would be ₹ 197.06. As such, the amount of compensation payable to his dependants will be arrived at in the following way:

(i) 50 per cent of ₹ 2,500 = 1,250

(ii) 1,250 x relevant factor (i.e.197.06)

= ₹ 2,46,325.00 (total compensation payable)

Compensation in Case of Permanent Total Disablement [Sec 4(1) (b)]

60 per cent of monthly wages of workman × relevant factor with

reference to the age of injured workman. Or 1,40,000 rupees of compensation. Whichever is more.

For above the calculation of the compensation in case of death or permanent partial disablement, the monthly wage of workman is limited to 4000 Rupees only. Or the government may prescribe and change the monthly wage amount for calculation of the compensation.

Example: Shyam, a worker aged 35 meets with an accident and suffers permanent total disablement while at work (i.e. in the course of employment). At the time she drew a monthly wage of ₹ 2,500. The amount of compensation payable will be arrived at as follows:

(i) 60 per cent of ₹ 2,500 = 1,500

(ii) 1,500 x relevant factor (i.e. 197.06)

= ₹ 2,95,590.00 (total compensation payable)

Compensation in Case of Permanent Partial Disablement [Sec 4(1) (c)]

The calculation of the compensation is same as in case of the permanent total disablement.

More injuries than One are Caused by the Same Accident

All injuries compensation caused by same accident will be added but compensation amount payable should not exceed more than what would have been payable in the case of permanent partial disablement.

Compensation in Case of Temporary Disablement [Sec 4(1) (d)]

Ramamurthy (Road sweeper employed on contract basis for Bangalore City Corporation) slipped and fell from a garbage truck and fractured his hand. He could not work for one month. This is temporary disablement.

In case of temporary disablement, payments equal to 25 per cent of the workers' ages shall be made at fortnightly intervals (every two weeks). [Sec 4(2)] In case the disablement lasts for more than 28 days, the employer should make the payment on the 16th day from the day of the disablement.

If the period of disablement lasts for less than 28 days, the payment shall be made after the expiry of 3 days. This wait for 3 days is to ascertain how long the temporary disablement will last—less than/equal to 28 days or more.

In case the employer makes any payment to the worker before the payment of this half monthly (every two weeks) or lump sum amount, it shall be deducted from any lump sum or half-monthly payments. [Section 4 (2) (a)]

[Sec 4(2A)]

The employee shall be reimbursed the actual medical expenditure incurred by him for treatment of injuries caused during course of employment.

If the Injury of the Workman Results in his Death [Sec 4(4)]

The employer shall, in addition to the compensation under sub-section (1), deposit with the Commissioner a sum of 2500 for payment of the same to the eldest surviving dependant of the workman towards the expenditure of the funeral of such workman or where the workman did not have a dependant or was not living with his dependant at the time of his death to the person who actually incurred such expenditure.

MATERNITY BENEFIT ACT, 1961

The Maternity Benefit Act aims to regulate of employment of women employees in certain establishments for certain periods before and after child birth and provides for maternity and certain other benefits.

The Act extends to the whole of India and is applicable to:

1. Every factory, mine or plantation (including those belonging to government) and
2. An establishment engaged in the exhibition of equestrian, acrobatic and other performances, irrespective of the number of employees, and
3. To every shop or establishment wherein 10 or more persons are employed or were employed on any day of the preceding 12 months.

However, the Act does not apply to any such factory/other establishment to which the provisions of the Employees' State Insurance Act are applicable for the time being.

Maternity Benefit

Every woman shall be entitled to, and her employer shall be liable for, the payment of maternity benefit, which is the amount payable to her at the rate of the average daily wage for the period of her actual absence.

Period for Which Benefit Allowed

The maximum period for which any woman shall be entitled to maternity benefit shall be 12 weeks in all whether taken before or after childbirth. However, she cannot take more than six weeks before her expected delivery.

Entitled to Maternity Benefit

(i) Every woman employee, whether employed directly or through a contractor, who has actually worked in the establishment for a period of at least 80 days during the 12 months immediately preceding the date of her expected delivery, is entitled to receive maternity benefit.

(ii) The qualifying period of 80 days shall not apply to a woman who has immigrated into the State of Assam and was pregnant at the time of immigration.

(iii) For calculating the number of days on which a woman has actually worked during the preceding 12 months, the days on which she has been laid off or was on holidays with wages shall also be counted.

(iv) There is neither a wage ceiling for coverage under the Act nor there is any restriction as regards the type of work a woman is engaged in.

Restriction on Employment of Pregnant Women

1. No employer should knowingly employ a woman during the period of six weeks immediately following the day of her delivery or miscarriage or medical termination of pregnancy. Besides, no woman should work in any establishment during the said period of six weeks.

2. Further, the employer should not require a pregnant woman employee to do an arduous work involving long hours of standing or

any work which is likely to interfere with her pregnancy or cause miscarriage or adversely affect her health, during the period of one month preceding the period of six weeks before the date of her expected delivery, and any period during the said period of six weeks for which she does not avail of the leave.

Discharge or Dismissal to be Void

Dismissal or discharge of a pregnant woman shall not disentitle her to the maternity benefit or medical bonus allowable under the Act except if it was on some other ground.

Other Benefits

Leave for Miscarriage and Illness

In case of miscarriage or medical termination of pregnancy, a woman shall, on production of the prescribed proof, be entitled to leave with wages at the rate of maternity benefit, for a period of six weeks immediately following the day of her miscarriage or medical termination of pregnancy.

Leave for Tubectomy Operation

In case of Tubectomy operation, a woman shall, on production of prescribed proof, be entitled to leave with wages at the rate of maternity benefit for a period of two weeks immediately following the day of operation.

Leave for Illness

Leave for a maximum period of one month with wages at the rate of maternity benefit are allowable in case of illness arising out of pregnancy, delivery, premature birth of child, miscarriage or medical termination of pregnancy or Tubectomy operation.

Medical Bonus

Every woman entitled to maternity benefit shall also be allowed a medical bonus of Rs 250, if no pre-natal confinement and post-natal care is provided for by the employer free of charge.

UNIT-VIII

Trade Unions Act, 1926

Standing Orders Act, 1946

Industrial Disputes Act, 1947

Minimum Wages Act, 1948

Payment of Wages Act, 1936

Equal Remuneration Act, 1976

Payment of Bonus Act, 1965

TRADE UNIONS ACT, 1926

Trade Unions are voluntary organisation of Workers as well as Employers formed to protect and promote the interest of their members. They are the most suitable organisations for balancing and improving the relations between the employer and the employees. The workers come together to maintain and improve their bargaining power on wages and working conditions.

The first organised Trade Union in India named as the Madras Labour Union was formed in the year 1918. From the beginning itself, Trade Unions were not confined to workers alone. From Nineteenth Century itself there were Employers' associations in the form of Chamber of Commerce, Industrial Associations, etc to protect and promote the interests of their members in a concerted manner. After independence, expansion of industrial activity and grouping workers' Trade Unions acted as a spur for strengthening and expansion of employers' organisation.

In industrially advanced countries, trade unionism has made a great impact on the social, political and economic life. India, being an agricultural country, trade unionism is restricted to industrial areas and it is still in a stage of growth. The earliest known trade unions in India were the Bombay Millhand's Association formed in 1890, the Amalgamated Society of Railway Servants of India and Burma formed in 1897, Printers' Union formed in Calcutta in 1905, the Bombay Postal Union which was formed in 1907, the Kamgar Hitwardhak Sabha Bombay formed in 1910.

Trade Union movement began in India after the end of First World War. After a decade following the end of First World War the pressing need for the coordination of the activities of the individual unions was recognised. Thus, the All India Trade Union Congress was formed in 1920 on a National Basis, the Central Labour Board, Bombay and the Bengal Trades Union Federation was formed in 1922. The All India Railwaymen's Federation was formed in the same year and this was followed by the creation of both Provincial and Central federations of unions of Postal and Telegraph employees.

The origin of the passing of a Trade Unions Act in India was the historic Buckingham Mill Case in which the Madras High Court granted an interim injunction against the Strike Committee of the Madras Labour Union forbidding them to induce certain workers to break their contracts of employment by refusing to return to work. Trade Union leaders found that they were liable to prosecution and imprisonment for bona fide union activities and it was felt that some legislation for the protection of trade union was necessary. In March, 1921, Shri N. M. Joshi, then General Secretary of the All India Trade Union Congress, successfully moved a resolution in the Central Legislative Assembly recommending that Government should introduce legislation for the registration and protection of trade unions. Opposition from employers to the adoption of such a measure was, however, so great that it was not until 1926 that the Indian Trade Unions Act was passed.

Indian Trade Unions Bill, 1925 having been passed by the Legislature received its assent on 25th March, 1926. It came into force on 1st June, 1927 as the Indian Trade Unions Act, 1926. By Section 3 of the Indian Trade Unions (Amendment) Act, 1964 the word "Indian" has been omitted and now it is known as The Trade Unions Act, 1926.

The main provisions made in this Act are as under

Trade Union means any combination, whether temporary or permanent, formed primarily for the purpose of regulating the relations between workmen and employers or between workmen and workmen or between employers and employers, or for imposing restrictive conditions on the conduct of any trade or business, and includes any federation of two or more trade unions.

Registration of Trade Union

The Act provides for the registration of the trade unions with the 'Registrars of Trade Unions' set up in different States. For registration of a trade union, seven or more members of the union can submit their application in the prescribed form to the Registrar of Trade Unions. The application shall be accompanied by a copy of the 'rules of the trade union' and a statement giving the following particulars:- (i) Names, occupations and addresses of the members making the application; (ii) The name of the trade union and the address of its head office; (iii) The titles, names, ages, addresses and occupations of the office bearers of the trade union as per the format given in the Act.

The Registrar, on being satisfied that the Union has complied with all the requirements of this Act, registers the Trade union.

Registration Certificate

On receipt of the application for registration, the Registrar issues a certificate of registration in the prescribed form as a conclusive evidence of registration of that Trade Union.

Cancellation of Registration

A certificate of Registration may be withdrawn or cancelled by the Registrar either after an application of a Trade Union or if the Registrar is satisfied that the certificate is obtained by fraud of mistake or that the trade union had ceased to exist or willfully and after notice from the Registrar contravene any provisions of the Act or rules, etc.

Annual Statutory Returns

The registered trade unions are required to submit annual statutory returns to the Registrar regarding their membership, general funds, sources of income and items of expenditure and details of their assets and liabilities, which in turn submits a consolidated return of their state in the prescribed proforma to Labour Bureau, Ministry of Labour and Employment. The Labour Bureau on receiving the annual returns from different States/Union Territories consolidates the all India statistics and disseminates them through its publication entitled the 'Trade Unions in India' and its other regular publications. Every trade union shall send annual returns to the Registrar in triplicate on or before the 1st day of June of the year succeeding the calendar year.

Uses of Funds

The general funds of a registered trade union shall not be spent on any other objects than those specified in the Act. Also, a registered trade union may constitute a separate fund, from contributions separately levied for or made to that fund, for the promotion of the civic and political interest of its members. No member shall be compelled to contribute to such fund and a member who does not contribute to the said fund shall not be excluded from any benefits of the trade union.

Maintenance of Accounts

The account books of a registered trade union and the list of members thereof shall be open to inspection by an office-bearer or member of the trade union at such times as may be provided for in the rules of trade union.

Disqualification

A person shall be disqualified for being chosen as, and for being a member of, the executive or any other office-bearer or registered trade union if- (i) he has not attained the age of eighteen years; (ii) he has been convicted by a court in India of any offence involving moral turpitude and sentenced to imprisonment, unless a period of five years has elapsed since his release.

The Trade Unions Act, 1926 has been amended from time to time and the most important being the Trade Unions (Amendment) Act, 2001.

This Act has been enacted in order to bring more transparency and to provide greater support to trade unionism in India. Some of the salient features of the Trade Unions (Amendment) Act, 2001 are:-

- No trade union of workmen shall be registered unless at least 10 per cent or 100, whichever is less, subject to a minimum of seven workmen engaged or employed in the establishment or industry with which it is connected are the members of such trade union on the date of making of application for registration.
- A registered trade union of workmen shall at all times continue to have not less than 10 per cent or 100 of the workmen, whichever is less, subject to a minimum of seven persons engaged or employed in the establishment or industry with which it is connected, as its members.
- A provision for filing an appeal before the Industrial Tribunal/ Labour Court in case of non-registration or for restoration of registration has been provided.
- All office bearers of a registered trade union, except not more than one-third of the total number of office bearers or five,

whichever is less, shall be persons actually engaged or employed in the establishment or industry with which the trade union is connected.

- Minimum rate of subscription by members of the trade union is fixed at ₹ 1 per annum for rural workers, three rupees per annum for workers in other unorganised sectors and ₹ 12 rupees per annum in all other cases.
- The employees who have been retired or have been retrenched shall not be construed as outsiders for the purpose of holding an office in the trade union concerned.
- For the promotion of civic and political interest of its members, unions are authorised to set up separate political funds.

Growth of Trade Union

On the basis of available information, Tamil Nadu accounted for the largest number of registered trade unions (8,793) followed by Rajasthan (4,593). Out of the total of 27,137 registered unions in the 13 states, as many as 27,063 unions (99.73 per cent) were Workers Unions and remaining 74 (0.27 per cent) were Employer Unions.

Income and Expenditure of Workers' Unions

The highest income and expenditure of Central Unions and as well as for State Unions were in Tamil Nadu.

MINIMUM WAGES ACT, 1948

Till 1948, there was no Act to regulate minimum wages and hence the workers of the industries where sweated labour was prevalent were exploited by the employers. The workers in these industries were paid extremely low wages. Further, there was a disparity in the rate of wages of similar kinds of work in unorganised industries. Accordingly, the Minimum Wages Act was passed in 1948, providing for the fixation/ revision of minimum rates of wages in respect of scheduled employment by the appropriate Government.

Objectives of the Act

The Minimum Wages Act was enacted in the year 1948 to give effect to the recommendations adopted by the International Labour

Conference in the year 1928. The objective of the Act is directed against exploitation of the ignorant, less organised and less privileged members of the society by the capitalists.

The objectives of the Act therefore are:

(i) To protect the unorganised worker so that he may not be subjected to unfair bargaining.

(ii) To see that the wages correspond to the amount of work done and there is no exploitation by the employer.

(iii) To see that wages are not below a certain minimum so that 'sweating in industry' may be prevented.

(iv) To see that in cases of less payment than the minimum fixed by the State Government, summary procedure is provided for the recovery of the balance with penalty and subsequent prosecution of the offending party.

(v) To see that there is a periodical revision of the wages.

Scope and Coverage

The Minimum Wages Act, 1948 extends to whole of India. It applies to employments which are enumerated in the schedule of the Act and in certain cases may extend to other employment added by the appropriate government.

Scheduled Employment [Section 2(g)]

'Scheduled Employment' means an employment specified in the Schedule or any process or branch of work forming part of such employment.

The Schedule is divided into two parts namely, Part I and II. Part II relates to employment in agriculture. It was realised that it would be necessary to fix minimum wages in many more employments to be identified in course of time. Accordingly, powers were given to the appropriate Government to add employments to the Schedule by following the procedure laid down in Section 27 of the Act. As a result, the State Governments and Central Government have made several additions to the schedule and it differs from State to State.

Fixation of Minimum Rates of Wages

Section 3(1) (a) of the Minimum Wages Act,1948 prescribes the manner in which appropriate Government shall fix, review and revise the minimum rates of wages payable to employees, employed in the employments specified in Part I and Part II of the Schedule. The appropriate Government may also add any employment to either part in respect of which minimum wages are to be fixed by notification under Section 27.

But regarding employees employed in an employment specified in Part II of the Schedule, the appropriate Government may, instead of fixing minimum rates of wages under section 3(1) (a) for the whole state, fix such rates for a part of the state or for any specified class or classes of such employment in the whole State or any part thereof.

The government may refrain from fixing minimum rates of wages in respect of any schedule employment in which there are less than one thousand employees. If at any time the government, after enquiry, finds that the number of employees in such employment has risen to one thousand or more, it shall fix the minimum rates of wages payable to the employees employed in such employment.

Review and Revision of Minimum Wages

Under Section 3(1) (b), the appropriate Government may review the minimum rates of wages so fixed at such intervals as it may think fit. Such intervals shall not exceed five years. The minimum rates of wages shall be revised on such review, if necessary. But when for sufficient reasons the appropriate Government is unable to review, it may review it even after five years. Till then, immediately before prevailing minimum rates shall continue to be minimum rates.

Manner of Fixation/Revision of Minimum Wages

Section 3 (2) empowers the appropriate Government to fix minimum rate of wages for:

(a) Time work, known as Minimum Time Rate;

(b) Piece work, known as a Minimum Piece Rate;

(c) A 'Guaranteed Time Rate' for those employed in piece work for the purpose of securing to such employees a minimum rate of wages on a time work basis;

(d) A 'Over Time Rate' i.e. minimum rate (whether a time rate or a piece rate) to apply in substitution for the minimum rate which would otherwise be applicable in respect of overtime work done by employee.

Under Section 3(3), different minimum rates of wages may be fixed for-

(i) Different scheduled employments;

(ii) Different classes of work in the same scheduled employments;

(iii) Adults, adolescents, children and apprentices;

(iv) Different localities.

The minimum rates of wages may be fixed by any one or more of the following wage periods, namely;

(i) By the hour,

(ii) By the day,

(iii) By the month, or

(iv) By such other large wage periods as may be prescribed.

Where such rates are fixed by the day or by the month, the manner of calculating wages for month or for a day as the case may be, may be indicated.

Minimum Rate of Wages (Section 4)

Section 4 (1) provides that any minimum rate of wages fixed or revised by the appropriate Government under Section 3 may consist of-

(i) A basic rate of wages and a special allowance at a rate to be adjusted, at such intervals and in such manner as the appropriate Government may direct to accord as nearly as practicable with the variation in the cost of living index number applicable to such worker (hereinafter referred to as the cost of living allowance); or

(ii) A basic rate of wages or without the cost of living allowance and the cash value of the concession in respect of supplies of essential commodities at concessional rates where so authorised; or

(iii) An all inclusive rate allowing for the basic rate, the cost of living allowance and the cash value of the concessions, if any.

Under Section 4 (2), the cost of living allowance and the cash value of the concessions in respect of supplies of essential commodities at concessional rates shall be computed by the competent authority at such intervals and in accordance with such directions specified or given by the appropriate Government.

Procedure for Fixing and Revision of Minimum Wages

Section 5 lays down that in fixing minimum rates of wages in respect of any scheduled employment for the first time or in revising minimum rates of wages, the appropriate Government can follow either of the two methods mentioned below.

(i) Committee Method

The appropriate Government may appoint as many committees and sub-committees as it considers necessary to hold enquiries and advice it in respect of such fixation or revision as the case may be. After considering the advice of the committee or committees, the appropriate Government shall, by notification in the Official Gazette fix or revise the minimum rates of wages. The wage rates shall come into force from such date as may be specified in the notification. If no date is specified, wage fixed shall come into force on the expiry of three months from the date of the issue of the notification.

(ii) Notification Method

Under this method the appropriate Government when fixing minimum wages shall by notification, in the Official Gazette publish its proposals for the information of persons likely to be affected thereby and specify a date not less than two months from the date of notification on which the proposals will be taken into consideration. The representations received will be considered by the appropriate Government. The appropriate Government is also required to consult the Advisory Board constituted under Section 7 and thereafter fix or revise the minimum rates of wages by notification in the Official Gazette.

Composition of Committee/Advisory Board

Each of the committee, sub-committee and the advisory board shall consist of persons to be nominated by the appropriate Government representing employers and employees in equal number and the independent persons not exceeding one-third of its total members. The chairman is an independent person to be appointed by the government.

The Mode of Payment of Minimum Rates of Wages

The wages to the workers are paid either in cash or kind. However, where there is a custom to pay wages wholly or partly in kind, the appropriate Government may authorise the payment partly or wholly in kind by the issue of notification. Further if the appropriate Government is of the opinion that provision should be made for supply of essential commodities at concessional rates, it may authorise the supply of these articles at concessional rates. The cash value of wages in kind and of concessions in respect of supplies of essential commodities at concessional rates, in such cases, is to be estimated in the manner prescribed under the rules [Section 11].

Payment of Minimum Rates of Wages

The Act imposes an obligation upon the employer to pay minimum rates of wages without any deduction to the workers employed in a Scheduled employment, wherever, the appropriate Government has fixed such wages by notification under Section 5 with respect to that employment [Section 12].

Wages of Worker Who Work for Less than Normal Working Day

If a worker, whose minimum rates of wages has been fixed in a prescribed manner works for any day for a shorter period than a requisite number of hours constituting a normal working day for him then he would be entitled to receive wages for the full day from the employer except when he willfully fails to work for the normal working day without any fault on the part of the employer and for such default or other similar cases the rules provide that the wages may be deducted [Section 15].

Wages for Two or More Classes of Work

Where an employee does two or more classes of work to which a different rate of minimum wages is applicable then the employee is entitled to receive wages from his employer in proportion to the time occupied by him in each class of work, calculated on the basis of minimum rates fixed for each of the classes of work [Section 16].

Minimum Time Rate Wages for Piece Work

Where an employee is employed on piece work for which minimum rates has not been fixed but instead the appropriate Government has fixed minimum time rates of wages under this Act then the employer is required to pay to the employee engaged on piece work minimum wages at not less than minimum time rate wages [Section 17].

Maintenance of Records and Display of Notices

Every employer is required to maintain registers and records containing the following particulars:

(a) Particular of employees employed by him;

(b) The work performed by them;

(c) The wages paid to them;

(d) The receipts given by the employees; and

(e) Any other information as prescribed.

Claims and Procedure

The appropriate Government is empowered to appoint by notification in the Official Gazette an authority to hear and decide for any specific claims arising out of (i) payment of less than minimum rates of wages, (ii) overtime rates and (iii) payment for work done on a day of rest to the employees employed by an employer of that area [Section 20(1)].

Who can be appointed as Authority?

Any one of the following persons may be appointed as an Authority to decide any claims relating to the matters specified above

(a) Any Commissioner for Workmen's Compensation;

(b) Any officer of the Central Government exercising functions as a Labour Commissioner for any region;

(c) Any officer of the State Government not below the rank of Labour Commissioner; or

(d) Any officer with experience as a Judge of Civil or Stipendiary Magistrate.

(e) (i) the employee himself, or (ii) any practitioner, or (iii) any officer, of a registered Trade Union authorised in writing to Act of his behalf, or (iv) any inspector or any person acting with the permission of the Authority before whom the claim is preferred may make an application.

Time for Making Claims

The application for claim is required to be presented within six months from the date on which the minimum wages or other amount becomes payable. But application can be admitted after six months if the applicant satisfies the Authority that he could not make the application within prescribed time for 'sufficient cause'.

Procedure for Deciding Claims

When an application for the claim is entertained, the Authority is required to hear the applicant and the employer and afford them all reasonable facilities to present their case and hold any enquiry which he may deem necessary. If after holding an enquiry into the merit of the claim if the Authority comes to the conclusion that the employer has made a default then it may direct the employer to pay the difference between minimum wage payable to him and wages actually paid to him.

Recovery of Amount

The Authority before whom the claim is preferred by a worker against an employer is vested with a power to order the recovery of the amount due in favour of a worker as it was a fine imposed on the employer, in case, the Authority happens to be a Magistrate. But, in case, the Authority is other than a Magistrate then on the application of the Authority to the Magistrate vested with a power to decide a claim under the Act, the amount due to worker can be recovered on the orders of Magistrate like a fine [Section 20(5)].

EQUAL REMUNERATION ACT, 1976

Wage differentials on the basis of sex were very common in agricultural and industries. This was not in conformity in the Constitution. Article 14 of the Constitution of India enjoins the State not to deny equality before regarding equal treatment of law and equal protection of law. Article 16 (1) declares equality of opportunity in matter of employment of appointment to an office under the State.

Article 16 (2) prohibits discrimination on ground, only of religion, race, caste, sex, descent, place of birth, residence or any of them be ineligible for, or in respect of any employment or office under the State. The Directive Principles of State Policy under Article 39 (d) envisages that equal pay should be given to men and women doing equal work. Further in 1958, India ratified ILO Convention No. 111 on Equal Remuneration. To give effect to Constitutional Directive and ILO Convention, the Equal Remuneration Act, 1976 was enacted.

Objectives of the Act

The object of the Act is to prevent discrimination on the ground of sex against women in respect of remuneration and in matters of recruitment and promotion of men and women.

Scope and Application of the Act

The Equal Remuneration Act, 1976 extends to the whole of India. The Act is applicable to several employments and establishments. However, the Act does not apply –

(a) To cases affecting the terms and conditions of a women's employment in complying with the requirements of any law giving special treatment to women, or

(b) To any special treatment accorded to women in connection with-

   (i) The birth or expected birth of a child, or

   (ii) The terms and conditions relating to retirement, marriage or death or to any provision made in connection with the retirement, marriage or death.

   (iii) Duty of employer to pay equal remuneration to men and women workers for same work or work of a similar nature.

Section 4 prohibits the employer to:

1. Pay to any worker, employed by him at rates less favourable than those at which remuneration is paid by him to the workers of the opposite sex in such establishment or employment for performing the same work or work of a similar nature.
2. Reduce the rate of remuneration of any worker in the process of bringing parity in remuneration between men and women.
3. Where in an establishment or employment, the rates of remuneration payable before the commencement of this Act for men and women workers for the same work or work of similar nature are different only on the ground of sex, then the higher (in cases where there are more than two rates) of such rates shall be payable, on and from such commencement, to such men and women workers. This would, however, not entitle a worker to the revision of the rate of remuneration payable to him or her with reference to the service rendered by him or her before the commencement of this Act.

No Discrimination to be Made While Recruiting Men and Women Workers

Section 5 prohibits the employer to make any discrimination against women. While making recruitment for the same work or work of a similar nature or in any condition of service subsequent to recruitment such as promotions, training or transfer except where the employment of women in such work is prohibited or restricted by or under any law for the time being in force. However, this provision would not affect any priority or reservation for scheduled castes or scheduled tribes, ex-servicemen, retrenched employees or any other class or category or persons in the matter of recruitment to the posts in an establishment or employment.

Advisory Committee

1. For the purpose of providing increasing employment opportunities for women, the appropriate Government shall constitute one or more Advisory Committees to advice it with regard to the extent to which women may be employed in such establishments or employments as the Central Government may, by notification, specify in his behalf.
2. Every Advisory Committee shall consist of not less than ten persons, to be nominated by the appropriate Government, of which one-half shall be women.
3. In tendering its advice, the Advisory Committee shall have regard to the number of women employed in the concerned establishment or employment, the nature of work, hours of work, suitability of women for employment, as the case may be, the need for providing increasing employment opportunities for women, including part-time employment, and such other relevant factors as the Committee shall regulate its own procedure.
4. The Advisory Committee shall regulate its own procedure.
5. The appropriate Government may, after considering the advice tendered to it by the Advisory Committee and after giving to the persons concerned in the establishment or employment an opportunity to make representations, issue such directions in respect of employment of women workers, as the appropriate Government may think fit.

Authorities for Hearing and Deciding Claims and Complaints

1. Section 7 empowers the appropriate Government, to appoint such officers not below the rank of a Labour Officer as it thinks fit, to be the authorities for the purpose of hearing and deciding-

(a) Complaints with regard to the contravention, appoint such officers not below the rank of a Labour Officer as it thinks fit, to be the authorities for the purpose of hearing and deciding.

(b) Claim arising out of non-payment of wages at equal rates to men and women workers for the same work or work of a similar nature.

2. Every complaint or claim shall be made in the prescribed manner.

3. If any question arises as to whether two or more workers are of the same nature or of a similar nature, it shall be decided by the authority appointed under Sub-section (1).

4. Where a complaint or claim is made to the authority appointed under Sub-section (1) it may, after giving the applicant and the employer an opportunity of being heard, and after such inquiry as it may consider necessary, direct–

   (i) In the case of a claim arising out of non-payment of wages at equal rates to men and women workers for the same work or work of similar nature, that payment be made to the worker of the amount actually paid.

   (ii) In the case of complaint, the adequate steps are taken by the employer so as to ensure that there is no contravention of any provision this Act.

5. Every authority appointed under Sub-section (l) shall have all the powers of Civil Court under the Code of Civil Procedure, 1908, for the purpose of taking evidence and of enforcing the attendance of witnesses and compelling the production of documents and every such authority shall be deemed to be a Civil Court for all the purposes of Section 195 and Chapter XXVI of the Code of Criminal Procedure, 1973.

6. Any employer or worker aggrieved by any order made by an authority appointed under Sub-section (1) on a complaint or claim may, within 30 days from the date of the order, prefer and appeal to such authority as the appropriate Government may by notification specify in this behalf, and that authority may, after hearing the appeal, confirm, modify or reverse the

order appealed against and no further appeal shall lie against the order made by such authority.

PAYMENT OF WAGES ACT, 1936

Before the enactment of the Payment of Wages Act, 1936, delays in the payment of wages and making unauthorised deductions from the wages were quite prevalent.

The Payment of Wages Act, 1936 was enacted with a view to ensuring that wages payable to employed persons covered by the Act are disbursed by the employers within the prescribed time limit and without arbitrary fines and unauthorised deductions.

Objectives of the Act

The main objectives of the Payment of Wages Act, 1936 is to regulate the payment of wages to certain classes of persons employed in specified industries/establishments.

Specifically, the Act aims to achieve the following objectives:

(a) The wages of workers must be paid at the proper time.

(b) The wages of workers must be paid in the form prescribed for the purpose.

(c) The wages of workers must be paid without any unauthorised deductions.

Application of the Act

The Payment of Wages Act, 1936 extends to the whole of India. It came into operation on 28th March, 1937. It applies to payment of wages to persons employed in:

(i) Any factory

(ii) Railways by a railway administration

(iii) Industrial or other establishment specified in sub-clauses (a) to (g) of section 2(ii).

The Act covers persons drawing less or equal to six thousand five hundred rupees per month.

Responsibility for Payment of Wages

As per Section 3, every employer is responsible for the payment of all wages required to be paid under this Act to persons employed by him. Quite apart from this the following persons shall also be responsible for the payment of wages under this Act:

(i) In a factory, a person named as manager of a factory under the Factories Act, 1948.

(ii) In industrial or other establishments, a person responsible to the employer for the supervision and control of the industrial or other establishments.

(iii) Upon railways (otherwise than in factories), if the employer is the railway administration and the person nominated in this behalf for the local area concerned.

Fixation of Wage-Period

Section 4 imposes an obligation on every person responsible for the payment of wages under section 3, to fix periods in respect of which such wages shall be payable. No wage-period shall exceed one month. Wages can also be paid on daily, weekly, fortnightly basis.

Time of Payment of Wages

Section 5 of the Act lays down that the wages of every person employed upon or in:

(a) Any railway, factory/industrial or other establishment upon or in which less than one thousand persons are employed shall be paid before the expiry of the seventh day.

(b) Any other railway, factory/industrial or other establishment, shall be paid before the expiry of the tenth day after the last day of the wage-period in respect of which the wages are payable.

(c) In the case of persons employed on a dock/wharf/jetty/mine (the balance of wages found due on completion of a final tonnage account of the ship or wagons loaded or unloaded, as the case may be) shall be paid before the expiry of the seventh day from the day of such completion.

(d) Where the employment of any person is terminated by or on behalf of the employer, the wages earned by him shall be paid before the expiry of the second working day from the day on which his employment is terminated.

Exemption from Compliance with the Time Limit for Payment of Wages

The appropriate Government may, by general or special order, exempt the person responsible for the payment of wages from the operation of the above said provisions in certain cases specified in the Act.

(a) All payment of wages shall be made on a working day.

(b) All wages shall be paid in current coin or currency notes or in both.

However, the employer may, after obtaining the written authorisation of the employed person, pay him the wages either by cheque or by crediting the wages in his bank account.

Deduction from Wages (Sec.7)

The following shall be deemed to be deduction from wages:

(i) Every payment made by the employed person to the employer or his agent.

Any loss of wages resulting from the imposition, for good and sufficient cause, upon a person employed, of any of the following penalties, namely:

- the withholding of increment or promotion (including the stoppage of increment at an efficiency bar);
- the reduction to a lower post or time scale or to a lower stage in a time scale; or
- suspension;

shall not be deemed to be a deduction from wages.

B. Deductions which may be Made from Wages

Deductions authorised under the Act are enumerated in section 7(2). Any other deduction is unauthorised. Further, the authorised deductions can be made only in accordance with the provisions of the Act. Deductions may be made of the following kinds only, namely:

(a) Fines;

(b) Deduction for absence from duty;

(c) Deductions for damage to or loss of goods expressly entrusted to the employed person for custody, or for loss of money for which he is required to account, where such damage or loss is directly attributable to his neglect or default;

(d) Deduction for house-accommodation supplied by the employer or by government of any housing board set up under any law for the time being in force (whether the government or the board is the employer or not) or any other authority engaged in the business of subsidising house- accommodation which may be specified in this behalf by the State Government by notification in the Official Gazette;

(e) Deductions for such amenities and services supplied by the employer as the State Government or any officer specified by it in this behalf may, by general or special order, authorise;

(f) Deductions for recovery of advances of whatever nature and the interest due in respect thereof;

(ff) Deductions for recovery of loans made from any fund constituted for the welfare of labour in accordance with the rules approved by the State Government, and the interest due in respect thereof;

(fff) Deductions for recovery of loans granted for house building or other purposes approved by the State Government, and the interest due in respect thereof;

(g) Deductions of income tax payable by the employed person;

(h) Deductions required to be made by the order of a court;

(i) Deductions for subscription to, and for payment of advances from a provident fund;

(j) Deductions for payment to co-operative societies as approved by the appropriate Government or any other officer specified by it in this behalf;

(k) Deductions made with the written authorisation of the person employed for payment of any premium on his life insurance policy to the Life Insurance Corporation of India;

(kk) Deductions made with the written authorisation of the employed persons, for the payment of his contribution to any fund constituted by the employer or a trade union registered under the Trade Union Act, 1926;

(kkk) Deductions made with the written authorisation of the employed person, for the payment of the fees payable by him for the membership of a registered trade union;

(l) Deductions; for payment of insurance premium on Fidelity Guarantee Bonds;

(m) Deductions for recovery of losses sustained by a railway administration on account of acceptance by the employed person of counterfeit or base coins or mutilated or forged currency notes;

(n) Deductions for recovery of losses sustained by a railway administration on account of failure of the employed person to invoice, to bill, to collect or to account for the appropriate charge due to that administration;

(o) Deductions for recovery of losses sustained by a railway administration on account of any rebates or funds incorrectly granted by the employed person where such loss is directly attributable to his neglect or default;

(p) Deductions made with the written authorisation of the employed person, for contribution to the Prime Minister's National Relief Fund or to such other fund as the Central Government may specify;

(q) Deductions for contributions to any insurance scheme framed by the Central Government for the benefit of its employees.

Limits on the Total Amount of Deductions

Section 7(3) lays down that the total amount of deductions in any wage-period from the wages of any employed person shall not exceed

(i) In cases where such deductions are wholly or partly made for payment to the co-operative societies - seventy-five per cent of such wages; and

(ii) In any other case - fifty per cent of such wages.

Fines [Section 7(2) (a) and 8]

1. The fine shall be imposed on any employed person only for acts and omissions which has received approval of the appropriate Government or of the prescribed authority, and has been specified by notice under Sub-Section (2).
2. A notice specifying such acts and omissions shall be exhibited in the prescribed manner in which the employment is carried on or in the case of persons employed upon a railway (otherwise than in a factory), at the prescribed place or places.
3. The fine shall not be imposed on any employed person unless he has been given an opportunity of showing cause against the fine.
4. The total amount of fine which may be imposed in any one wage-period on any employed person shall not exceed an amount equal to three per cent of the wages payable to him in respect of that wage-period.
5. No fine shall be imposed on any employed person who is under the age of fifteen years.
6. No fine imposed on any employed person shall be recovered from him by installments or after the expiry of ninety days from the day on which it was imposed.
7. Every fine shall be deemed to have been imposed on the day of the Act or omission in respect of which it was imposed.
8. All fines and all realisations shall be recorded in a register to be kept by the person responsible for the payment of wages and all such realisations shall be applied only to such purposes beneficial to the persons employed in the factory or establishment as are approved by the prescribed authority.

Deductions for Absence from Duty [Sections 7(2) (B) and 9]

The Act authorises the employer to make deduction from wages of employed person when he remains absent from any place or places of duty where he is required to work. This absence may be for the whole day or any part of the period during which he is required to work.

Amount of Deductions

In case of individual absenteeism, the amount of such deduction from wages will be in the same proportion which period of absence bears to the total period within such wage period during which, he was required to work by the terms of his employment.

However, if ten or more employed persons, acting in concert, absent themselves without due notice which is required under the terms of their contracts of employment, and without reasonable cause, such deduction, from such persons, may include such amount, not exceeding his wages for eight days, as may be due to the employer in lieu of due notice.

Deductions for Damage or Loss of Goods or for Loss of Money

Section 7(2)(c) authorises deductions from the wages can be made (i) for damage or loss of goods expressly entrusted to the employed person for custody, or (ii) for loss of money for which an employed person is required to account, where such damage or loss is directly attributable to his neglect or default. However, before making any such deduction employed person shall be given an opportunity to show cause against the deductions or if any other prescribed procedure has been laid down in this respect the same must be followed. The deductions are subject to the provisions laid down in Section 10, namely:

1. The total amount of deductions under this head should not exceed the actual amount of the damage or loss caused to the employer due to the negligence or default of the employed person [Section 10(10].
2. The person responsible for payment of wages under Section 3 should record all such deductions and realisations thereof, in a register to be kept in such form as may be prescribed.

Deductions for House-Accommodation [Section 7(2) (D) and 11]

1. A deduction under clause (d) or clause (e) of Section 7(2) shall not be made from the wages of such an employed person, unless the house accommodation, amenity or service has been accepted by him as a term of employment or otherwise.
2. Such deduction shall not exceed an amount equivalent to the value of the house accommodation, amenity or service supplied.
3. A deduction under the said clause (e) shall be subject to such conditions as the appropriate Government may impose.

Deductions for Recovery of Advances [Sections 7(2) (i) and (12)]

Section 7(2) (f) deals with the following deductions:

(i) The recovery of advances of whatever nature,

(ii) The interest due on such advance, or

(iii) For adjustment of over-payment of wages.

Conditions

The deductions under Section 7(2) (f) are subject to the following conditions:

1. The recovery of the advance of money given before employment shall be made from the first payment of wages is respect of a complete wage period, but no recovery shall be made of such advances given for travelling expenses [Section 12 (a)].
2. The recovery of an advance given after employment shall be subject to such conditions, as imposed by the appropriate Government.
3. Deductions for the recovery of such advances not already earned should be subject to any rules made by the appropriate Government. Such rules may provide (i) the extent to which such advances may be given, and (ii) the installments by which they may be recovered [Section 12(b)].

Maintenance of Registers and Records (Sec.13)

1. Every employer shall maintain such registers and records giving such particulars of persons employed by him, the work performed by them, the wages paid to them, the deductions made from their wages, the receipts given by them and such other particulars and in such form as may be prescribed.
2. Such registers shall be preserved for a period of three years after the date of last entry made therein.

Authorities under the Payment of Wages Act

Section 15 empowers the State Government to appoint an authority by the issue of notification for a specified area to hear and decide and dispose of all claims arising out of deduction from wages, or delay in payment of wages of persons employed or paid in the area including all matters incidental to such claims.

(i) Who may be appointed?

The following persons may be appointed as an authority for the above purposes namely:

(i) Presiding officers of a Labour Court or Industrial Tribunal constituted under the Industrial Disputes Act, 1947 or under any corresponding law relating to the investigation and settlement of industrial disputes in force in the State; or

(ii) Any Commissioner for Workmen's compensation; or

(iii) Other officer with experience as judge of a civil court or as a Stipendiary Magistrate.

(ii) Who may file the Application?

If the payment of wages is delayed beyond the due date or deductions are made from wages contrary to the provisions of the Act, an application for recovering the same can be filed either by an employee himself or legal practitioner or official of a registered Trade Union duly authorised in writing by the employee or by inspector or by any other person with the permission of the Authority hearing the claim. If there are several employees borne on the same establishment and if their wages for the same period have remained unpaid after the due date, a single claims application can be filed on behalf of all such employees. Similarly if several applications are filed by employees belonging to the same unpaid group, the Authority can deal with them as if it was a single application by an unpaid group.

Limitation

Every such application has to be presented within one year from the date on which the payment of wages was due or from the date on which deductions from wages were made. The Authority has, however, been given the powers to condone the delay in filing such application on its being satisfied that there was a 'sufficient cause' for not filing the application within the time prescribed.

THE PAYMENT OF BONUS ACT, 1965

Bonus is an incentive to increase production. It generally represents the cash incentive given on some conditions, e.g. attainment of certain standards of attendance and efficiency. Bonus is a gift, incentive or cash payment paid by an employer to an employee in addition to his salary or wage to reward performance. The concept of bonus first originated after the First World War referred to as 'War Bonus'. Subsequently, the term 'War Bonus' was substituted by special allowance.

Objectives of the Act

The objective of the Payment of Bonus Act is to provide for the payment of bonus to the employees in certain establishments on the basis of profits or production or productivity and for various matters connected therewith.

The specific objectives of the Payment of Bonus Act as per the judgement of the Honourable Supreme Court in *Jalan Trading Company* vs. *Mill Mazdoor Union* (1967) are as follows:

(i) To maintain peace and harmony between labour and capital.

(ii) To allow the employees to share the prosperity of the establishment.

(iii) to prescribe the minimum and maximum rates of bonus together with a scheme of 'set-off' and 'set-on' with a view to secure the right of labour to share in the prosperity of the establishment and to ensure a reasonable degree of uniformity.

(iv) To provide mechanism for enforcement of the liability for the payment of bonus.

Applicability of the Act

It extends to the whole of India. The Act applies to every factory and every other establishment in which 20 or more persons are employed on any day during an accounting year. However, the appropriate Government may extend the application of these provisions to any factory/establishment employing less than 20 but not less than 10 persons during the accounting year, after giving two months notice in the Official Gazette. While determining the number of persons employed in an establishment, all employees even those drawing ₹ 3, 500 must be taken into account.

Act Not to Apply to Certain Classes of Employees

According to Section 32 of the Act, the following categories of employees are excluded from the operation of the Payment of Bonus Act:

1. Employees employed by the Life Insurance Corporation of India;
2. Seamen as defined in clause (42) of Section (3) of the Merchant Shipping Act, 1958;
3. Employees registered or listed under any scheme made under the Dock Workers (Regulation of Employment) Act, 1948 and employed by registered or listed employers;
4. Employees employed by an establishment engaged in any industry carried on by or under the authority of any department of Central Government or a State Government or a local authority;
5. Employees employed by:
   (a) The Indian Red Cross Society or any other institution of a like nature;

   (b) Universities and other educational institutions;
   (c) Institutions established not for purposes of profit;
6. Employees employed by the Reserve Bank of India;
7. Employees employed by:
   (a) The Industrial Finance Corporation of India;
   (b) Any Financial Corporation established under Section 3, or any Joint Financial Corporation established under Section 3A of the State Financial Corporation Act, 1951;
   (c) The Deposit Insurance Corporation;
   (d) The National Bank for Agricultural and Rural Development;
   (e) The Unit Trust of India;
   (f) The Industrial Development Bank of India;
   (g) The Small Industries Development Bank of India established under Section 3 of the Small Industries Development Bank of India Act, 1989;
   (h) The National Housing Bank;
   (i) Any other financial institution being an establishment in public sector, which the Central Government may, by notification in the official Gazette specify, having regard to: (i) its capital structure; (ii) its objectives and the nature of its activities; (iii) the nature and extent of financial assistance or any concession given to it by the government; and (iv) any other relevant factor;
8. Employees employed by inland water transport establishments operating on routes passing through any other country.

Calculation of Amount Payable as Bonus

The Act prescribes the procedure for calculating the amount payable to the employees. For this purpose, first of all the available surplus in an accounting year is computed under Section 5. Out of this surplus, 67 per cent in case of company (other than a banking company) and 60 per cent in other cases shall be the 'allocable surplus' which would be available for payment of bonus to employees subject to maximum bonus permissible under the Act.

Computation of Available Surplus

Section 5 of the Act lays down that available surplus in respect of accounting year shall be calculated by making certain deductions from the 'gross profit' as per section 6 and by making certain additions to it.

Sums Deductible from Gross Profits

According to Section 6 of the Act, the following sums shall be deducted from the gross profits as prior charges:

(a) **Depreciation:** Any amount by way of depreciation admissible in accordance with the provisions of Section 32(1) of the Income Tax Act, 1961 or in accordance with the provisions of the agricultural income tax law, as the case may be.

(b) **Development Rebate:** Any amount of development rebate or investment allowance or development allowance which the employer is entitled to deduct from his income under the Income Tax Act, 1961.

(c) **Direct Tax:** Any direct tax calculated subject to the provisions of Section 7 which the employer is liable to pay for the accounting year.

(d) **Sums Specified in the Third Schedule of the Act:** This schedule specifies certain sums to be deducted from the gross profit as 'prior charges' for the different categories of employers, such as, non-banking company, banking company, corporation, co-operative society and any other employer.

Certain additions to the Gross Profit: In addition to the above said deductions, the difference between the following will be added to the gross profit in order to ascertain the amount of available surplus as per Section 5 of the Act.

(i) The direct tax calculated as per Section 7 in respect of gross profits of the employer for the immediately preceding accounting year; and

(ii) The direct tax calculated as per Section 7 in respect of gross profits of the employer for such preceding accounting year after deducting there from the amount of bonus.

Thus, the computation of the available surplus is as follows:

$$AS = GP - (D + DR + DT + SS) + TS$$

Where AS = Available surplus, GP= Gross profit, D= Depreciation, DR= Development rebate, DT= Direct tax, SS = Sums specified in the third schedule, TS= Tax saving calculated as per Section 7.

Eligibility for Bonus (Sec. 8)

Section 8 deals with the qualifying period of service of eligibility for bonus.

1. Every employee is eligible for bonus provided he has worked at least 30 working days in that year.
2. An employee is deemed to have worked in an establishment in the accounting year also on the days on which –
   (a) he has been laid off;
   (b) he has been on leave with salary or wage;
   (c) he has been absent due to temporary disablement caused by accident arising out of and in the course of his employment; and
   (d) the employee has been on maternity leave with salary or wage, during the accounting year (Section 14).
3. Where an employee has not worked for all the working days in any accounting year, the bonus payable to him shall be proportionately reduced.
4. The following categories of employees are entitled for bonus:
   (a) A temporary workman;
   (b) A probationer;
   (c) A piece rated worker;
   (d) A dismissed employee reinstated back with wages;
   (e) A part time employee;
   (f) A retrenched employee.

Disqualification for Bonus (Sec. 9)

An employee shall be disqualified from receiving bonus if he is dismissed from service for

(a) fraud; or

(b) riotous or violent behaviour while on the premises of the establishment; or

(c) theft, misappropriation or sabotage of any property of the establishment.

Payment of Minimum Bonus (Sec. 10)

1. Every employer is bound to pay to every employee a minimum bonus which shall be 8.33 per cent of his salary or wage or one hundred rupees, whichever is higher.
2. Minimum bonus is payable whether or not the employer has any allocable surplus in the accounting year.

Payment of Maximum Bonus (Sec. 11)

Section 11 which regulates the payment of maximum bonus provides

(i) Where in respect of any accounting year referred to in Section 10, the allocable surplus exceeds the amount of minimum bonus, the employer shall in lieu of such minimum bonus be bound to pay to every employee bonus which shall be an amount in proportion to the salary or wage earned by the employee during the accounting year subject to a maximum of twenty per cent of such salary or wage.

(ii) In computing the allocable surplus under this section, the amount set on or the amount set off under the provisions of Section 15 shall be taken into account.

Illustration

Basic wage Rs 1500, DA 75 per cent of basic, HRA @20 per cent of basic, Medical allowance 200 / month. He worked from May 2007 to Feb. 2008. Is he eligible for bonus? If yes, how much should be the minimum and maximum bonus.

Sol. Basic: ₹ 1500

DA: 75 per cent of basic = 1500 × 75 per cent = ₹ 1125

HRA: 20 per cent of basic = 1500 × 20 per cent = ₹ 300

Medical Allowance: 200/month

Since the employee has worked for more than 30 days continuously in the organisation and the employees' salary (Basic + DA) which is 2,625 and within the stipulated limit of Rs 3,500 as per the Bonus Act, 1965.

The employee is eligible to receive bonus.

Minimum bonus = 8.33 per cent × 2625 = Rs 2186.62

Maximum bonus = 20 per cent × 2625 = Rs 5250

Set-On and Set-Off of Allocable Surplus

Section 15 which provides for 'set-on' and 'set-off' reads:

1. Where for any accounting year, the allocable surplus exceeds the amount of maximum bonus payable to the employees in the establishment under Section 11, then, the excess shall, subject to a limit of twenty per cent of the total salary or wage of the employees employed in the establishment in that accounting year, be carried forward for being set on in the succeeding accounting year and so on up to and inclusive of the fourth accounting year to be utilised for the purpose of payment of bonus in the manner illustrated in the Fourth Schedule.
2. Where for any accounting year, there is no available surplus or the allocable surplus in respect of that year falls short of the amount of minimum bonus payable to the employees in the establishment under Section 10, and there is no amount or sufficient amount carried forward and set on under sub-section (1) which could be utilised for the purpose of payment of the minimum bonus, then, such minimum amount or the deficiency, as the case may be, shall be carried forward for being set off in the succeeding accounting year and so on up to and inclusive of the fourth accounting year in the manner illustrated in the Fourth Schedule.
3. The principle of set-on and set-off as illustrated in the Fourth Schedule shall apply to all other cases not covered by sub-section (1) or sub-section (2) for the purpose of payment of bonus under this Act.

4. Where in any accounting year, any amount has been carried forward and set-on or set-off under the section, then, in calculating bonus for the succeeding accounting year, the amount of set-on or set-off carried forward from the earliest accounting year shall first be taken into account.

Time Limit for Payment of Bonus

1. The amount of bonus payable under the Act shall be paid in cash within a period of eight months from the close of the accounting year.

   However, the aforesaid period of eight months can be extended by the appropriate Government or authority provided the total period so extended does not exceed two years.
2. Where there is a dispute regarding payment of bonus pending before any authority under Section 22, within a month from the date on which the award becomes enforceable or the settlement comes into operation, in respect of such dispute.

Recovery of Bonus due from an Employer

Section 21 of the Payment of Bonus Act provides that where any money is due to an employee by way of bonus from his employer under a settlement or an award or agreement, the employee himself or any other person authorised by him in writing in this behalf, or in the case of the death of the employee, his assignee or heirs may, without prejudice to any other mode of recovery made an application to the appropriate Government for the recovery of the money due to him, and if the appropriate Government or such authority as the appropriate Government may specify in this behalf is satisfied that any money is so due, it shall issue a certificate for that amount to the Collector who shall proceed to recover the same in the same manner as an arrear of land revenue.

Time Limit for Filing an Application

Every such application shall be made within one year from the date on which the money became due to the employee from the employer. However, any such application may be entertained after the expiry of the said period of one year, if the appropriate Government is satisfied that the applicant had sufficient cause for not making the application within the said period.

INDUSTRIAL EMPLOYMENT (STANDING ORDERS) ACT, 1946

There are 'service conditions' or 'service rules' for various employees like Government employees, bank employees, LIC employees, etc. The Industrial Employment (Standing Orders) Act, 1946 is designed to provide service rules to workmen.

The objective of the Act is to require employers in industrial establishments to formally define conditions of employment under them.

What are 'Standing Orders' - 'Standing Orders' means rules of conduct for workmen employed in industrial establishments. 'Standing orders' means rules relating to matters set out in the schedule to the Act. [Section 2(g)]. The schedule to the Act requires that following should be specified in Standing Orders -

(a) Classification of workmen i.e. temporary, badli, casual, permanent, skilled, etc.

(b) Manner of intimating to workmen working hours, shift working, transfers, etc.

(c) Holidays

(d) Attendance and late coming rules

(e) Leave rules

(f) Leave eligibility and leave conditions

(g) Closing and reopening of sections of industrial establishment

(h) Termination of employment, suspension, dismissal, etc. for misconduct and acts or omissions which constitute misconduct

(i) Retirement age

(j) Means of redressal of workmen against unfair treatment or wrongful exactions by employer

(k) Any other matter that may be prescribed.

Coverage of Act - The Act is applicable to all 'industrial establishments' employing 100 or more workmen. [Section 1(3)].

'Industrial establishment' means (i) an industrial establishment as defined in section 2(i) of Payment of Wages Act (ii) Factory as defined in section 2(m) of Factories Act (iii) Railway (iv) Establishment of contractor who employs workmen for fulfilling contract with owner of an industrial establishment. [Section 2(e)].

The term 'industrial establishment' includes factory, transport service, construction work, mines, plantation, workshop, building activity, transmission of power, etc.

Workman - 'Workman' has meaning assigned to it under section 2(s) of Industrial Disputes Act. [Section 2(i)]. Thus, 'workman' includes skilled, unskilled, manual or clerical work. However, 'workman' does not include employees engaged in managerial or administrative capacity or supervisory capacity. 'Workman' does not include workers subject to Army Act, Navy Act or Air Force Act or to police or prison services.

Approval of Standing Orders - Every employer covered under the Act has to prepare 'Standing Orders', covering the matters required in the 'Standing Orders'. Five copies of these should be sent to Certifying Officer for approval. [Section 3(1)]. 'Certifying Officer' means Labour Commissioner and any officer appointed by government to be 'Certifying Officer'. [Section 2(c)].

The Certifying Officer will inform the Union and workmen and hear their objections. After that, he will certify the 'Standing Orders' for the industrial establishment. [Section 5]. Till standing orders are certified, 'Model Standing Order' prepared by government will automatically apply. [Section12A].

Standing order should be displayed in English and local language on special notice boards at or near entrance of the establishment. [Section 9]. Modifications of Standing Order shall be done by following similar procedure. [Section 10].

Once the 'Standing Orders' are certified, they supersede any term and condition of employment, contained in the appointment letter. If there is inconsistency between 'Standing Order' and 'Appointment Letter', the provisions of 'Standing Order' prevail - *Eicher Goodearth Ltd.* v. *R K Soni* - (1993)

Standing orders are binding on employer and employee. These are statutorily imposed conditions of service. However, they are not statutory provisions themselves (meaning that the 'Standing Orders' even when approved, do not become 'law' in the sense in which Rules and Notifications issued under delegated legislation become after they are published as prescribed.) - *Rajasthan SRTC* v. *Krishna Kant* - AIR 1995

Model Standing Orders - The Act has prescribed Model Standing Orders. These are automatically applicable till employer prepares his own 'Standing Orders' and these are approved by 'Certifying Officer'. [Section 12A].

Disciplinary Action - The most important use of 'Standing Orders' is in case of disciplinary action. A workman can be punished only if the act committed by him is'misconduct' as defined under the 'Standing Orders'. The 'Model Standing Orders' contain such acts like insubordination, disobedience, fraud, dishonesty, damage to employer's property, taking bribe, habitual absence or habitual late attendance, riotous behaviour, habitual neglect of work, strike in contravention of rules, etc. as misconducts. The 'Certified Standing Orders' may cover other acts as 'misconduct', if approved by 'Certifying Officer'.

Subsistence Allowance – Where a workman is suspended by employer pending investigation or enquiry into complaints or charges of misconduct against him, the workman shall be paid subsistence allowance equal to 50 per cent of wages for first 90 days of suspension and 75 per cent of wages for remaining period till completion of disciplinary proceedings. [Section 10A (1)]. - 'Wages' has same meaning as under section 2(rr) of Industrial Disputes Act. [Section 2(i)].

THE INDUSTRIAL DISPUTES ACT, 1947

The objective of the Industrial Disputes Act is to secure industrial peace and harmony by providing machinery and procedure for the investigation and settlement of industrial disputes by negotiations. This Act deals with the retrenchment process of the employees, procedure for layoff, procedure and rules for strikes and lockouts of the company.

Introduction

Industrial Disputes have adverse effects on industrial production, efficiency, costs, quality, human satisfaction, discipline, technological and economic progress and finally on the welfare of the society. A discontent labour force, nursing in its heart mute grievances and resentments, cannot be efficient and will not possess a high degree of industrial morale. Hence, the Industrial Dispute Act of 1947 was passed as a preventive and curative measure.

Scope and Objectives

The Industrial Dispute Act of 1947 came into force on the first day of April, 1947. Its aim is to protect the workmen against victimisation by the employers and to ensure social justice to both employers and employees. The unique objective of the Act is to promote collective bargaining and to maintain a peaceful atmosphere in industries by avoiding illegal strikes and lock outs. The Act also provides for regulation of lay off and retrenchment. The objective of the Industrial Disputes Act is to secure industrial peace and harmony by providing machinery and procedure for the investigation and settlement of industrial disputes by negotiations.

Appropriate Government [Sec. 2(a)]: Appropriate Government means the Central Government in relation to any industrial dispute concerning any industry carried on by or under the authority of the Central Government, any industry carried on by a Railway Company, any controlled industry specified by the Central Government, The Unit Trust of India, Corporations under the Central Statutes, Banking company, Insurance company, Mines, Oil field, Cantonment board, Major ports, etc. In relation to any other industrial dispute, the appropriate Government is the State Government.

Award [Sec 2 (b)]: It means an interim or a final determination of any industrial dispute or of any question relating thereto by any Labour Court, Industrial Tribunal or National Tribunal and includes an arbitration award made under section 10A.

Industry [Sec. 2(j)]: Industry means any business, trade, undertaking, manufacture or calling of employers and includes any calling, service, employment, handicraft or industrial occupation or avocation of workmen.

Industrial Dispute [Sec. 2(k)]: Means any dispute or difference between employers and employers, or between employers and workmen, or between workmen and workmen, which is connected with the employment or non-employment or the terms of employment or with the conditions of labour, of any person.

Settlement [Sec. 2(p)]: Settlement means a settlement arrived at in the course of conciliation proceeding and includes a written agreement between an employer and a workman arrived at otherwise than in the course of conciliation proceeding where such agreement has been signed by the parties thereto in such manner as may be prescribed and a copy thereof has been sent to an officer authorised by the Appropriate Government and the Conciliation Officer.

Wages [Sec. 2(rr)]: Wages mean all remuneration capable of being expressed in terms of money, which would, if the terms of employment, express or implied were fulfilled, be payable to a workman in respect of his employment or of the work done in such an employment and includes:

(i) Such allowances (including dearness allowance) as the workman is for the time being entitled to;

(ii) The value of any house accommodation, or of supply of light, water, medical attendance or other amenity or of any service or of any concessional supply of food grains or other articles;

(iii) Any travelling concession.

But the followings are excluded:

(a) Any bonus.

(b) Any contribution paid or payable to any pension fund or provident fund, or for the benefit of the workman under any law for the time being in force.

(c) Any gratuity payable on the termination of his service.

2(n) "Public Utility Service" means -

(i) Any railway service or any transport service for the carriage of passengers or goods by air;

(ia) Any service in, or in connection with the working of, any major port or dock;

(ii) Any section of an industrial establishment, on the working of which the safety of the establishment or the workmen employed therein depends;

(iii) Any postal, telegraph or telephone service;

(iv) Any industry which supplies power, light or water to the public;

(v) Any system of public conservancy or sanitation;

(vi) Any industry specified in the First Schedule which the appropriate Government may, if satisfied that public emergency or public interest so requires, by notification in the Official Gazette, declare to be a public utility service for the purposes of this Act, for such period as may be specified in the notification.

First Schedule

Industries which may be declared to be public utility services under sub-clause (vi) of clause (n) of section 2

1. Transport (other than railways) for the carriage of passengers or goods by land or water.
2. Banking.
3. Cement.
4. Coal.
5. Cotton textiles.
6. Foodstuffs.
7. Iron and steel.
8. Defence establishments.
9. Service in hospitals and dispensaries.
10. Fire brigade service.
11. India Government Mints.
12. India Security Press.
13. Copper Mining.
14. Lead Mining.

15. Zinc Mining.
16. Iron Ore Mining.
17. Service in any oil field.
18. Omitted.
19. Service in uranium industry.
20. Pyrites mining industry.
21. Security Paper Mill, Hoshangabad.
22. Services in Bank Note Press, Dewas.
23. Phosphorite mining.
24. Magnesite Mining.
25. Currency Note Press.
26. Manufacture or production of mineral oil (crude oil), motor and aviation spirit, diesel oil, kerosene oil, fuel oil, diverse hydrocarbon oils and their blends including synthetic fuels, lubricating oils and the like.
27. Service in the International Airports Authority of India.
28. Industrial establishments manufacturing or producing Nuclear Fuel and Components, Heavy Water and Allied Chemicals and Atomic Energy.

Dispute Settlement Authorities under the Act

The I.D. Act provides elaborate and effective machinery for the investigation and amicable settlement of industrial disputes by setting up the various authorities. These are:

1. Works Committee;
2. Conciliation Officer;
3. Conciliation Board;
4. Court of Enquiry;
5. Labour Court;
6. Industrial Tribunal;
7. National Tribunal;
8. Arbitrators;
9. Grievances Settlement Authority.

Dismissal, Discharge, etc. of an Individual Workman to be Deemed to be an Industrial Dispute. [Sec 2a]

Difference in between the workman and his employer connected arising out of following activities shall be deemed to the industrial dispute.

- Dismissal of workman
- Discharge of workman
- Retrenchment of the workman
- Termination of workman from his services

[Sec 2A (2)]

Workman having the disputes can make a application to the conciliation officer to settle the dispute. After the expiry of three months of time conciliation officer fails to settle the dispute, workman can make a direct application to labour courts or tribunals for adjudication.

[Sec 2A (3)]

Workman should make an application to labour courts or tribunals for adjudication before the expiry of three years from the date of discharge, dismissal, retrenchment or otherwise termination of service of workman.

Works Committee [Sec. 3]: In the case of an industrial establishment in which 100 or more workmen are employed, the appropriate Government may require the employer to constitute a 'Work Committee'. It consists of equal number of representatives of employers and workmen engaged in the establishment. The representatives of the workmen shall be chosen from amongst the workmen engaged in the establishment and in consultation with the registered trade union, if any. Works committee deals with the workers problem arising day to day in the industrial establishment.

Conciliation Officer [Sec. 4]: The appropriate Government is empowered to appoint any number of persons, as it thinks fit, to be conciliation officers. The conciliation officer having duty of mediating and acts as the mediators in between the parties to resolve the dispute.

In the case of public utility services matters like strikes and lockouts the conciliation officer can initiate the conciliation proceeding and tries to settle the dispute in between the parties.

If the conciliation officer fails to resolve the dispute between the parties, he should report to the appropriate Government. If necessary the dispute shall be referred to the Board, Labour Court, Tribunal or National Tribunal, by the appropriate Government. [Sec 12 (5)]

Duties of Conciliation Officers [Sec 12]

- Hold conciliation proceedings relating to strikes and lockouts procedural matters of public utility services.
- Investigate the matters of the disputes.
- Conciliation officers shall induce the parties to come to a fair and amicable settlement of the dispute.
- Duty to send the report of settlement of dispute and memorandum of the settlement signed by the parties to the dispute to the government or his superior.
- In case of failure of settlement of dispute in between parties, duty to send them to the government or his superior, report of facts and circumstances relating to the disputes and in his opinion, a settlement could not be arrived at.
- Duty to send the report to the government or his superior within 14 days from the commencement of the proceeding or within such shorter period as may be fixed by the appropriate Government.

Conciliation Board [Sec. 5]: Appropriate Government is also authorised to constitute a Board of Conciliation for promoting the settlement of an industrial dispute. It consists of a chairman who shall be an independent person, and two or four other members. The members appointed shall be in equal numbers to represent the parties to the dispute. On the dispute being referred to the Board it is the duty of the Board to do all things as it thinks fit for the purpose of inducing the parties to come to fair and amicable settlement.

If there are many parties relating to or in the dispute the government may appoint the conciliation board consisting of the above said members.

According to [Sec 10 (2)], when parties in the industrial dispute apply to the government to refer dispute to the Conciliation Board and if government satisfies it shall make the reference to the Conciliation Board.

Duties of Board [Sec 13]

- It shall be the duty of the Board to endeavour to bring about a settlement of dispute.
- Investigate the matters relating to the dispute between parties and inducing the parties to come to a fair and amicable settlement of the dispute.
- In case of failure of settlement of dispute in between parties, duty to send to the government the report of facts and circumstances relating to the disputes and board opinion, a settlement could not be arrived at.
- The Board shall submit its report under this section within two months of the date on which the dispute was referred to it or within such shorter period as may be fixed by the appropriate Government.

Court of Enquiry [Sec. 6]: Government can initiate a Court of Inquiry. This Court of Inquiry was to find out matters connected with or relevant to an industrial dispute. Where a Court consists of two or more members, one of them shall be appointed as the chairman.

A Court of Inquiry looks into only matters which are referred to it by government and submits its report to the government ordinarily within certain period from the date of reference.

Adjudication

Labour Court [Sec. 7]: The appropriate Government is empowered to constitute one or more Labour Courts. Its function is the adjudication of industrial disputes relating to any matter specified in the Second Schedule.

Matters within the Jurisdiction of Labour Courts

Second Schedule

1. The propriety or legality of an order passed by an employer under the standing orders;

2. The application and interpretation of standing orders;
3. Discharge or dismissal of workmen including reinstatement of, or grant of relief to, workmen wrongfully dismissed;
4. Withdrawal of any customary concession or privilege;
5. Illegality or otherwise of a strike or lock-out; and

According to [Sec 10 (1) (c)], matters specified in Third Schedule, dispute not effecting more than 100 workers can be referred to labour court.

According to [Sec 10 (2)], when parties in the industrial dispute apply to the government to refer dispute to the labour court and if government satisfies it shall make the reference to the labour courts.

According to [Sec 10 (6)], no Labour Court or Tribunal shall have jurisdiction to adjudicate upon any matter which is under adjudication before the National Tribunal.

A Labour Court consists of one person only. A person is qualified to be appointed as presiding officer of a Labour Court, if:

(a) He is, or has been a judge of a High Court, or
(b) He has been a District Judge or an Additional District Judge for at least three years, or
(c) He has held the office of the chairman or any other member of the Labour Appellate Tribunal or of any Tribunal for at least two years, or
(d) He has held any judicial office in India for not less than seven years, or
(e) He has been the presiding officer of a Labour Court constituted under any Provincial Act or State Act for at least five years.
(f) He is or has been a Deputy Chief Labour Commissioner (Central) or Joint Commissioner of the State Labour Department, having a degree in law and at least seven years' experience in the labour department after having acquired degree in law including three years of experience as Conciliation Officer.
(g) As the case may be, before being appointed as the presiding officer; or (g) he is an officer of Indian Legal Service in Grade III with three years' experience in the grade.

Industrial Tribunal [Sec. 7A]: The appropriate Government may, by notification in the Official Gazette, constitute one or more Industrial Tribunals for the adjudication of industrial disputes relating to any matter, whether specified in the Second Schedule or the Third Schedule and for performing such other functions as may be assigned to them under this Act.

Third Schedule

1. Wages, including the period and mode of payment;
2. Compensatory and other allowances;
3. Hours of work and rest intervals;
4. Leave with wages and holidays;
5. Bonus, profit sharing, provident fund and gratuity;
6. Shift working otherwise than in accordance with standing orders;
7. Classification by grades;
8. Rules of discipline;
9. Rationalisation;
10. Retrenchment of workmen and closure of establishment; and
11. Any other matter that may be prescribed.

According to [Sec 10 (2)], when parties in the industrial dispute apply to the government to refer dispute to the industrial tribunal and if government satisfies it shall make the reference to the industrial tribunal.

According to [Sec 10 (6)], no Labour Court or Tribunal shall have jurisdiction to adjudicate upon any matter which is under adjudication before the National Tribunal.

A Tribunal consists of one person only

For appointment as the presiding officer of a Tribunal

- He is, or has been, a Judge of a High Court; or
- He has, for a period of not less than three years, been a District Judge or an Additional District Judge;
- He is or has been a Deputy Chief Labour Commissioner (Central) or Joint Commissioner of the State Labour

Department, having a degree in law and at seven years' experience in the labour department after having acquired degree in law including three years of experience as Conciliation Officer.

Provided that no such Deputy Chief Labour Commissioner or Joint Labour Commissioner shall be appointed unless he resigns from the service of the Central Government or State Government, as the case may he, before being appointed as the presiding officer; or he is an officer of Indian Legal Service in Grade III with three years' experience in the grade.

National Tribunal [Sec. 7 (B)]: The Central Government may, by notification in the Official Gazette, constitute one or more National Industrial Tribunals. Its main function is the adjudication of industrial disputes which involve questions of national importance or affecting the interest of two or more States.

According to [Sec 10 (1-A)], dispute involves any question of national importance or is of such a nature that industrial establishments situated in more than one State, whether it relates to any matter specified in the Second Schedule or the Third Schedule, the government will order in writing refer to National Tribunal for adjudication.

According to [Sec 10 (2)], when parties in the industrial dispute apply to the government to refer dispute to the National Tribunal and if government satisfies it shall make the reference to the National Tribunal.

The Central Government shall appoint a National Tribunal consisting of one person only.

- A person to be appointed a presiding officer of a National Tribunal must be, or
- must have been, a judge of a High Court, or
- must have held the office of the chairman, or
- any other member of the Labour Appellate Tribunal for a period of not less than two years.

The Central Government may appoint two persons as assessors to advise the National Tribunal.

Arbitration

Voluntary Reference of Disputes to Arbitration [Sec. 10 (A)]: An arbitrator is appointed by the government. Whether the dispute is before Labour Court, or Industrial Tribunal or National Tribunal, the parties can go to arbitration by written agreement. The arbitrators conduct the investigation into the dispute matters and give arbitration award (final decision or settlement or decree) as for making reference of an industrial dispute. If an industrial dispute exists or is apprehended and the employer and the workman agree to refer the dispute to an arbitration, they may refer the dispute to an arbitration. But such reference shall be made before the dispute has been referred under Sec. 19 to a Labour Court or Tribunal or National Tribunal by a written agreement. The arbitrator may be appointed single or more than one in number. The arbitrator or arbitrators shall investigate the dispute and submit to the appropriate Government the arbitration award signed by the arbitrator or all the arbitrators, as the case may be.

Grievance Settlement Authority [Sec. 9 (c)]: This Section is incorporated as a new chapter II B of the Act. As per this Section, the employer in relation to every industrial establishment in which fifty or more workmen are employed or have been employed on any day in the preceding twelve months, shall provide for, in accordance with the rules made in that behalf under this Act, a Grievances Settlement Authority.

9C. Every industrial establishment employing 20 or more workmen shall have one or more Grievance Redressal Committee for the resolution of disputes arising out of individual grievances.

The Grievance Redressal Committee shall consist of equal number of members from the employer and the workmen.

The chairperson of the Grievance Redressal Committee shall be selected from the employer and from among the workmen alternatively on rotation basis every year.

The total number of members of the Grievance Redressal Committee shall not exceed more than six: Provided that there shall be, as far as practicable, one woman member if the Grievance Redressal Committee has two members and in case the number of members is more than two, the number of women members may be increased proportionately.

The Grievance Redressal Committee may complete its proceedings within forty-five days on receipt of a written application by or on behalf of the aggrieved party.

The workman who is aggrieved of the decision of the Grievance Redressal Committee may prefer an appeal to the employer against the decision of Grievance Redressal Committee and the employer shall, within one month from the date of receipt of such appeal, dispose off the same and send a copy of his decision to the workman concerned.

Nothing contained in this section shall apply to the workmen for whom there is an established Grievance Redressal Mechanism in the establishment concerned.

Awards (decree) [Sections 16, 17, 17A]

The award of a Labour Court or Tribunal or National Tribunal shall be in writing and shall be signed by its presiding officer. [Sec 16(2)].

Every arbitration award and every award of a Labour Court, Tribunal or National Tribunal shall, within a period of 30 days from the date of its receipt by the appropriate Government, be published in such manner as the appropriate Government thinks fit. [Sec 17(1)].

The award published shall be final and shall not be called in question by any Court in any manner whatsoever. [Sec 17 (2)].

An award (including an arbitration award) shall become enforceable on the expiry of thirty days from the date of its publication [Sec 17A (1)].

Where the award has been given by a National Tribunal, that it will be inexpedient (not advisable or not practicable) on public grounds affecting national economy or social justice to give effect to the whole or any part of the award, the appropriate Government, or as the case may be, the Central Government may, by notification in the Official Gazette, declare that the award shall not become enforceable on the expiry of the said period of thirty days. [Sec 17A (1) (b)].

The appropriate Government or the Central Government may, within 90 days from the date of publication of the award under Section 17, make an order rejecting or modifying the award, to legislature of state or parliament [Sec 17A (2)] and if no pursuance has made, the order become enforceable after the expiry of 90 days. [Sec 17A (3)].

Any award as rejected or modified laid before legislature of state or parliament, shall become enforceable on the expiry of 15 days from the date on which is so laid. [Sec 17A (3)].

Award declared becomes enforceable on the specified date if mentioned, if no date mentioned award becomes enforceable according to above rules.

Period of Operation of Settlements and Awards [Sec 19]

A settlement shall come into operation on such date as is agreed upon by the parties to the dispute, and if no date is agreed upon, on the date on which the memorandum of the settlement is signed by the parties to the dispute.

An award shall remain in operation for a period of one year from the date on which the award becomes enforceable under Section 17A: Provided that the appropriate Government may reduce the said period and fix such period as it thinks fit:

> the appropriate Government may, before the expiry of the said period, extend the period of operation by any period not exceeding one year at a time as it thinks fit, so however, that the total period of operation of any award does not exceed three years from the date on which it came into operation.

Strikes and Lockouts

Strike [Sec. 2 (q)]: Strike means "a cessation of work by a body of persons employed in any industry acting in combination or a concerted refusal under a common understanding of any number of persons who are or have been so employed, to continue to work or to accept employment". Mere stoppage of work does not come within the meaning of strike unless it can be shown that such stoppage of work was a concerted action for the enforcement of an industrial demand.

Lockout [Sec. 2(1)]: Lockout means "the temporary closing of a place of employment, or the suspension of work, or the refusal by an employer to continue to employ any number of persons employed by him". Lockout is the antithesis of strike.

- It is a weapon of the employer while strike is that of the workers.
- Just as a strike is a weapon in the hands of the workers for enforcing their industrial demands, lockout is a weapon available to the employer to force the employees to see his points of view and to accept his demands.
- The Industrial Dispute Act does not intend to take away these rights.
- However, the rights of strikes and lockouts have been restricted to achieve the purpose of the Act, namely peaceful investigation and settlement of the industrial disputes.

Procedure of Strikes

According to Sec. 22(1)

Worker should follow the rules mentioned below for doing strike. The rules are as follows:

(a) Issue of notice of strike is mandatory;

(b) The date of strike must be within six weeks from the date of issue of strike notice;

(c) The day of strike must not be within 14 days from the date of notice;

(d) There should be no strike on any day before the date specified in the strike notice;

(e) There should be no strike during the pendency of conciliation proceedings and seven days after the conclusion of said proceedings.

Procedure of Lockouts

Section 22 (2) of the Act provides that no employer carrying on any public utility service shall lock out any of his workmen:

1. Issue of notice of lockout is mandatory;

2. Without giving them notice of lockout as hereinafter provided, within six weeks before locking out; or
3. Within 14 days of giving notice; or
4. Before the expiry of the day of lockout specified in any such notice as aforesaid; or
5. During the pendency of any conciliation proceedings before a Conciliation Officer and seven days after the conclusion of such proceedings.

Illegal Strikes and Lockouts [Sec 24]

A strike or a lockout shall be illegal, if employers or worker who ever disobeys or fails to follow the rules [Sec 22, 23, 10(3), 10-A (4-A)] for commencing strikes or lockout, those strikes and lockout are said to illegal.

General Prohibition of Strike, and Lockouts [Sec. 23]: No workman who is employed in any industrial establishment shall go on strike in breach of contract and no employer of any such workman shall declare a lockout in the following circumstances.

(a) During the pendency of conciliation proceedings before a Board and seven days after the conclusion of such proceedings;

(b) During the pendency of proceedings before a Labour Court, Tribunal or National Tribunal and two months after the conclusion of such proceedings;

(c) During the period of operation of a Settlement or Award in respect of any of the matters covered by the Settlement or Award.

Unfair Labour Practices

Fifth Schedule

I - On the Part of Employers and Trade Unions of Employers

1. To interfere with, restrain from, or coerce, workmen in the exercise of their right to organise, form, join or assist a trade union or to engage in concerted activities for the purposes of collective bargaining or other mutual aid or protection, that is to say, -

(a) threatening workmen with discharge or dismissal, if they join a trade union;

(b) threatening a lockout or closure, if a trade union is organised; and

(c) granting wage increase to workmen at crucial periods of trade union organisation, with a view to undermining the efforts of the trade union at organisation.

2. To dominate, interfere with or contribute support, financial or otherwise, to any trade union, that is to say:-

(a) an employer taking an active interest in organising a trade, union of his workmen; and

(b) an employer showing partiality or granting favour to one of several trade unions attempting to organise his workmen or to its members, where such a trade union is not a recognised trade union.

3. To establish employer-sponsored trade unions of workmen.

4. To encourage or discourage membership in any trade union by discriminating against any workman, that is to say:-

(a) discharging or punishing a workman, because he urged other workmen to join or organise a trade union;

(b) discharging or dismissing a workman for taking part in any strike (not being a strike which it deemed to be an illegal strike under this Act);

(c) changing seniority rating of workmen because of trade union activities;

(d) refusing to promote workmen to higher posts on account of their trade union activities;

(e) giving unmerited promotions to certain workmen with a view to creating discord amongst other workmen, or to undermine the strength of their trade union;

(f) discharging office bearers or active members of the trade union on account of their trade union activities.

5. To discharge or dismiss workmen -

(a) by way of victimisation;

(b) not in good faith, but in the colourable exercise of the employer's rights;

(c) by falsely implicating a workman in a criminal case on false evidence or on concocted evidence;

(d) for patently of false reasons;

(e) on untrue or trumpet up allegations of absence without leave;

(f) in utter disregard of the principles of natural justice in the conduct of domestic enquiry or with undue haste;

(g) for misconduct of a minor or technical character, without having any regard to the nature of the particular misconduct or the past record of service of the workman, thereby leading to a disproportionate punishment.

6. To abolish the work of a regular nature being done by workmen, and to give such work to contractors as a measure of breaking a strike.

7. To transfer a workman mala fide from one place to another, under the guise of following management policy.

8. To insist upon individual workmen, who are on a legal strike to sign a good conduct bond, as a precondition to allowing them to resume work.

9. To show favouritism or partiality to one set of workers regardless of merit.

10. To employ workmen as "badlis" casuals or temporaries and to continue them as such for years, with the object of depriving them of the status and privileges of permanent workmen.

11. To discharge or discriminate against any workman for filing charges or testifying against an employer in any enquiry or proceeding relating to any industrial dispute.

12. To recruit workmen during a strike which is not an illegal strike.

13. Failure to implement award, settlement or agreement.

14. To indulge in acts of force or violence.

15. To refuse to bargain collectively, in good faith with the recognised trade unions.

16. Proposing or continuing a lock-out deemed to be illegal under this Act.

II - On the Part of Workmen and Trade Unions of Workmen

1. To advise or actively support or instigate any strike deemed to be illegal under this Act.

2. To coerce workmen in the exercise of their right to self-organisation or to join a trade union or refrain from joining any trade union, that is to say –

(a) for a trade union or its members to picketing in such a manner that non-striking workmen are physically debarred from entering the work places;

(b) to indulge in acts of force or violence or to hold out threats of intimidation in connection with a strike against non-striking workmen or against managerial staff.

3. For a recognised union to refuse to bargain collectively in good faith with the employer.

4. To indulge in coercive activities against certification of bargaining representative.

5. To stage, encourage or instigate such forms of coercive actions as willful "go slow", squatting on the work premises after working hours or "gheraos" of any of the members of the managerial or other staff.

6. To stage demonstrations at the residences of the employers or the managerial staff members.

7. To incite or indulge in willful damage to employer's property connected with the industry.

8. To indulge in acts of force or violence or to hold out threats of intimidation against any workman with a view to prevent him from attending work.

Lay-Off and Retrenchment

Lay-off [Sec. 2(kkk)]: Lay-off means "the failure, refusal or inability of an employer on account of shortage of coal, power or raw materials or the accumulation of stocks or the breakdown of machinery or for any other reason to give employment to a workman whose name is borne on the muster rolls of his industrial establishment and who has not been retrenched".

Retrenchment [Sec. 2(oo)]: Retrenchment means the termination by the employer of the service of a workman for any reason whatsoever otherwise than as a punishment indicated by way of disciplinary action.

Rights of Workman Laid Off for Compensation [Sec. 25c]

A workman who is laid off is entitled to compensation only if he complies with the following conditions:

(i) He must not be a badli or a casual workman.
"Badli workman" means a workman who is employed in an industrial establishment in the place of another workman whose name is borne on the muster rolls of the establishment.

(ii) His name must be borne on the muster rolls of the industrial establishment.

(iii) He must have completed at least one year of continuous service.

(iv) A worker is entitled to lay-off compensation for the period of his lay off other than for weekly holidays which may intervene.

(v) The rate of compensation must be equal to 50 per cent of the total of the basic wage and dearness allowance that might have been payable to him.

(vi) No compensation can be claimed for more than forty-five days during the period of twelve months.

Workmen Laid Off Not Entitled to Compensation [Sec. 25e]

No compensation shall be paid to a workman who has been laid off:

(i) If he refuses to accept any alternative employment in the same or any other establishment belonging to the same employer situated in the same town or village or within a radius of five miles and it does not require any special skill or previous experience, provided the same wages are offered.

(ii) If he does not present himself for work at the appointed time during normal working hours at least once a day.

(iii) If lay off in the consequence of strike or slowing down of production by the workers in another part of the establishment.

Close Down Any Undertaking [Sec 25ffa]

An employer who intends to close down an undertaking shall serve, at least 60 days before the date on which the intended closure.

A notice is required to give to the appropriate Government stating clearly the reasons for the intended closure of the undertaking.

Provided that nothing in this section shall apply to –

An undertaking in which less than 50 workmen are employed or less than 50 workmen were employed on an average per working day in the preceding twelve months. An undertaking set up for the construction of buildings, bridges, roads, canals, dams or for other construction work or project.

Retrenchment of Worker [Section 25C]

If lay-off exceeds 45 days only the management or owner can retrench the workers by following below said rules. The reason for compelling and restricting 45 days period of lay-off before doing retrenchment of employee is:

lay-off is considered to be a unique situation created by reasons beyond the control of employer, it is supposed to be a temporary situation contingent on the grounds mentioned in the definition of layoffs in the section 2(kkk). However, if this contingency is prolonging beyond a reasonable time, say 45 days, it will be matter of serious concern both to the employer and to employees because both of them put to a loss of 50 per cent wages by employees and loss of earnings by employer due to temporary stoppage of work, which employer would have earned if there was no laid-off for the reasons mentioned in section 2 (kkk).

In the case if an employer is not able to restore the situation which compelled him to lay off employees; he can retrench employees after the expiry of 40 days in stuff continuing layoffs.

Procedure for Retrenchment [Sec. 25G]

LIFO (Last in First Out) method should be followed while retrenchment of workers, a worker who has joined last shall be retrenched first.

Conditions Precedent to Retrenchment of Workmen [Sec. 25F]

Worker who has completed one year of service and continuing in service must be retrenched by the owner by following rules.

1. One month notice of retrenchment should be given to the worker by the owner.
2. Notice should include the reasons for the retrenchment of the concerned worker.

Retrenchment Compensation [Sec 25F (b)]

Retrenchment worker can claim compensation from the worker under following procedure

- 15 days of salary drawn for every year of service completed E.g.: last drawn salary of worker = 10000 - Number of years of service = 5 years

So, retrenchment compensation calculated as follows

Salary drawn is = 10000, for 15 days salary is half of the amount = 5000 × number of service years = 5. = 25000 is the retrenchment compensation.

Re-Employment of Retrenched Workmen [Sec. 25h]

This Section provides priority for a retrenched workman in the case of reemployment. In case the employer proposes to re-employ any person, he is under an obligation to offer first priority to the persons who have been retrenched.

During Pendency of Proceedings [Sec 33]

During the pendency of any conciliation proceeding before a

conciliation officer or a Board or of any proceeding before an arbitrator or a Labour Court or Tribunal or National Tribunal in respect of an industrial dispute, employer should not do the following-

- For any misconduct connected with the dispute, discharge or punish, whether by dismissal or otherwise, any workmen concerned in such dispute,
- Alter the term of contract according to standing orders,
- Take action against the protected workman.

If employer wants to take above actions against the employee, employer should makes an application to a Conciliation officer, Board, an Arbitrator, a Labour Court, Tribunal or National Tribunal.

Penalties

Sec	***Reasons***	***Punishment***
25U	Unfair labour practice	Punishable with imprisonment for a term which may extend to six months or with fine which may extend to 1000 rupees or with both.
26	Illegal Strikes	Punishable with imprisonment for a term which may extend to one month, or with fine which may extend to 50 rupees, or with both.
26	Illegal Lockouts	Punishable with imprisonment for a term which may extend to one month, or with fine which may extend to 1000 rupees, or with both.
27	Any person who instigates or incites others to take part in, or otherwise acts in furtherance of, a strike or lockout which is illegal under this Act	Punishable with imprisonment for a term which may extend to six months, or with fine which may extend to 1000 rupees, or with both.
28	Giving Financial Aid to Illegal Strikes and Lockouts	Punishable with imprisonment for a term which may extend to six months, or with fine which may extend to 1000 rupees, or with both.
30	Disclosing Confidential Information	Punishable with imprisonment for a term which may extend to six months, or with fine which may extend to 1000 rupees, or with both.

30A	Closure of Establishment Without Notice	Punishable with imprisonment for a term which may extend to six months, or with fine which may extend to 5000 rupees, or with both.
31	Contravenes the Provisions of Section 33	Punishable with imprisonment for a term which may extend to six months, or with fine which may extend to 1000 rupees, or with both.

UNIT-IX

Labour Welfare:

Meaning

Definition

Scope

Theories

Principles and Approaches

Statutory and Non-statutory Labour Welfare

Intra and Extra Mural Welfare

Agencies of Labour Welfare:

State

Employer

Trade Unions

Voluntary Agencies

MEANING OF LABOUR WELFARE

Welfare includes anything that is done for the comfort and improvement of employees and is provided over and above the wages. Welfare helps in keeping the morale and motivation of the employees high so as to retain the employees for longer duration. The welfare measures need not be in monetary terms only but in any kind/forms. Employee welfare includes monitoring of working conditions, creation of industrial harmony through infrastructure for health, industrial relations and insurance against disease, accident and unemployment for the workers and their families. Labour welfare entails all those activities of employer, which are directed towards providing the employees with certain facilities and services in addition to wages or salaries.

DEFINITION

Labour Welfare means working out things for the well-being of the labours, knowing there wants and enabling them to fulfill their wants.

In the Report II of the ILO Asian Regional Conference, it has been stated that worker's welfare may be understood to mean "such services, facilities and amenities, which may be established outside or in the vicinity of undertakings, to enable the persons employed therein to perform their work in healthy and congenial surroundings and to provide them with the amenities conducive to good health and high morale."

The Labour Investigation Committee (1944-46) includes under labour welfare activities "anything done for the intellectual, physical, moral and economic betterment of the workers, whether by employers, by government or by other agencies, over and above what is laid down by law or what is normally expected as per of the contractual benefits for which the workers may have bargained."

The Report of the Committee on Labour Welfare (1969) includes under it "such services, facilities and amenities as adequate canteens, rest and recreation facilities, sanitary and medical facilities, arrangements for travel to and from work and for the accommodation of workers employed at a distance from their homes and such other services, amenities and facilities including social security measures as contribute to improve the conditions under which worker are employed."

SCOPE

The subject of labour welfare facilities is a very broad one covering a wide field of amenities and activities. In order to obtain a clearer understanding of its scope, we may examine the ways in which labour welfare is classified. Labour welfare work can be broadly divided into two categories: (a) statutory and non-statutory or voluntary and (b) intra-mural and extra-mural welfare facilities.

THEORIES OF LABOUR WELFARE

The form of labour welfare activities is flexiblc, elastic and differs from time to time, region to region, industry to industry and country to country depending upon the value system, level of education, social customs, degree of industrialisation and general standard of the socio-economic development of the nation. Seven theories constituting the conceptual framework of labour welfare activities are the following:

1. **The Police Theory:** This is based on the contention that a minimum standard of welfare is necessary for labourers. Here the assumption is that without policing, that is, without compulsion, employers do not provide even the minimum facilities for workers. Apparently, this theory assumes that man is selfish and self-centred and always tries to achieve his own ends, even at the cost of the welfare of others.

   According to this theory, owners and managers of industrial undertakings get many opportunities for exploitation of labour. Hence, the state has to intervene to provide minimum standard of welfare to the working class.

2. **The Religious Theory:** This is based on the concept that man is essentially "a religious animal." Even today, many acts of man are related to religious sentiments and beliefs. These religious feelings sometimes prompt an employer to take up welfare activities in the expectation of future emancipation either in this life or after it.

3. **The Philanthropic Theory:** This theory is based on man's love for mankind. Philanthropy means "Loving mankind." Man is believed to have an instinctive urge by which he strives to remove the suffering of others and promote their well-being. In fact, the labour welfare movement began in the early years of the industrial revolution with the support of philanthropists.
4. **The Trusteeship Theory:** This is also called the Paternalistic Theory of Labour Welfare. According to this the industrialist or employer holds the total industrial estate, properties, and profits accruing from them in a trust. In other words, the employer should hold the industrial assets for himself, for the benefit of his workers, and also for society. The main emphasis of this theory is that employers should provide funds on an ongoing basis for the well-being of their employees.
5. **The Placating Theory:** This theory is based on the fact that the labour groups are becoming demanding and militant and are more conscious of their rights and privileges than ever before. Their demand for higher wages and better standards of living cannot be ignored. According to this theory, timely and periodical acts of labour welfare can appease the workers. They are some kind of pacifiers which come with a friendly gesture.
6. **The Public Relation Theory:** This theory provides the basis for an atmosphere of goodwill between labour and management, and also between management and the public. Labour welfare programmes under this theory, work as a sort of an advertisement and help an organisation to project its good image and build up and promote good and healthy public relations.
7. **The Functional Theory:** This is also called the Efficiency Theory. Here, welfare work is used as a means to secure, preserve and develop the efficiency and productivity of labour, it is obvious that if an employer takes good care of his workers, they will tend to become more efficient and will thereby step up production. This theory is a reflection of contemporary

support for labour welfare. It can work well if both the parties have an identical aim in view; that is, higher production through better welfare. And this will encourage labour's participation in welfare programmes.

PRINCIPLES AND APPROACHES

The success of welfare activities depends on the approach which has been taken into account in providing such activities to the employees. Welfare policy should be guided by idealistic morale and human value. Every effort should be made to give workers/ employees some voice in the choice of welfare activities so long as it does not amount to dictation from workers.

There are employers who consider all labour welfare activities as distasteful legal liability. There are workers who look upon welfare activities in terms of their inherent right. Both parties have to accept welfare as activities of mutual concern. Constructive and lasting progress in the matter of social justice can be achieved only if welfare activities are accepted as essential factors in the progress of the business organisation.

Labour welfare is dependent on certain basic principles. The following are the principles on which successful implementation of welfare programmes depends:

1. **Adequacy of Wages:** Labour welfare measures cannot be a substitute for wages. Workers have a right to adequate wages. But high wage rates alone cannot create healthy atmosphere, nor bring about a sense of commitment on the part of workers. A combination of social welfare, emotional welfare and economic welfare together would achieve good results.
2. **Social Liability of Industry:** Industry, according to this principle, has an obligation or duty towards its employees to look after their welfare. The constitution of India also emphasises this aspect of labour welfare.
3. **Impact on Efficiency:** This plays an important role in welfare services, and is based on the relationship between welfare and efficiency, though it is difficult to measure this relationship. Programmes for housing, education and training,

the provision of balanced diet and family planning measures are some of the important programmes of labour welfare which increases the efficiency of the workers, especially in underdeveloped or developing countries.

4. **Increase in Personality:** The development of the human personality is given here as the goal of industrial welfare which, according to this principle, should counteract the baneful effects of the industrial system. Therefore, it is necessary to implement labour welfare services. Both inside and outside the factory, that is, provide intra-mural and extra-mural labour welfare services.
5. **Totality of Welfare:** This emphasises that the concept of labour welfare must spread throughout the hierarchy of an organisation. Employees at all levels must accept this total concept of labour welfare programme will never really get off the ground.
6. **Co-ordination or Integration:** This plays an important role in the success of welfare services. From this angle, a coordinated approach will promote a healthy development of the worker in his work, home and community. This is essential for the sake of harmony and continuity in labour welfare services.
7. **Democratic Values:** The co-operation of the worker is the basis of this principle. Consultation with, and the agreement of workers in the formulation and implementation of labour welfare services are very necessary for their success. This principle is based on the assumption that the worker is "a mature and rational individual." Industrial democracy is the driving force. Workers also develop a sense of pride when they are made to feel that labour welfare programmes are created by them and for them.
8. **Responsibility:** This recognises the fact that both employers and workers are responsible for labour welfare. Trade unions are also involved in these programmes in healthy manner. Labour welfare belongs to the domain of trade union activity. Further, when responsibility is shared by different groups, labour welfare work becomes simpler and easier.

9. **Accountability:** This may also be called the Principle of Evaluation. Here, one responsible person gives an assessment or evaluation of existing welfare services on a periodical basis to a higher authority. This is very necessary, for then one can judge and analyse the success of labour welfare programmes.
10. **Timely:** The timeliness of any service helps in its success. To identify the labour problem and to discover what kind of help is necessary to solve it and when to provide this help are all very necessary in planning labour welfare programmes. Timely action in the proper direction is essential in any kind of social work.

Approaches

Moreover the various approaches to labour welfare reflect the attitudes and beliefs of the agencies, which are engaged in welfare activities. The different approaches to labour welfare reflect the evolution of the concept of welfare.

Researchers (Railkar, 1990; Kohli and Sharma, 1997) have noted the following approaches to labour welfare:

Paternalistic Approach

The Paternalistic Approach to labour welfare can be traced back to the beginning of the modern industrial system where there was hardly any difference between management and ownership. The owners could have first hand information of the living and working conditions of the workers. The employers felt that they were responsible for the moral and material well-being of persons employed by them. The underlying assumption of this approach is that it takes for granted that the workers belong to a different and inferior social category, in need of help and charity. This assumption colours the nature of welfare schemes. These schemes are imposed from above (managers being wiser than workers) and the attitude of the employer seems to be 'I have done so much for you, now you should respect me and be loyal to me'. It may work in the initial stages of the factory system where the workers come from the villages. But with the changes in the attitudes of the people in general and industrial workers in particular, this attitude is resented and welfare measures are not accepted as charity.

Atomistic Approach

This approach demanded that every individual should be left as free as possible. Every individual can attain his own best interest only under the conditions of maximum freedom. Therefore in the matters of labour welfare this view was completely opposed to any welfare promoting activities undertaken by the government or any social or public agency. According to this view, the scope of labour welfare activities should be as little as possible. This hypothesis is based on three important principles, which are as follows:

Society in its natural form is made up of individuals. They are un-organised and un-coordinated. Under such a natural society every individual is self-centred.

Such an individual always acts in a calculated manner. An individual always need a secure life. He is engaged in the activities of self-preservation. He will therefore act in such a manner that his self or personal interest will always be maximised.

Every individual throughout the life will act in such a manner that helps to promote his self-interest. He is always in the pursuit of this objective. He fulfills it to the best of his ability.

Mechanistic Approach

With the beginning of the twentieth century labour welfare and labour relations have been moving towards a more sympathetic approach. Efforts to increase efficiency of labour have become a matter of fundamental importance. It was observed that if labour administration is more scientifically managed then there is considerable scope for improving efficiency of labour. Such an approach to scientific management of the industry leads to the 'mechanistic' view about, labour welfare. It treats worker as 'labour' performed in some 'mechanical units' such as 'hours of work', 'man — days', 'man — hours'. Its emphasis is on the scientific and effective methods of production.

Such an approach is greatly favoured by the employers and management. However, it is strongly opposed to by the trade union organisation. This approach is based on the 'stimulus and response' relationship. The essence of the scientific management and mechanistic approach is the 'carrot and stick' method that it advocates. Under this approach welfare activities such as social security measures, better economic justice or healthy and hygienic atmosphere at the place of work are not found necessary in order to promote over all development of the personality of workers. Therefore, this approach takes a highly restrictive view of labour welfare activities.

Humanistic Approach

The Australian sociologist Elton Mayo advocated this approach. Mayo finds that what is more important is to treat labour as a human element of production. Therefore it was necessary to take a fresh and more sympathetic view of labour welfare.

Humanistic approach is based on human relationships, which was missing in the earlier approaches to labour welfare. The human factor was particularly missing in the administration of the industry and Mayo discovered the importance of informal relations between groups of workers and stressed sociality of man. The approach considered human personality, attitudes and sentiments of workers, while promoting labour welfare. Therefore, the humanistic approach to labour welfare takes an enlightened view about labour welfare.

STATUTORY AND NON-STATUTORY LABOUR WELFARE

Organisations provide welfare facilities to their employees to keep their motivation levels high. The employee welfare schemes can be classified into two categories viz. statutory and non-statutory welfare schemes. The statutory schemes are those schemes that are compulsory to provide by an organisation as compliance to the laws governing employee health and safety. These include provisions provided in industrial acts like Factories Act, 1948; Dock Workers Act, (safety, health and welfare) 1986; Mines Act, 1962. The non-statutory schemes differ from organisation to organisation and from industry to industry.

The Factories Act, 1948

The welfare facilities provided under this act are as follows:

1. Adequate, suitable and clean washing facilities separately for male and female workers.
2. Facilities for storing and drying clothes.
3. Canteens, if more than 250 workers are employed.
4. Shelter, rest rooms and lunch rooms if there are more than 150 workers.
5. Welfare officer, whenever more than 500 workers are employed.

The Plantation Labour Act, 1951

The welfare facilities provided under this act are as follows:

1. A canteen wherever 150 or more than workers are employed.
2. A crèche, if employing 50 or more women workers.
3. Recreational facilities for the workers and their children.
4. Educational arrangements.
5. Housing facilities for every worker and his family residing in the plantation.
6. Medical aid to workers and their families.
7. Sickness allowance and maternity allowance.
8. Appointment of welfare officer in plantations employing 300 or more.

The Mines Act, 1952

The mines owners are required to make provisions for:

1. Creches if 50 or more women are employed.
2. Shelters for taking food and rest, wherever 150 or more workers are employed.
3. First aid boxes for first aid room in mines employing more than 150 workers.
4. Pit head baths equipped with shower bath, sanitary and lockers etc.

The Motor Transport Workers Act, 1961

The welfare facilities provided under this act are as follows:

1. Canteens for prescribed standards.
2. Clean, ventilated, well lighted and comfortable rest rooms at every place where motor transport workers are required to halt at night.
3. Uniforms, raincoats to drivers, conductors and time checkers for protection against rain and cold.
4. Prescribed medical facilities.

The Contract Labour Act, 1970

The welfare facilities provided under this act are as follows:

1. A canteen in every establishment employing 100 or more workers.
2. Rest rooms or other suitable alternatives accommodation where the contract labour is required.
3. Washing facilities.
4. First aid boxes.

INTRA AND EXTRA MURAL WELFARE

Labour welfare is of two types: 1. Intra-mural and 2. Extra-mural

1. **Intra-mural:** Intra-mural activities consist of such welfare schemes provided within the factories as provision for creches and canteens, supply of drinking water, washing and bathing facilities, sufficient lighting, first aid appliances, fire extinguishers etc.
2. **Extra-mural:** These services are provided outside the establishment. These consist of housing accommodation, transport, sports, fields, holiday homes, maternity benefits etc.

AGENCIES FOR WELFARE WORK

The following are the main welfare agencies. These are: 1. Central

Government, 2. State Government, 3. Employers, 4. Trade unions and 5. Other agencies. These are discussed below:

1. **Central Government:** The Central Government tries to extend its helping hand through various acts covering the safety, health and welfare of workers. These are mainly Factories Act, 1948; Mines Act, 1952; Shipping Act, 1948; Plantation Labour Act, 1951.
2. **State Government:** State Government in different states and unions territories offer welfare facilities to workers. In Assam, a statutory welfare fund is created for offering medical, educational, and other facilities to plantation workers.
3. **Employers:** "The employers in general looked upon welfare work as fruitless and barren though some of them indeed had done pioneering work". Enlightened employers like HUL, Godrej, L&T, TISCO, Siemens, Voltas, Bajaj, Birla, Sandoz, Philips, HMT, LIC, BHEL, etc. have undertaken welfare activities in the interest of workers.
4. **Trade Unions:** The contribution of trade unions in India towards labour welfare activities is not significant. Poor finances, multiple unionisms, often significant come in the way of undertaking labour welfare work enthusiastically. There are certain exception to this- like the Ahmedabad Textile Labour Association, Mazdoor Sabha of Kanpur and the Indian Federation of Labour.
5. **Other Agencies:** In addition to the above agencies Bombay Social Service League, Seva Sadan Social Service League, Bombay Women's Societies, Assam Seva Samity, Y.M.C.A. etc. also provide services to the working class on a voluntary basis.

UNIT – X

Labour Market:

- Features
- Demand and Supply of Labour
- Nature and Composition of Indian Labour Force
- Unemployment and Underemployment

Concepts of Wages

State Regulation of Wages

Fixation of Wages

Wage Theories

Wage Differentials

Labour Market: A labour market is the place where workers and employees interact with each other. In the labour market, employers compete to hire the best, and the workers compete for the best satisfying job.

FEATURES

The different features of labour markets are as follows:

(i) A labour market is viewed as a process by which supplies of a particular type of labour and demands for that type of labour are balanced.

(ii) The relationship between a seller and a buyer is important in a labour market.

(iii) There is a lack of perfect mobility in a labour market which gives rise to a diversity of wage rates for the same type of work and we do not find a normal wage rate to which the market rate naturally tends. In other words, labour market is essentially an imperfect market.

(iv) Wage fixing is an essential characteristic of the labour market where the buyer of labour normally sets the price.

(v) In labour market the price tends to be fixed for some length of time. Employers do not want wage rates to fluctuate with every change in demand and supply conditions.

(vi) The labour market is far more complex than the commodity market.

(vii) The essential characteristic of the labour market of an expanding economy is that the vast majority of individuals are employees while relatively small minorities function either as employing persons or as employed managers of employing units.

(viii) As a result of industrialisation the average employing unit has become larger in size, its bargaining power has expanded while at the same time, the bargaining power of the individual worker has shrinked and become almost meaningless for all practical purposes.

(ix) Another feature of the labour market what Prof. Kerr has termed as 'Balkanisation' (i.e., degree of isolation) of the markets. It refers to the development of institutional rules within the labour markets. The overall effect of 'balkanisation' is to contribute to the growing imperfections of competition within labour markets.

(x) It should be noted that the labour market seems to perform more adequately during periods of full employment than during periods of depression. This is so because in periods of full employment more jobs are open than it is during the periods of widespread unemployment. This provides an explanation for the narrowing of wage differentials during periods of full employment.

(xi) The labour market is characterised by stability and lack of fluidity and diversity of rates for similar jobs. A rise in the price of labour offered by a particular employer does not cause employees of other firms receiving fewer wages to leave their jobs and go to high wage employer.

(xii) We have noted that a labour market may be viewed as definite geographic area. But it is not easy to define the boundaries of labour markets.

(xiii) The labour market for some workers is national in scope (even international) while mobility of some workers is highly restricted. The extent of a market depends in part upon the worker's education and skill. Highly trained professionals like engineers and doctors are likely to find suitable employment in many different localities. Such workers are likely to move to another job which pays better. Workers without specialised skill like clerks, unskilled workers, etc. find it difficult to get employment in various areas. The boundaries of their labour markets are likely to be restricted to home area.

(xiv) Age is also an important factor in the mobility of labour. In general, young workers tend to be more mobile than their older counterparts in the labour force.

DEMAND AND SUPPLY OF LABOUR

Although labour has certain peculiarities and cannot be regarded as a commodity, still wages are very largely determined by the interaction of the forces of demand and supply.

Demand for Labour

The demand for labour is a derived demand. It is derived from demand for the commodities it helps to produce. The greater the consumers' demand for the product, the greater the producers' demand for the labour required in making it. Hence an expected increase in the demand for a commodity will increase the demand for the type of labour that produces this commodity.

The elasticity of demand for labour depends, therefore, on the elasticity of demand for its output. Demand for labour will generally be inelastic if their wages form only a small proportion of the total wages. The demand, on the other hand, will be elastic if the demand for the commodity it produces is elastic or if cheaper substitutes are available.

The demand for labour also depends on the prices of the co-operating factors. Suppose the machines are costly, as is the case in India, obviously more labour will be employed. The demand for labour will increase. Another factor that influences the demand for labour is the technical progress. In some cases, labour and machinery are used in a definite ratio. For instance, the introduction of automatic looms reduces the demand for labour.

After considering all relevant factors, e.g., demand for the products, technical conditions, and the prices of the co-operating factors, the wages are governed by one fundamental factor, viz., marginal productivity.

Suppose an entrepreneur employs workers one by one. After a point, the law of diminishing marginal returns will come into operation. Every additional worker employed will add to the total net production at a decreasing rate. The employer will naturally stop employing additional workers at the point at which the cost of employing a worker just equals the addition made by him to the value of the total net product.

Thus, the wages that he will pay to such a worker (the marginal unit of labour) will be equal to the value of this additional product or marginal productivity. This is all about the demand side of labour. Now let us consider the supply side.

Supply of Labour

By the supply of labour, we mean the various numbers of workers of a given type of labour which would offer themselves for employment at various wage rates.

The supply of labour may be considered from two view-points:

(a) Supply of labour to the industry and

(b) Supply of labour to the entire economy.

For an industry, the supply of labour is elastic. Hence, if a given industry wants more labour, it can attract it from other industries by offering a higher wage. The supply of labour for the industry is subject to the law of supply, i.e., low wage, small supply and high wage, large supply. Hence, the supply curve of labour for an industry rises upwards from left to right.

The supply of labour for the entire economy depends on economic, social and political factors or institutional factors, e.g., attitude of women towards work, working age, school and college leaving age and possibilities of part-time employment for students, size and composition of the population and sex distribution, attitude to marriage, the size of the family, birth control, standard of medical facilities and sanitation, etc.

The supply of labour may be decreased by workers refusing to work for a time. This happens when labour is organised into trade unions. The workers may not accept wages offered by the employer if such wages do not ensure the maintenance of a standard of living to which they are accustomed.

But, as we shall see, it is only when higher wages are justified by higher marginal productivity that high wages will be paid. Thus, workers with low marginal productivity cannot demand high wages merely on the basis of their standard of living. On the whole, we might say that, the number of potential workers being given, the supply of labour may be defined as the schedule of units of labour at the prevailing rates of wages.

This depends on two factors:

(a) The number of workers who are willing and able to work at different wages;

(b) The number of working hours that each worker is willing and able to put in at different wages.

In case the workers have no saying power and the only alternative to work is starvation, the supply of labour in general will be perfectly inelastic. Over a short period, reduction in wages may not cause any reduction in the supply of labour. For any industry over a long period, the supply curve will slope upwards from left to right. In other words, supply will be somewhat elastic in the long run.

NATURE AND COMPOSITION OF INDIAN LABOUR FORCE

Workers can either be working in either (a) agriculture and allied activities, or (b) the non-agriculture sector then we can observe a clear contrast in the composition of labour force. While some people may not be surprised to find that the agriculture sector is predominantly concentrated in rural India, it is interesting to note the agricultural sector employs women labourers more intensively. On the other hand, the non-agricultural sector is mostly urban and comprises of relatively more males.

The following table (taken from the NSS report on informal sector) details the distribution of workers:

Table: Per 1000 distribution of workers by industry groups/divisions during 2009-10

Category	*Agriculture*	*Agr allied activities*	*Non-agriculture*	*Total*
All male	450	22	528	1000
All female	595	92	313	1000
All total	**491**	**41**	**468**	**1000**
Rural male	603	26	371	1000
Rural female	690	103	207	1000
Rural total	**630**	**50**	**320**	**1000**
Urban male	49	10	941	1000
Urban female	102	36	862	1000
Urban total	**59**	**16**	**925**	**1000**

UNEMPLOYMENT AND UNDEREMPLOYMENT

Unemployment rates are higher for urban persons as compared to rural persons. Urban females have the highest unemployment rates at 9.22 per cent and rural females have the lowest rates at 7.31 per cent.

A state-wise analysis for unemployment trends reveals that comparatively developed states such as Goa and Kerala have the highest unemployment rates of 11.39 per cent and 9.13 per cent respectively. Whereas lowest unemployment rates of 0.48 per cent and 0.77 per cent are found in less developed states such as Uttarakhand and Chhattisgarh.

Unemployment is highest for the age categories of 10 to 24 corroborating the view that youth unemployment is on the rise in India.

The unemployment rate is seen to increase, with an increase in educational attainment and is particularly high after the secondary level of education. Unemployment rate among educated females, in both urban and rural areas, is the highest.

Estimation of underemployment levels reveals that under-employment is widespread among females in general and rural females in particular.

Underemployment levels calculated across the employment status shows that self-employed and casual labour categories have the highest levels of underemployment. Among the regular wage/ salaried labour, underemployment is negligible.

CONCEPTS OF WAGES

The committee on Fair Wages (1948) and the 15th session of The Indian Labour Conference (1957) put forward certain Wage Concepts:

The committee on Fair Wages (1948) defined-

1. Minimum Wage
2. Fair Wage
3. Living Wage
4. Need-based Minimum Wage

1. Minimum Wages

It is amount of remuneration, which is just sufficient to enable an average worker to fulfill all his obligations. It is applicable to workers across the country and is governed by the Minimum Wages Act 1948. The law states that an employer who cannot pay the minimum wage has no right to engage labour and no justification to run a firm. The current minimum wage in India is ₹ 66 per day to all the workers in scheduled employment. It is revised every five yrs. The committee on Fair wage has defined minimum wage as "the wage must provide not merely for the bare sustenance of life, but for the preservation of the efficiency of the workers. For this purpose, minimum wage must provide some measures of education, medical requirements and amenities".

2. Fair Wages

Workers performing work of equal skills, difficulty or unpleasantness should receive equal or fair wages. The basis of fair wage is the minimum wage, within the capacity of the organisation to pay. Fair wage should be related to the productivity of the labour. It should match the prevailing rates of wages in the same or neighbouring localities. It should reflect the level of national income and its distribution. Fair wage, according to the committee on Fair Wage, is the wage which is above the minimum wage but below the living wage. Factors affecting the fair wage are as follows:

While the lower limit of the fair wage obviously is the minimum wage, the upper limit is equally set by what may broadly be called the capacity of industry to pay. Between these two limits the actual wage would depend on

(a) The Productivity of Labour;

(b) The prevailing rates of wages;

(c) The level of national income and distribution;

(d) The place of the industry in the economy of the country.

3. Living Wages

It represents a standard of living which is provided not merely for a bare physical sustenance but decency, protection against ill-health, requirements of essential social needs and some insurance against the more important misfortunes including old age.

Living wages should enable the male earner to provide for himself and his family, not only the bare essentials of food, clothing and shelter, but also a measure of frugal comfort including:

(i) Education for the children;

(ii) Protection against ill-health;

(iii) Requirements of essential social needs;

(iv) A measure of insurance against the more important misfortunes including old age.

4. Need-based Minimum Wage

The minimum wage should be need-based and "should ensure the minimum human needs of the industrial worker, irrespective of any other consideration."

The basis for calculating Need-based minimum wage is as follows:

(a) The standard working-class family taken to consist of three consumption units for one earner; earnings of women, children and adolescents should be disregarded.

(b) Minimum food requirements-net intake of 2700 calories for an average Indian adult.

(c) Clothing requirements- 18 yards per annum (Average worker's family of 4 = 72 yards/annum).

(d) Housing- minimum rent charged by government in any area for houses provided under subsidised industrial housing scheme for low-income group.

(e) Fuel, Lighting and other miscellaneous items- 20 per cent of total minimum wage.

STATE REGULATION OF WAGES

The government has adopted various methods to regulate wages in India such as prescribing minimum rates of wages, regulating payment of wages, settlement of wage-related disputes through adjudication process, setting up of wage boards, etc.

FIXATION OF WAGES

Under Section 5 of Minimum Wages Act, 1948 there are basically two method of fixation/revision of Minimum Wages (1) Committee Method (2) Notification Method. Revision of Minimum Wages should not exceed an interval of five years. Section 3 empowers appropriate Government to fix the minimum rates of wages in the scheduled employments.

Minimum rate of the wages fixed or revised consists of the following:

* A basic rate of wages and a special allowance, viz., cost of living allowance;
* A basic rate of wages with or without cost of living allowance and cash value of concessions for supplies of essential commodities;
* An all inclusive rate, i.e. basic rate, cost of living allowance and cash value of concessions.

The Minimum Wage rate may be fixed at (a) time rate, (b) piece rate, (c) guaranteed time rate and (d) overtime rate.

The Act provides that different Minimum Wage rate may be fixed for (a) different scheduled employments, (b) different works in the same employment, (c) adult, adolescent and children, (d) different locations or (e) male and female.

Also, government may fix such Minimum Wage by (a) an hour, (b) day, (c) month, or (d) any other period as may be prescribed by the notified authority.

WAGE THEORIES

1. **Subsistence Theory:** This theory was propounded by David Ricardo. Ricardo states that "The labourers are paid to enable them to subsist and perpetuate the race without increase or diminution". This theory is also known as "Iron Law of Wages". According to this theory, if the wage fall below the subsistence level, the number of workers would decrease as many of them would die of hunger, disease, malnutrition. This would make the wage rates go up as labour will become

scarce. However, if the workers are paid more than the subsistence wages, they would marry and procreate. This would increase their number and bring down the rate of wages.

2. **Wage Fund Theory:** This theory was propounded by Adam Smith. According to him, wages are paid out of a predetermined fund of wealth. If the fund is large, wages would be high; if it is small, wages would be reduced to the subsistence level.

3. **Surplus Value Theory:** This theory was propounded by Karl Marx. According to Marx, the price of any product was determined by the labour time needed for producing it. The labour was not paid in proportion to the time spent on work but subsistence wages which is much less and the surplus went to the capitalist.

4. **Residual Claimant Theory:** This theory was propounded by Francis A. Walker. According to Walker, there are four factors of production namely, land, labour, capital and organisation. Wages represent the amount of value created in the production which remains after payment of the other three factors of production namely, land, capital and organisation.

5. **Marginal Productivity Theory:** This theory was propounded by Henry Wicksteed and John Clark. According to this theory, workers are paid what they are economically worth. As long as each additional worker contributes more to the total value than the cost in wages, the employer will continue to hire workers. The employer will stop hiring when it becomes uneconomical for him to do so.

6. **Bargaining Theory:** This theory was propounded by John Davidson. According to this theory, wages are determined by the relative bargaining power of employers and employees. According to this theory, there is an upper limit and a lower limit on wage rates and the actual rates between these limits are determined by the bargaining power of the employers and the workers. The upper limit makes the highest wages the employers would be willing to pay, whereas, the lower limit

indicates the minimum wages prescribed under the strength of resistance of the workers at the subsistence wages below which they will not available for work.

7. **Demand and Supply Theory:** Alfred Marshall, the chief exponent to this theory, explained the complexity of the economic world tried to provide a less rigid and deterministic theory. According to him, the determination of wages is affected by the whole set of actors which govern demand for and supply of labour. They demand price of labour, however, determined by the marginal productivity of the individual worker.
8. **The Purchasing Power Theory:** This theory was propounded by Keynes. According to him, wages are not only the cost of production for an employer but also incomes for the wage earners who constitute a majority in the total working population. A major part of the products of an industry is consumed by the same workers and their families. Hence, if the wage rates are high they will have more purchasing power, which would increase the aggregate demand for goods and the level of output. Conversely, if the wage rates are low, their purchasing power would be less, which would bring about a fail in the aggregate demand.

WAGE DIFFERENTIALS

The wage paid to workers varies greatly. These wage differentials are mostly the result of differences in worker ability and the workers' effort in performing the job. There are also wage differentials across occupations, because of differences in the demand and supply of labourers for particular job or occupation. These differences arise primarily because of differences in the amount of education or training required and in the desirability of the job itself.

The five causes of wage differentials are as follows: 1. Occupational Differences, 2. Inter-firm Differentials, 3. Regional Differences, 4. Inter-Industry Differences, and 5. Personal Wage Differences.

As there are individual differences, so are wage differentials also. An organisation offers different jobs, thus, differentials in wages for different jobs are inevitable. Wage differentials are also known as inter-industry, inter-firm, inter-area or geographical differentials.

Wage differentials may be due to following causes:

1. Occupational Differences

Occupations in an organisation widely differ from one another in terms of skill requirement and the extent of requirement and the extent of responsibility. Accordingly, wages vary from occupation to occupation. Such differences in occupations induce people/workers to undertake more challenging jobs, encourage workers to develop their skills by way of education and training. It is varying skill requirement for different occupation that shapes the manpower planning in an organisation-be it an industrial organisation or educational institution.

2. Inter-firm Differentials

There are wage differentials of workers in different plants in the same area and occupation. Factors like differences in quality of labour employed by different firms, imperfections in the labour market and differences in the efficiency of equipment's and supervision result in inter-firm wage differentials. Added to these are differences in technological advance, managerial efficiency, financial capability, firm's age and size, availability of raw material, power and transport facilities also account for differences in wages among firms.

3. Regional Differences

Not only wages differ among occupations, but these also differ in case of workers working in the same occupation at different geographical regions. These differences are the result of working conditions prevalent in different regions of the country. For example, the Central Government employees serving in the remote and disturbed areas like the North Eastern States of India are paid additional remuneration in the form of the Remote Area Allowance. Sometimes, such wage differentials are used to attract people to serve in particular regions.

4. Inter-Industry Differences

These differences in wages surface in case of workers working in the same occupation and the same area but in different industries.

These differences are the result of varying skill requirements, level of unionisation, nature of product market, ability to pay, the stage of development of an industry, etc.

5. Personal Wage Differences

These differences arise because of the differences in the personal characteristics (age or sex) of workers working in the same unit and occupation. Though provision of 'equal pay for equal work' is certainly there, but it is still not the reality. Instances are there when woman worker is paid less than her male counterpart for doing the same job. Of course, there are other reasons also which cause wage differentials between male and female workers.

Amendments and Latest Provisions Related Under Labour Laws

1. **The Factories Act, 1948:** Lot of changes under such as in Welfare Measures i.e. Canteen, Creche etc., Appointment of Safety Officers etc.
2. **The ESI Act, 1948: 1.**Wage ceiling for coverage of employees is up to ₹ 15,000 per month. **2.** Conveyance Allowance is excluded under the part of wage. **3.** Maintenance of Previous Records for Inspection up to 5 years only.
3. **The EPF Act, 1952: 1.** Under EDLI - The Benefit has been extended from Rs 1,00,000 to Rs 1,30,000.
4. **The Workmen Compensation Act, 1923:** Compensation under **1.** Death i.e. Minimum is 1,20,000, Maximum is ₹ 4,25,000, **2.** Permanent Disablement-Minimum-₹ 1,40,000, Maximum is 5,40,000, 2. Computation for calculation of compensation on wages has been extended from ₹ 4,000 to ₹ 8,000, **3.** The Act can be amended as Employees Compensation Act and **4.** Casual Labour are also covered under the act as per latest amendment.
5. **The Payment of Wages Act, 1936:** Wages to be paid either through deposit in Bank or by cheque.
6. **The Payment of Bonus Act, 1965:** Amendment has been proposed to extend wage ceiling from ₹ 10,000 to ₹ 15,000 and also for computation of Bonus from ₹ 3,500 to ₹ 5,000

Minimum Bonus has also extended from 8.33 per cent to 11 per cent.

7. **The Payment of Gratuity Act, 1972: 1.** Maximum Payment under Gratuity has been extended from ₹ 3,50,000 to ₹ 10,00,000, **2.** Compulsory Insurance coverage for employees under Gratuity Act.

8. **The Industrial Dispute Act, 1947:** U/s 11a and impact of Sec 2a, any workmen will directly approaches to Labour Court and Tribunal Directly without conciliation, if they are discharged, dismissed, terminated from service.

9. **The Contract Labour Act, 1970:** Non-Compliance under statutory provisions, contract labour to be deemed as employees of the principal employer.

Index

A

Abraham Maslow, 23, 27, 134
Adam Smith, 84, 133, 335
Administrative Participation, 206
Advisory Committees, 268
Ahmedabad, 218, 219, 324
Alfred Marshall, 85, 336
All India Trade Union Congress (AITUC), 219, 220, 223, 224, 255
All India Trade Union Federation (AITUF), 220
Amalgama Society, 222
American Society for Training and Development (ASTD), 127
Analysing Organisational Plans, 63
Andrea Gabor, 30
Aptitude Tests, 73
Arbitrator, 311
Armand V. Feigenbaum, 120
Asian Regional Conference, 314
Asian, 230
Assam, 251, 324
Associative Participation, 206
Australian, 133

B

B.P. Wadia, 222
Badli workman, 308
Bajaj, 324
Balkanisation, 326
Bangalore City Corporation, 249
Bargaining Theory, 335
Behaviour Description Questionnaire, 159
Behaviour modification, 157
Behavioural Anchored Rating Scale, 110
Behavioural Sciences, 134
Behavioural Specifications, 59
Behaviourally Anchored Rating Scales (BARS), 110
Bengal Trades Union Federation, 254
Bengal, 220
Bernard Bass, 168
Bethlehem Steel Plant, 16
Bharatiya Mazdoor Sangh (BMS), 223
BHEL, 118, 324
Birla, 324
Bombay Millhand's Association, 219, 222, 254
Bombay Postal Union, 254
Bombay Textile Mills, 222
Brainstorming technique, 145
Buckingham Mill Case, 254
Buddy Referral, 73
Business Process Management, 118

C

C. B. Gupta, 38
Calcutta, 254
Central Government, 299
Central Legislative Assembly, 255
Central Trade Union Organisations, 220
Chamber of Commerce, 254
Change Management, 67
Charisma, 170
Chester Barnard, 29, 134
Chhattisgarh, 331
Chicago, 24
Chris Argyris, 122
Clayton P. Alderfer, 156
Coal Mines Provident Fund, 230
Collective Bargaining, 201
Common Metric Questionnaire (CMQ Model), 60
Compensation and Benefits, 67
Computer Data Banks, 72
Conciliation Officer, 195
Conciliation, 194
Consultative Participation, 206
Continuum Leadership Behaviour, 167
Critical Incident Technique, 59

D

Dale Yoder, 184
David Mc Cellan, 134
David Ricardo, 84, 334
Decisive Participation, 206
Delphi method, 63
Delphi technique, 146
Demand Forecasting, 63
Democratic Values, 318
Deniel Katz, 32
Deputy Chief Labour Commissioner, 298, 299
Dickson, 25
Dinabandhu, 222
Direct Observation Method, 59
Discharge, 294
Dismissal, 294
Donald Kirkpatrick, 127
Douglas McGregor, 28, 94, 152
Dr. Manmohan Singh, 212
Dr. Rensis Likert, 160
Dunn, 72

E

Econometrics Models, 65
Economic factors, 184
Edwin B. Flippo, 44
Elton Mayo, 133
Emotional and Social Specifications, 59
Employee Referrals, 70
Employer Unions, 258
Employment Agencies, 70
Employment Interview, 75
England, 230
Equal Remuneration Act, 266
European, 230
Extended Sickness Benefit (ESB), 243
Extended Sickness Benefit, 243

F

Factor Comparison, 87
Fatigue, 176
First World War, 209, 254, 279
Fleishman Job Analysis System (FJAS Model), 61
Forced Labour Convention, 211
Francis A. Walker, 84, 335

Fred E. Fiedler, 164
Frederick Herzberg, 134, 150
Frederick Winslow Taylor, 16, 17
Fredrick Winslow Taylor, 133
Free Form method, 108
Full-fledge Enquiry, 93
Functional Job Analysis (FJA Model), 60
Functional Theory, 316

G

Gandhian Approach, 217
Gandhian Trusteeship Approach, 189
Gazette, 238
Geneva, 209
George C. Homans, 143
George Odiome, 113
German Sociologist Max Weber, 133
Germany, 203
Giri Kamgar Union, 218
Goa, 331
Godrej, 324
Governing Body, 210
Great Britain, 30
Grievance Committee, 90
Grievance Redressal Committee, 300, 301
Grievance Redressal Mechanism, 301
Grievance Settlement Authority, 300

H

H. Koontz, 38
H. Weihrich, 38
Harold Stieglitz, 56
Harvard Professor, 133
Harvard University, 188
Hawthorne, 24, 28
Henri Fayol, 17, 18, 19, 134
Henry Fayol, 35, 38
Henry Gantt, 17
Henry Murray, 152
Henry Wicksteed, 84, 335
Hero-Honda, 154
Hind Mazdoor Panchayat, 223
Hind Mazdoor Sabha (HMS), 223
Hiring Hall, 221
HMT, 324
Honourable Supreme Court in Jalan Trading Company, 279
Hot-Stove Rule, 94
HUL, 324
Human Relations Approach, 188
Humanistic approach, 321
Hyderabad, 118

I

Incentive Wage Plan, 88
Indian Factories Act, 219
Indian Labour Conference (ILC), 207
Indian Labour Conference, 78, 200, 331
Indian Labour Force, 330
Indian Legal Service, 299
Indian National Congress, 222
Indian National Trade Union Congress (INTUC), 220, 222, 223
Indian Nationalism, 231
Indian Trade Unions Act, 255
Indian Trade Unions Bill, 255
Industrial Associations, 254
Industrial Dispute Act, 193, 194, 200, 289, 290
Industrial Disputes Act, 193, 194, 289
Industrial Relations System, 185
Industrial Tribunal, 197, 199, 290, 300
Industrial Tribunal/Labour Court, 257

Industrial Truce Resolution, 212
Institutional factors, 184
Intellectual Breadth, 159
Intelligence Test, 73
International Labour Conference (ILC), 209
International Labour Office (ILO), 86
International Labour Office, 211
International Labour Organisation (ILO), 208, 209, 229
International Labour Organisation, 203, 209
International Trade, 192
International Uniformity, 229
Interview Method, 59
Iron Law of Wages, 84

J

J. Loy, 114
J. Richard, 114
J. T. Dunlop, 188
J.D. Thompson, 32
Jamshedpur Labour Union, 218
Jane Mouton, 160
Japan, 41, 117
Jeanneret, 60
John Clark, 84, 335
John Davidson, 85, 335
John Humble, 113
John Storey, 49
Joint Management Council (JMC), 202
Joseph M. Juran, 120
Juan Somavia, 211

K

Kamgar Hitwardhak Sabha, 222, 254
Kan Ban System, 42
Kaoru Ishikawa, 118
Karl Marx, 84, 335
Keith Davis, 203
Kenneth Blanchard, 163
Kerala, 331
Keynes, 336
Kirloskar Oil Engines, 118
Kurt Goldstein, 149
Kurt Lewin, 139

L

Labour Bureau, 256
Labour Commissioner, 299
Labour Court, 197, 199, 290, 295, 300, 301, 304, 311
Labour courts, 197
Labour Investigation Committee, 314
Labour Welfare Officer, 201
Lawrence J. Henderson, 32
Leadership-Member Exchange (LMX), 168
Leonard Nadler, 98, 99
LIC, 324
Lok Sabha, 238, 240
Lombardo, 159
Ludwing Von Bertalanfty, 32

M

Madeline Heilman, 107
Madras High Court, 254
Madras Labour Union, 222, 254, 255
Mahatma Gandhi, 196, 219
Mahindra, 118
Management Information System, 66
Management information systems (MIS), 32
Managerial Judgement, 63
Marginal Productivity Theory, 84
Maruti-Suzuki, 154

Marxist Approach, 187
Mary Parker Follett, 35, 134
Maslow, 28, 149, 150
Maternity Benefit Act, 230, 250
Matrix structure, 54
Mazdoor Sabha of Kanpur, 324
McCall, 159
McCarthy, 168
McClelland, 152
McCormick, 60
McFarland, 52
Mecham, 60
Mechanical Test, 73
Mechanistic Approach, 320
Medical Benefit Council, 239, 240
Mental Specifications, 58
Mica Mines Labour Welfare Fund Act, 230
Mill Mazdoor Union, 279
Minimum Wages Act, 79, 258, 260, 332, 334
Ministry of Labour and Employment, 256
Model Standing Order, 288
Motorola, 120
Mr. M.M. Lokhande, 222
Mr. N. N. Joshi, 219

N

National Economy, 229
National Industrial Tribunals, 299
National Relief Fund, 274
National Trade Union Organisation, 219
National Tribunal, 197, 198, 199, 290, 295, 297, 299, 300, 301, 304, 311
National tribunals, 197
Negotiation, 214
Nepotism, 72
Noetic Outcomes Consulting, 180
Nominal Group Technique (NGT), 146

O

Objective Test, 74
Official Gazette, 262, 292, 301
Onward Industry, 20
Opinion Surveys, 90
Organisational behaviour, 132, 136
Organisational Climate Analysis, 124
Over Time Rate, 261

P

Partial disablement, 247
Paternalistic Theory, 316
Paul Hersey, 163
Payment Linked Wage System, 88
Peace Conference, 209
People Oriented Behavioural Leaders, 159
Performance Appraisal Technique, 112
Permanent Disablement Benefit (PDB), 244
Philanthropic Theory, 316
Philips, 324
Physical Examination, 75
Physical Specifications, 58
Piece Rate System, 88
Pluralistic Approach, 187
Position Analysis Questionnaire (PAQ Model), 60
Praja Socialist Party, 223
Preliminary Interview, 74
Professor Elton Mayo, 24
Professor T. V. Rao, 100
Professor Udai Pareek, 100

Projective Test, 74
Psychological Approach, 187
Psycho-motor Test, 73
Public Relation Theory, 316
Punjab, 220
Purchasing Power Theory, 336

Q

Quality Function Deployment, 119
Questionnaire Method, 60

R

R K Soni, 288
Rajasthan, 258
Rajya Sabha, 238, 240
Ramachandrapuram, 118
Rangnekar, 153
Ratio Trend Analysis, 64
Recruiting Skilled Employees, 67
Red Tapism, 22
Reducing Fatigue, 178
Refreezing, 181
Rensis Likert, 171
Residual Claimant Theory, 84
Richard E. Walton, 115
Robert Blake, 160
Robert House, 162
Robert L. Kahn, 32
Robert McNamara, 31
Roethlisberger, 25
Rowntree Company, 21

S

S.H. Slithers, 217
Salary Administration, 78
Sandoz, 324
Satyagraha, 189
Scheduled Employment, 259
Schmidt, 166, 168
Second Schedule, 299
Selection Tests, 74
Self-Actualisation Needs, 149
Self-imposed discipline, 91
Shri N. M. Joshi, 255
Shri. Narasimha Rao, 212
Siemens, 324
Situation Test, 74
Social Factors, 83
Social Security Legislations, 230
Social Service League, 222
Sociological Approach, 187
Sorabji Shaparji, 222
Standing Labour Committee (SLC), 207
State Government, 299
State Labour Advisory Boards, 203
State Labour Department, 299
Stephen, 72
Surplus Value Theory, 84, 335
System Approach, 188

T

T. Venkateswara Rao, 98
Tactical plans, 36
Taft-Hartley Act, 221
Tamil Nadu, 258
Tannenbaum, 166, 168
Task Management, 161
Technological factors, 184
Temporary Disablement Benefit (TDB), 244
Ten Management Roles, 42
Textile Labour Association, 218, 324
T-Group Training, 122
Theo Haimann, 40

Theodore Newcomb, 144
Third Party Methods, 72
Third Schedule, 299
Tiffen, 109
Time Rate System, 88
TISCO, 324
Totality of Welfare, 318
Toyota, 41
Trade Union Act, 214
Trade Union Organisation, 224
Trade Union, 254
Trade Unions Act, 230, 254, 257
Training and Development, 68
Tribunal, 295, 300, 301, 304, 311
Tripartite Bodies, 203
Trusteeship Theory, 316

U

Unfreezing, 181
Union Territories, 237
Unitary Approach, 186
United Nations System, 208, 210
United Nations, 209
United Trade Union Congress (UTUC), 223
Urwick, 153
Uttarakhand, 331

V

Victor Vroom, 155
Voltas, 324
Voluntary Arbitration, 196
Voluntary Organisations, 72

W

W. Buckley, 32
W. Edwards Deming, 120
W.G. Scott, 32
Wage Fund Theory, 84
Warwick University, 46
West Bengal, 142
West Germany, 205
Western Pennsylvania, 150
William Ouchi, 34
William R. Spriegel, 92
William Spriegel, 174
Work Committee, 294
Work Method Analysis, 59
Work Profiling System (WPS Model), 60
Work Sample Tests, 74
Workplace Diversity, 67
World War II, 30

Y

Yugoslavia, 203, 205